POWER AND THE PEOPLE

THUCYDIDES' *HISTORY* AND THE AMERICAN FOUNDING

THE McDONALD
CENTER FOR
AMERICA'S FOUNDING
PRINCIPLES

MERCER
UNIVERSITY

THE A. V. ELLIOTT CONFERENCE SERIES

The Thomas C. and Ramona E. McDonald Center
for America's Founding Principles

Guided by James Madison's maxim that "a well-instructed people alone can be permanently a free people," the McDonald Center exists to promote the study of the great texts and ideas that have shaped our regime and fostered liberal learning.

Directors
Will R. Jordan and Charlotte C. S. Thomas

Published Volumes

Charlotte C. S. Thomas, ed., *No Greater Monster nor Miracle than Myself: The Political Philosophy of Michel de Montaigne* (2014)

Charlotte C. S. Thomas, ed., *Of Sympathy and Selfishness: The Moral and Political Philosophy of Adam Smith* (2015)

Will R. Jordan and Charlotte C. S. Thomas, ed., *The Most Sacred Freedom: Religious Liberty in the History of Philosophy and America's Founding* (2016)

Will R. Jordan, ed., *Promise and Peril: Republics and Republicanism in the History of Political Philosophy* (2017)

Will R. Jordan, ed., *When in the Course of Human Events: 1776 at Home, Abroad, and in American Memory* (2018)

Charlotte C. S. Thomas, ed. *Power and the People: Thucydides' History and the American Founding* (2019)

Forthcoming

Will R. Jordan, ed., *Essays on the Federalist and Anti-Federalist Papers* (2020)

Charlotte C. S. Thomas, ed., *Liberty and Tyranny in Plato* (2021)

POWER AND THE PEOPLE

Thucydides' History and the American Founding

Edited by Charlotte C. S. Thomas

MERCER UNIVERSITY PRESS
Macon, Georgia
1979–2019
40 Years of Publishing Excellence

MUP/ P578

Published by Mercer University Press
1501 Mercer University Drive
Macon, Georgia 31207

9 8 7 6 5 4 3 2 1

Books published by Mercer University Press are printed on acid-free paper that meets the requirements of the American National Standard for Information Sciences—Permanence of Paper for Printed Library Materials.

ISBN 978-0-88146-659-9
Cataloging-in-Publication Data is available from the Library of Congress

CONTENTS

CONTRIBUTORS

Bernard Dobski, Assumption College

Norman Fischer, Clark Atlanta University

Steven Forde, University of North Texas

Sarah Gardner, Mercer University

Laurie Johnson, Kansas State University

Allison Levy, St Johns College, Santa Fe

Clifford Orwin, University of Toronto

Devin Stauffer, University of Texas

Charlotte C. S. Thomas, Mercer University

Karl Walling, US Naval War College

Ann Ward, Baylor University

ACKNOWLEDGMENTS

A collection of essays such as this one requires the support of many people, all of whom deserve special recognition for their generous contributions to this volume. Each of the essays is adapted from presentations made at Mercer University's 2016 A. V. Elliott Conference on Great Books and Ideas, organized by the Thomas C. and Ramona McDonald Center for America's Founding Principles. The Elliott and McDonald families' magnanimous support of the work of the McDonald Center made that conference and this volume possible, and we will perennially be in their debt both for their financial support and for the gift of their confidence in our vision for the Center. Mercer University's institutional support for the McDonald Center has likewise been remarkable. President William D. Underwood supported our work from its earliest inchoate stages and enabled us to develop as a stable and permanent part of Mercer's institutional landscape. Former Provost Wallace McDaniel was a very important part of that process, as well, as were the three Deans with whom we have worked over the years: Lake Lambert, Keith Howard, and Anita Gustafson. Dean Lambert played a particularly important role in the Center's development, without which we simply would not have been able to proceed, and for that we are particularly grateful. I must save my highest praise, though, for Will Jordan, with whom I co-direct the McDonald Center. His unwavering vision and indefatigable will are almost as impressive to me as his thoughtful and generous spirit. One must have a good partner to do work such as this, but what one wants really is a friend. Everything good that happens at the McDonald Center has more than a bit of Will Jordan in it, including this volume, and for that I am deeply grateful.

The authors of the essays in this volume were wonderful guests when we congregated in Macon for our conference in the Spring of 2016, and they have continued to be a joy to work with throughout the process of bringing the book to print. Norman Fischer, Allison Levy, Ann Ward, Bernard Dobski, Michael Palmer, Steven Forde, Devin Stauffer, Sarah Gardner, Laurie Johnson, and Karl Walling were model partners in this endeavor. My sincere thanks go out to all of them. I would also like to thank our undergraduate student panelists from the conference: Anna Bates, Jacob Harvey, Justin Kasian, Cody Moran, and Joseph Payne. It takes great courage for an undergraduate to deliver an essay to a crowd filled with visiting scholars, and these students comported themselves wonderfully. Thanks is owed to you all for rising to the occasion and proving once again how impressive Mercer University students are.

One of the most enjoyable parts of my role as co-director of the McDonald Center is to participate in reading groups that convene throughout the year to prepare an interdisciplinary group of faculty and students for the books and authors on which our Spring conference will be focused. In this case, we took the whole 2015-16 academic year to read Thucydides' *History* together cover to cover. Will Jordan, Sarah Gardner, Tom Scott, Gordon Johnston, Eric O'Dell, Kevin Honeycutt, Amy Nichols-Belo, Luke Buffenmeyer, Jacob Harvey, Jaz Buckley, Joseph Payne, Cody Moran, Justin Kasian, Eliza Guta, Anna Bates, Daniel Crum all deserve special recognition for their diligence and lively participation. We consumed a lot of pizza, laughed until it hurt, and taught each other a great deal about Thucydides that year. It was a real joy.

Thanks are also due to Holly Cooper and Cody Moran for their assistance in editing and indexing this volume.

Mercer University Press has been a perfect partner in the work of bringing these essays into print. Marc Jolley makes every part of the process enjoyable and produces beautiful, well-made books. His staff is great, and his editors are smart and careful and kind. The scholarly world is full of horror stories about the difficulty of bringing edited volumes into the world, but I have none of those to add. Since 2012, my experience with Mercer University Press has been unwaveringly positive.

Finally, I would like to thank my son, Isaiah, who has never complained about me coming home late after dinners with our visiting lecturers, and who usually does not mind eating leftover pizza for dinner when I bring it to him after reading groups. Thanks for being such a great kid. I love you more.

INTRODUCTION

Charlotte C. S. Thomas

In his introduction to the 1959 edition of Hobbes's translation of Thucydides' *The Peloponnesian War*, Bertrand de Jouvenel writes:

> The study of history would be unnecessary for political education if the lessons to be drawn from great historic events could be summed up in a few trenchant sentences. We would then need no more than these final sentences. But political prudence does not consist in recipes which can be conveyed: it is a virtue which has to be acquired the hard way. The greatest possible economy of effort is achieved if a very competent guide takes you through the important experiences of others. He tells you just enough and not too much: why this step was taken and how it turned out to be disastrous. It is for you to think out why it turned out to be disastrous and how it might have been avoided: it is only by such personal speculation that one gains political education; in that realm, as in all others, one only learns by thinking for oneself. [1]

For Jouvenel, the paradigmatic historian was Thucydides, and his most attentive student was Thomas Hobbes. In the same introduction quoted above, Jouvenel writes that Hobbes claimed to learn political science from Thucydides and that some of the most fundamental tenets of Hobbesian political theory can be traced back to his understanding of Thucydides' *History*. Specifically, he argues that Hobbes's commitment to a unifying and "over-awing" political authority comes at least in part from his appreciation of Thucydides' critique of the democratic Assembly of the Athenians.

One need not be a Hobbesian to see that Hobbes was right about Thucydides' power as a historian, political theorist, and political educator. Whether one comes away from the *History* as a critic of democratic institutions or as a defender of them against the corrupting power of imperial expansion, one's understanding of political institutions cannot escape being deepened by a careful reading of Thucydides' *History*. And one would be hard pressed to attend carefully to the speeches and accounts of political ac-

---

[1] Thucydides, *The Peloponnesian War: The Complete Hobbes Translation*, ed. David Grene, (Chicago: University of Chicago Press, 1959).

tion in *The Peloponnesian War* without developing a richer understanding of political prudence.

John Adams seems to have shared Hobbes's and Jouvenel's deep admiration for Thucydides. As his August 11, 1777 letter to 10-year-old John Quincy Adams attests, Thucydides' *History* was an important part of his political education and a text well known to the founding generation for its deep insight and contemporary relevance.

> My dear Son,
>
> As the War in which your Country is engaged will probably hereafter attract your Attention, more than it does at this Time, and as the future Circumstances of your Country, may require other Wars, as well as Councils and Negotiations, similar to those which are now in Agitation, I wish to turn your Thoughts early to such Studies, as will afford you the most solid Instruction and Improvement for the Part which may be allotted you to act on the Stage of Life.
>
> There is no History, perhaps, better adapted to this usefull Purpose than that of Thucidides, an Author, of whom I hope you will make yourself perfect Master, in original Language, which is Greek, the most perfect of all human Languages. In order to understand him fully in his own Tongue, you must however take Advantage, of every Help you can procure and particularly of Translations of him into your own Mother Tongue.
>
> You will find in your Fathers Library, the Works of Mr. Hobbes, in which among a great deal of mischievous Philosophy, you will find a learned and exact Translation of Thucidides, which will be usefull to you.
>
> But there is another Translation of him, much more elegant, intituled "The History of the Peloponnesian War, translated from the Greek of Thucidides in two Volumes Quarto, by William Smith A.M. Rector of the Parish of the holy Trinity in Chester, and Chaplain to the Right Honourable the Earl of Derby."
>
> If you preserve this Letter, it may hereafter remind you, to procure the Book. You will find it full of Instruction to the Orator, the Statesman, the General, as well as to the Historian and the Philosopher. You may find Something of the Peloponnesian War, in Rollin.
>
> I am with much Affection your Father,
> John Adams[2]

[2] https://founders.archives.gov/documents/Adams/04-02-02-0247.

John Adams's admiration for Thucydides is clear in this little letter, as is his familiarity with the text. In fact, he indicates that he had at least four versions of Thucydides in his library: a Greek edition, a translation by the "mischievous" Thomas Hobbes, a "more elegant" translation by William Smith, and the abridgement contained in Rollin's *Ancient History*. Adams encourages young John Quincy to read all of these editions and translations together in order to make himself "the perfect master" of Thucydides' writings. A serious assignment indeed.

Lest we think that John Adams understood Thucydides to be appropriate only for children and only for didactic purposes, consider this line from the January 21, 1812 letter he wrote to Thomas Jefferson:

> I have given up newspapers in exchange for Tacitus & Thucydides, for Newton & Euclid; & I find myself much the happier. sometimes indeed I look back to former occurrences, in remembrance of our old friends and fellow laborers, who have fallen before us. of the signers of the Declaration of Independence I see now living not more than half a dozen on your side of the Patomak, and, on this side, myself alone. you & I have been wonderfully spared and myself with remarkable health, & a considerable activity of body & mind. I am on horseback 3. or 4. hours of every day; visit 3. or 4. times a year a possession I have 90 miles distant, performing the winter journey on horseback. I walk little however; a single mile being too much for me; and I live in the midst of my grandchildren, one of whom has lately promoted me to be a great grandfather.[3]

Thomas Jefferson and John Adams are both in their seventies, most of the founding generation is already gone, and Adams describes his retirement to Jefferson as riding horses, playing with his grandchildren . . . and reading Thucydides. This letter suggests not only that Adams loved Thucydides throughout his life, but also that he thought of his love of Thucydides as something Jefferson would appreciate and understand. Through Hobbes and directly, it seems that Thucydides was a part of the intellectual backdrop of the American Founding. But, what did he contribute?

This collection of essays attempts to draw more clearly the connections between Thucydides' *History* and the eighteenth-century statesmanship and political theory that informed the founding of the American republic. In its attempt to deepen our understanding of a book that was important to the American Founders, this volume instantiates the central work of the

[3] https://founders.archives.gov/documents/Jefferson/03-04-02-0334.

McDonald Center for America's Founding Principles: to take a deep and serious look at the books and ideas that influenced the American Founding. When a book (such as Thucydides' *History*) not only brings us greater historical clarity, but also gives us new lenses through which to see our contemporary American political landscape, we find the epicenter of our ambitions for the McDonald Center. This book and the 2016 conference on which it is based, sit right there at the heart of our hopes.

****

The ten essays in this volume consider from very different perspectives the value of Thucydides' *History* for helping make sense of the American Founding. Some of the essays engage Thucydides in his own context or put him in conversations with other ancient authors. Others draw more direct connections from Thucydides to the figures and ideas of the American Founding. Still others look at the legacy of Thucydides for the inheritors of the founding in the nineteenth century through the contemporary era. All of the included essays share a commitment to careful reading of Thucydides' *History*, though, and a consensus regarding his value for our ongoing education in political action and theory.

Clifford Orwin's essay, "The Impossible Synthesis? A Thucydidean Perspective on Liberal Democracy," looks to Thucydides' foundational influence on Hobbes and Hobbes's foundational influence on the American Founders. Orwin argues that Thucydides is "encoded in our political DNA." He does not mean that North Americans know and credit Thucydides' influence in our thinking but that, through, Hobbes, Thucydides has made his way into our thoughts mainly unattributed. This claim reminded me immediately of Alexis de Tocqueville's quip that (early nineteenth-century) Americans were Cartesian on instinct, although most of them had never heard of Descartes. Perhaps it is not too far a stretch to characterize Orwin's account as an exploration of the ways in which we are, in the contemporary political world, Thucydidean on instinct. But the essay is also an exploration of how Thucydides might provide us with helpful critiques of contemporary liberal democracy. The analogies between the massive expansion of Athenian power after the Persian Wars and the even more massive expansion of American power after the Second World War are uncannily clear. An understanding of how to frame a contemporary account analogous to Thucydides' implicit recommendation for responding to the ancient conundrum is less obvious; but Orwin makes a compelling case.

In "Political Science and Political Medicine: Thucydides, the *Federalist Papers*, and the New World Order," Karl Walling constructs a dialogue between Thucydides, the authors of the *Federalist Papers*, and contemporary scholars of international relations and American foreign policy. Political medicine, in this context, refers to the ways in which politics can treat natural human maladies, perhaps even cure them. Through this imaginary dialogue, Walling considers three deeply varied notions of what politics can and can't accomplish in response to natural human frailty. By putting Thucydides into conversation with the American founders, Walling gets to the heart of what this volume hopes to be. By extending the lessons of that dialogue to the contemporary milieu, he gets ultimately to what we hope the McDonald Center will be, that is, a place where the books and ideas that informed the Founders may also inform our own understanding of what it means to be a free and responsible citizen of the contemporary American republic.

Steven Forde, in "The Virtues and Vices of Individualism," traces the idea of Athenian individualism throughout Thucydides' *History*. Forde argues that Athenian individualism is anomalous in the ancient world and that an account of its evolution and decay thread through the entire work. Individualism is also, of course, a deep concern of those interested in the health of the polities in the contemporary world, especially the United States. Forde works through the ways that Athenian individualism and American individualism are alike, but also provides an account of some important differences between them, including the modern commitment to individual rights, which may be a republican pathway to avoiding a contemporary repeat of Athens's ancient tragedy.

Allison Levy's essay, "Piety and Athenian Imperialism in Thucydides' Peloponnesian War," works to understand the hopes that animate Athenian imperial expansion and the military conquests it entails, especially the Sicilian expedition. How does Thucydides characterize the ambition that sends the Athenians to Sicily? How should one make sense of the indictment of Alcibiades and the Athenian refusal to relieve an ill and ill-suited Nicias from his command in light of these ambitions and hopes? Perhaps those familiar with the *History* will not be surprised that Levy finds eros to be more of an animating force than piety for the Athenians, but the case is neither simple nor obvious. Levy's inquiry takes us to the heart of Thucydides' portrayal of the character of the Athenians and its manifestations in the classical world.

Ann Ward's "Love, Beauty, and the Problem of Politics: Alcibiades in Thucydides and Plato," looks at the portrayal of Alcibiades both in Thucydides' account of the Sicilian expedition and in Plato's *Symposium*. Looking at Diotima's "ladder of love" in the *Symposium*, she considers Alcibiades' character, what seems to move him erotically, and his political ambition, especially in relation to the way that the philosopher's character and erotic nature is described in the same section of Plato's text. Ward then looks to Thucydides' portrayal of Alcibiades in light of Plato's presentation of his character. Finally, she brings Thucydides' historical details back into conversation with Plato's account in order to think more concretely about the political lessons the story of Alcibiades suggests.

In "Nikias' Virtue," Norman Fischer begins with a detail gleaned from his careful and close reading of Hobbes's translation of the *History*. Hobbes, as it turns out, omitted an extremely important sentence in Thucydides' paean to Nikias' character and lamentation over his awful death. Hobbes includes the famous line that Nikias "least deserved to fall into so great a misfortune," but he leaves out the reason Thucydides gives for him being least deserving of a bad death, i.e. that he lived a virtuous life. (Thucydides' reasoning is more complicated and subtle than that, but I will leave Fischer's essay to manage the nuance.) What is the nature of Nikias' virtue? How does his virtue, whatever it might entail, inform his place in the Athenian political order and his successes and failures as a general? How does the case of Nikias reflect more generally on Thucydides' presentation of Athenian character? Fischer takes up all of these important questions, and he closes with a few comparisons to Alexis de Tocqueville's presentation of American character.

In "Separation of Powers in History? Thucydides on the Measured Virtue of the Five Thousand," Bernard Dobski begins with the 1777 letter from John Adams to John Quincy Adams quoted above in this introduction, and to the same point. Statesmen, to their great profit have been looking to Thucydides for guidance for centuries. As Dobski argues, political theorists perhaps should look to him more often. His particular theoretical focus in this essay is the question of political liberty and the case of the short-lived rule of the Five Thousand in 410 BCE. While political liberty does not, at first glance, appear to be one of Thucydides' central themes in the *History*, even a cursory consideration of the presentation of the rule of the Five

Thousand suggests we should take a closer look. Dobski gives an account of why Thucydides may be so enamored of the constitution of the Five Thousand, what its lessons might have been for Athens, and what they might be for us.

Devin Stauffer, in "Thucydides and the New Political Science of the American Founding," focuses on one passage from Alexander Hamilton's *Federalist #9* to explore an important sense in which the American Founders differed from Thucydides in their understanding of the perils and promises of republican government. He argues that while Hamilton shared much of Thucydides' diagnosis of the maladies of republics, innovations in political science made new remedies available. Such measures as the separation of powers, checks and balances, an independent judiciary, more sensible schemes of representation, and the expansion of the sphere of government were all generally well understood. All were either poorly known or not known at all to Thucydides. Stauffer explores how Thucydides' still vibrant and meaningful analysis might best be understood through the lens of these modern institutional innovations.

Sarah Gardner's essay, "A Philologist in the American Civil War," takes up the case of Basil L. Gildersleeve, a Johns Hopkins philologist and former Confederate officer whose "A Southerner in the Peloponnesian War," positioned the relevance of Thucydides' *History* for gilded age Americans. Rather than escaping into his classical education, Gildersleeve employed Thucydides' teachings in order to face reconstruction and reconciliation. But, this does not mean that he worked to construct parallels between the American Civil War and the Peloponnesian War; arguing from such comparisons, according to Gildersleeve, rarely gets to the heart of things. As Gardner argues, Gildersleeve's use of Thucydides is far subtler than that, and so too should ours be.

While most of the essays in this volume nod in one way or another to the contemporary relevance of Thucydides' History, Laurie Johnson takes that topic up explicitly in her essay, "Why Our Democracy Needs Thucydides Now More than Ever." From "fake news" to Twenty-First century presidential politics to free market capitalism, Johnson looks at contemporary issues head-on and asks what help we might find in Thucydides to understand them. Then, in the end, she steps back to consider the kind of writing Thucydides did, its importance to his contemporaries and to us, and the value of having such writers in our world to help us see the moral and political landscape more clearly.

Collectively, these essays exhibit the remarkable range of ways Thucydides' *History* may inform our attempts to understand both the American Founding and our contemporary political experience. They push toward some of the deepest and most controversial issues debated in the scholarship of Thucydides as a political philosopher, but they are all accessible to the novice reader. We hope that the volume will be useful to all who read Thucydides whether their interest is scholarly or personal. And we hope it will make this sometimes-intimidating text seem a bit more approachable. Reading Thucydides is among the most powerful ways I know to accelerate one's education in political prudence, a virtue that the American republic very much needs its citizens to develop. And, as Jouvenel reminds us, ". . . political prudence does not consist in recipes which can be conveyed: it is a virtue which has to be acquired the hard way." Perhaps this volume may make the hard way, if not less difficult, at least a little more enjoyable.

THE IMPOSSIBLE SYNTHESIS? A THUCYDIDEAN PERSPECTIVE ON LIBERAL DEMOCRACY

Clifford Orwin

In the course of its now long history, liberal democracy has often found itself beleaguered, and so finds itself today. Its prospects, which looked dim in 1862, 1917, 1940, and 1949, equally alarm certain observers now. Consider this from the thoughtful Canadian journalist Terry Glavin.

> On a scale that exceeds anything since the darkest moments of the Cold War era, a belligerent authoritarian internationalism is corrupting the world's democracies and undermining the institutions of freedom and the rule of law from Hong Kong to Hungary and from Washington to Warsaw. .... [Consider] Syria's Bashar Assad, [or] the Philippines' Rodrigo Duterte, Hungary's Viktor Orban, Venezuela's Nicolas Maduro or any of the other theocrats, gangsters and generals whose systems of kleptocracy, mass murder and oppression are soaring in the ascendant at the moment, everywhere.[1]

Glavin may exaggerate, but he may not. Liberal democracy is beset by low confidence and declining attachment to it, especially among the young.[2] While the challenges facing it are obvious, its determination to meet them is not. Consider only the most obvious problems. The "end of history" euphoria of the Nineties has subsided and the "Third Wave" of democratization appears to be ebbing. The global economy, that linchpin of the liberal system, has proved more volatile than expected, while the environmental crisis

---

[1] *National Post*, August 2, 2017, http://nationalpost.com/opinion/terry-glavin-if-trudeau-is-the-free-worlds-last-hope-the-free-world-is-doomed/wcm/f8feca58-1f3c-4d3a-b3fc-548dac0c9451.

[2] With all respect to Graham Allison, the real "Thucydides trap" that China poses to America and her allies may lie in its promotion of an illiberal politics. Yascha Mounk and Roberto Stefan Foa, "Yes, people really are turning away from liberal democracy," *Washington Post*, December 8, 2016. https://www.washingtonpost.com/news/wonk/wp/2016/12/08/yes-millennials-really-are-surprisingly-approving-of-dictators/?utm_term=.6af85d2deb83. Mounk and Foa have elaborated their views in "The Signs of Deconsolidation," *Journal of Democracy* 28.1 (January 2017), 5-16. http://www.journalofdemocracy.org/sites/default/files/02_28.1_Foa%20%26%20Mounk%20pp%205-15.pdf.

poses many questions both economic and political. Then there is the global refugee crisis, which has strained both liberal and illiberal regimes to the utmost. There is the emphatically non-liberal democratic model of China, which now clearly rivals liberal democracy for prominence on the world scene.[3] Not to forget the challenge of such different but equally illiberal republics as those of Iran and Turkey. Closer to home the rise of populism dishevels mature democracies as well as immature ones. Under these circumstances we liberal democrats are called on to make ever greater efforts of self-understanding.

Can the study of Thucydides further such self-understanding? This might seem doubtful. For one thing there might seem a tension between this task and the priority that Thucydides accords to foreign policy. The difference that the regime makes is less obvious in foreign affairs than in domestic ones, and so the careful analysis of regimes may seem less required for it. Were not war and diplomacy Thucydides' first concerns? And might we not say of "state actors" that they bow to the imperatives of the "international system"? That in so doing they pursue not principles but interests, which as such do not vary according to their respective regimes?

Fortunately for our project, the answers to these last questions all prove to be no. In the first place, even if it were true that all states agreed in jostling among themselves for the same basket of goods, they would still at least differ in the priorities they assigned to them. This is true today and was so in Thucydides' time. Consider the speech of the Corinthians at 1.66-71, which contrasts the uniquely blithe indifference of the Athenians to safety with the uniquely intense Spartan preoccupation with it. While ultimately hyperbolic (cf. the reply of the Athenian envoys at 1.72-78), there is certainly much to this contrast. Thucydides' narrative attests not only to what is common to cities in their endless jostling among themselves, but to what distinguishes them. And while we can't deny the impact on their behavior of many other influences, the regime clearly matters. For Thucydides as for Aristotle (cf. *Politics* 3.1-6), every city is a regime in disguise; a part of the city that, having seized the right to speak for the whole, effectively impersonates it. And while regimes may have much in common (above all of course their respective determination to perpetuate themselves), they also differ widely. They display different assets and liabilities in foreign policy just as they do in do-

---

[3] Allison, *Destined for War: Can America and China Escape Thucydides' Trap*? (New York: Houghton Mifflin Harcourt, 2016)

mestic affairs; sometimes even, as with Athens and Sparta, different concerns.

The regime would therefore remain a crucial issue for Thucydides even if we did take him to be primarily concerned with foreign rather than domestic policy. Yet we may also doubt the adequacy of this last view. His very first characterization of the war that furnishes his subject is that it was the greatest motion ever, and motion proves as pervasive in domestic as in foreign politics. The persistent counterpart of wars among cities is strife or faction (*stasis)* within them. The narrative stresses the interpenetration of the domestic and foreign sphere[s], thereby suggesting that this Thucydides' comprehensive theme, rather than either sphere as distinct from the other. What is true of Athens and Sparta proves true of all the cities in the work: that neither of these spheres of their policy can be understood apart from the other. Athens's failure in the war is an aspect of her regime, reflecting her inferiority to Sparta in coping with *stasis.* Her greater propensity to error abroad reflects her greater susceptibility to faction at home. Yet this last is itself due largely to the unbridled ambition of her leading citizens, which as such mirrors the city's aggressive stance toward the world.

In recognizing the primacy of the regime, Thucydides anticipates Plato and Aristotle. Unlike them he considers only actual cities or regimes, not ones in speech (cf. the *Republic*) or to be prayed for (cf. the *Politics,* Books Seven and Eight). Instead of ascending to the question of the best regime in principle, he settles for that of the best in practice. Or to be precise, that of the best of actual known regimes. Or to be more precise still, the best of the actual regimes in his own actual city during his own actual lifetime (8.97). Whatever else we may say about him, Thucydides practices a certain epistemic modesty.

It is with this question of the regime in mind that we will undertake our Thucydidean assessment of liberal democracy. In so doing I must enter two further demurrers. I make no claim to have understood everything in Thucydides' book, but merely to have applied what I have understood from it. Nor therefore can I claim to have seen liberal democracy (or anything else) just as he would have seen it. When dealing with so great a writer, you take the little that you know and you do the best you can.[4]

[4] Bill Staines, "The Quiet Faith of Man" https://www.youtube.com/watch?v=jNF1SKrAiZY. Although philosophy is not Staines's theme, this has always seemed to me good advice for its students.

Thucydides and the Hobbesian Basis of Modern Liberal Democracy

It was the United States that afforded the first example of liberal democracy, although the term would not exist for many more decades. It was the first regime that owed its design not just to practice (the failure of the Articles of Confederation, the experience of the various state governments, and so on) but to theory. This latter spilled forth from a crowd of pamphleteers, from a handful of second tier thinkers, and from one source that loomed above them: the vast and craggy peak that is Montesquieu. As the author of a quasi-republican interpretation of the large commercial monarchy of England, Montesquieu offered useful advice on many great questions of institutional design. He followed most of his modern predecessors in deprecating the utility of the ancient Greek *polis* as a model for modern politics: if any ancient model preoccupied him it was no Greek city, but rather Rome. For this reason Thucydides did not loom large in his discussions or in those of the American Founders. They were republicans, certainly, but their preferred republican alternative did not resemble any of the regimes that figure in Thucydides. Instead it embodied that new kind of regime we call liberal democracy. If anything, democracy in the ancient sense figured as their whipping boy, a Petri dish for the political pathologies that they aspired to avoid.

Let us stipulate then, as the lawyers say, that the foundations of modern republican politics owe little to imitation of the examples of Athens, Sparta, Argos, or Syracuse. This does not mean, however, that they owe little to the influence of Thucydides. That influence is deeply embedded in modern politics because of the dependence of all subsequent modern political thought (and *a fortiori* all modern liberal thought) on Thucydides' greatest modern reader, Thomas Hobbes, who published in 1628 at age 40, his complete and unabridged translation. He was also so helpful as to provide his own introduction to the work. While this preceded the publication of his own schematic political writings (the first of which, the *Elements of Law*, he would complete only in 1640) certain features of those writings are already discernible in the Introduction. Yet it is, not surprisingly, only in those later political writings that the full impact of Hobbes's reading of Thucydides becomes apparent. One way of approaching his overall project is as a reconfiguration of crucial elements in Thucydides. This project and hence this reconfiguration would persist through the changes wrought on Hobbes by such thinkers as Locke and Montesquieu in whom liberal democracy becomes fully recognizable. We could thus describe Thucydides as encoded in our political DNA. [5]

That there is a distinctly modern politics, and that it arose out of many particular circumstances unforeseeable by Thucydides, is undeniable. The resulting combinations have been vastly different from anything he knew. This does not preclude, of course, the persistence of the very underlying elements discerned by Thucydides, or family resemblances among modern regimes to those of Athens and Sparta. As already suggested, however, there was a further (and crucial) element in the emergence of theoretical modernity that Thucydides would not have foreseen. This was that his presentation of the world should inspire the philosophical generation of a new politics intended to overcome the shortcomings of all previous political regimes -- clearly including all of those those expounded by him. Yet this is exactly what happened with Hobbes. The great Leviathan, that baggy protoliberal monster, an authoritarian monarchy of a new sort but at the same time at least the stepfather of modern liberal democracy, owes an enormous debt to Thucydides.

To see this we might as well begin with a passage of Hobbes that clearly draws on Thucydides.

> So that in the nature of man we find three principal causes of quarrel: first, competition; secondly, diffidence; thirdly, glory. ...The first maketh men invade for gain; the second, for safety; and the third, for reputation. (*Leviathan,* Chapter 16, paras 6-7)

As so often noted, Hobbes has lifted his three principal natural causes of quarrel from Thucydides; more precisely, from some of Thucydides' characters, the Athenian spokesmen at the First Lacedaemonian Conference in Sparta. Compelled to speak before the Spartans and their allies in extenuation of the Athenian Empire, they offer among other things the following.

---

[5] On the relationship between Hobbes and Thucydides see now Ioannis D. Evrigenis, *Images of Anarchy: The Rhetoric and Science in Hobbes's State of Nature (*New York: Cambridge University Press, 2014), 15-43; Kinch Hoekstra, "Hobbes's Thucydides," in A.P. Martinich and Hoekstra, ed. *Oxford Handbook of Hobbes* (Oxford: Oxford University Press, 2016), 547-574; Timothy W. Burns, "Hobbes and Dionysius of Halicarnassus on Thucydides, Rhetoric, and Political life," *Polis* 31 (2014), 387-424. All these treatments are compelling in illuminating different aspects of Hobbes's debt to Thucydides. They unite in questioning the conventional distinction between the supposedly "humanist" early Hobbes of the Thucydides translation and the later one of the political treatises.

> [From the outset] we were compelled to advance our empire to its present state, [swayed] first of all by fear, although later by honor too and lastly also by profit…." (1.75)[6]

Later in the speech they restate their position as follows:

> So we have done nothing to be wondered at, or off the beaten track for human beings, in accepting an empire that was offered us and in not relinquishing it, overcome by the greatest things, honor and fear and profit. (1.76)

Clearly the Hobbes of Chapter 13 follows these Athenians. Decisive for understanding the fundamental human political situation are the passions of fear, honor, and interest, on which human beings cannot but act and which must lead to conflict among them. Hobbes dubs this conflict a war of all against all, which he further describes as the state of nature because it follows inevitably from men's natural subjection to these passions.

True, there are significant differences of both substance and intention between Hobbes's statement of these three compulsions and that of Thucydides' Athenians. What Thucydides' Athenian envoys allege only of cities, Hobbes applies first and foremost to individuals. Hobbes will, admittedly, go on to declare that the state of nature also describes the situation that prevails among sovereigns or as we would say among state actors, but the focus of his argument will remain the individual. More subtle is that while the Athenians present honor as no less compulsory for human beings than fear or interest—in the second of their enumerations they actually list honor first among the three compulsions—Hobbes's argument will stand or fall on the premise that honor can be repressed or redefined to render it innocuous. Whereas according to the Athenians honor impels to empire, the liberal tradition will redefine it as implying only independence from others, not rule over them. Honor is ambiguously promoted and reduced to (universal human) dignity.[7] It is Hobbes's peculiar form of individualism—this portrayal of human beings in the State of Nature as free and independent but also highly volatile and dangerous—which would ground not only his peculiar moralism but subsequent liberal versions of it including that of the American founders.

---

[6] Translations from Thucydides are my own.

[7] This expresses what Devin Stauffer describes in his contribution to this volume as the greater optimism of Hobbes and the liberal tradition.

By applying to individuals what Thucydides' Athenians apply only to cities, Hobbes is able to introduce another revolutionary premise that would inform the liberal democratic tradition: the equality of all human beings. This is (as it must be, given Hobbes's 'moral realism') an equality of power from which political equality necessarily follows. All being both mortal and endowed with an equal capacity of inflicting mortal harm on others, each brings equal cards to the political table. If the goal of political life were the common good, then this argument would not be good, for claims to rule would depend, as in Plato and Aristotle, on men's naturally unequal capacities to contribute to the good specified. Hobbes, however, debunks all notions of a common good—indeed of a substantive good of any sort, the good being merely the semblance of the pleasant and so radically relative to persons, times, and circumstances (*Leviathan,* Chapter 6, paras. 7-8). Insofar as the good is real it is inconsiderable. Insofar as it is considerable it is not real, but an illusion of our vanity.

Hobbes thus attempts a fundamental reorientation of human life, away from that pursuit of imaginary goods with which, following Machiavelli, he taxes the ancients, and toward the avoidance of only too real evils. For all practical purposes the political good is redefined as security against these evils. It is this that the Hobbesian sovereign supplies at our behest (for we are to conceive him as entirely our creation, our agent and therefore our representative). While thus presenting civil peace as the goal of political life, Hobbes already defines this peace expansively as including comfort and prosperity (*Leviathan,* ch.30, para. 1). At the same time, he makes it clear that we are not to understand it as a means to a virtue that transcends it or to any higher human purpose. We are 95% of the way to liberal democracy.

The final 5% mattered of course. Hobbes's promotion of absolutism, so incongruous to us today, provoked lively expostulations from the likes of Spinoza, Locke, and Montesquieu. All seized the opportunity of stressing what really was a significant difference between them and the much-reviled Hobbes, while at the same time distracting attention from their considerable agreements with him. They agreed among themselves in identifying the basic contradiction in Hobbes's thought. On the one hand, he claimed that no condition was so ill as to find ourselves at the discretion of other human beings whose power was equal to or greater than our own. On the other, his proposed remedy, the great Leviathan, would place each of us at the discretion of one or an assembly of such beings whose power was vastly greater than our own. Hobbes regarded this dilemma as insoluble: to curb the sovereign's power to oppress was to curb his power to protect. These later thinkers strove to create institutions that would succeed in squaring this Hobbesian circle. Thus did their thought undergird liberal contrivances familiar to us, including the American constitutions both state and federal.

Hobbes's Thucydidean Synthesis

Thus far I have suggested that Hobbes's conception of the political problem owed something to Thucydides. It remains to argue that his and subsequent liberal solutions to it can be understood as implying a synthesis of Thucydidean elements. For this we must begin by recalling the two peak political alternatives as Thucydides presents them: the Athenian manner and the Spartan one. It is these two regimes that are the great antagonists of his work. For all the remarkable individuals whom we encounter in reading Thucydides, his focus is on the virtues and corresponding vices of these two outstanding political alternatives.

Athens emerges from the pages of Thucydides as the regime of daring and innovation, of democracy, yes, but also of empire. As a naval power her glance embraces the whole of the Mediterranean: her most dangerous but also most illustrative son, Alcibiades, will dream of an empire stretching from Asia Minor to the Pillars of Hercules (6.15.2, 6.90.2-3). Her quasi-universalism on the level of politics supports a greater openness to the whole in thought: as she would rule, so also she thinks, where no city has gone before. At least among her more thoughtful and educated citizens, not ancestral piety but a probing rationalism defines their outlook on the world, and through its articulation in forums of public deliberation, shapes the outlook of ordinary Athenians as well. Athens aspires to the highest virtue, collectively and as individuals; but Pericles, the greatest teacher of this virtue, does his utmost to justify it through reason. Some of the citizens, most notably Diodotus, rise to a perspective above that of the city, achieving through their reason a theoretical transcendence of it. Others, most notably again Alcibiades, radicalize the Periclean vision but thereby bring the city into question. Ultimately her laudable attempt to come to terms with her imperialism will subvert her domestic politics: the double standard of rule abroad and equal citizenship at home proves impossible to sustain. If Athens aims higher than Sparta, she falls lower: it is because she falls prey to the cancer of civil strife at home that she will lose the war to Sparta which avoids such strife (2.65.8-13).

Sparta, by contrast, is the conservative power that aims not to add to what it has but merely to retain it in the face of the challenge posed by the rising power of Athens. She is a city not of outstanding individuals or of the rational individualism that supports them but of deep traditionalism. She deviates from her customs only with the greatest reluctance, which is in tension with rationalism as usually understood. And indeed she persists in her old ways longer than any reason will warrant (8.96). Yet there is a certain reason to this very stubbornness, as the Spartans hold that their long record of success supports it; these usages have been tested by time and through circumstances of perpetual adversity (1.84). There is, moreover, an overall guiding concern of the Spartans, never explicitly stated by any of their spokesmen but inferred and declared by Thucydides himself: meeting the perpetual threat to the existence of their regime and themselves posed by their horde of helots (4.80).

Not the pursuit of any resplendent good but the avoidance of an overwhelming evil thus guides Spartan policy, and enables us to make sense of a regime the grounds of which would otherwise remain obscure. If Sparta is an outlier, it is because her straits are so narrow as to leave her no leeway—hence the *agōgē*, that strict civic and military education that instills iron discipline (1.84). For their counterpart to that virtue that the Athenians (according to Pericles) practice spontaneously (2.39), the Spartans rely on rigorous habituation.

As Thucydides presents these regimes, each is capable of much that the other is not, including a distinctive nobility. Yet each is also marred by grave vices that are the obverse of its virtues. The excellence of the Spartans as a group is inseparable from their mediocrity as individuals,[8] while that of the best Athenians as individuals entails their unreliability as citizens. Sparta's superior resistance to evils is inseparable from her negative orientation and so her indifference to lofty aspirations. Athens's openness to these is inseparable from her greater vulnerability to faction in domestic affairs and to overreaching in foreign ones. Athenian imperialism, for all its problems, displays a certain noble candor and magnanimity, while Sparta's focus on her own safety, however salutary, drives her to extremes of hypocrisy as she enforces what is expedient for her as obligatory on others (3.68). You can't have eve-

[8] As nature abhors subjection to convention, there are exceptions to the rule of the mediocrity of Spartan citizens, including the spectacular one of Brasidas, the focus of Michael J. Palmer's paper delivered at the 2016 A. V. Elliott Conference at Mercer University.

rything. No regime could combine the loftiness, rationalism, and individualism of Athens with the enduring solidity of Sparta.

Yet Hobbes, that profound reader of Thucydides, aimed at just such a synthesis of incompatibles. And because he set the agenda for the liberal project, liberal democracy remains the heir of this attempt. Hobbes aspired to bring Athenian daring (and the rationalism and individualism that were its highest expressions) to the support of Spartan diffidence and wariness. He harnessed the power of reason to puncture all higher human pretensions (including, above all, the ambition to rule), the better to establish that the only sensible orientation is a negative one.

How does Hobbes accomplish his intended synthesis? By seeking to universalize that drag on irrational exuberance that Thucydides had identified as the anchor of the Spartan regime. He recasts the merely local but very real threat that the helots had posed to the Spartans as the threat that every human being poses to every other. His most vivid portrayal of this threat is of course his account of the state of nature. That account has two parts, of which the most celebrated is his depiction of an imagined condition in which men live with no common authority over them. It includes the most famous sentence in the work.

> In such condition, there is no place for industry, because the fruit thereof is uncertain, and consequently, no culture of the earth, no navigation, nor use of the commodities that may be imported by sea, no commodious building, no moving or removing such things as require much force, no knowledge of the face of the earth, no account of time, no arts, no letters, no society, and which is worst of all, continual danger and fear of violent death, and the life of man solitary, nasty, brutish, and short. (Chapter 13, para. 9)

As the negation of all human goods, the state of nature or *summum malum* replaces the *summum bonum* as the supreme or authoritative (Aristotelian *kyrios*) guide to human activity, with the great advantage that while human beings cannot agree on the latter, they should be able to agree on the former. They must recognize, moreover that the quest for the *summum bonum* is not only useless but harmful from the point of view of avoiding evil, since its practical effect is only to aggravate the strife that continues to permeate society, as attested above all by the religious wars of Hobbes's day.

Yet Hobbes's depiction of a primal anarchy, as powerful as it is, is only half his story. He describes it as his inference from the human passions as he has expounded them in earlier chapters of the volume (6-12). Lest some remain unpersuaded by it, he follows it with an argument "from experience," i.e. from our experience of life *within* civil society, better, from our own behavior within society.

> Let him therefore consider with himself – when taking a journey, he arms himself, and seeks to go well accompanied; when going to sleep, he locks his doors; when even in his house, he locks his chests; and this when he knows there to be laws, and public officers, armed, to revenge all injuries shall be done him – what opinion he has of his fellow subjects, when he rides armed; of his fellow citizens, when he locks his doors; and of his children and servants, when he locks his chests? Does he not there as much accuse mankind by his actions, as I do by my words? (Chapter 13, para. 10).

In this decisive respect every society resembles Sparta beleaguered by her Helots. Danger is everywhere and everywhere imperfectly suppressed, for it is a function not, like the threat posed by the Helots, of particular political circumstances, but of human nature itself. Hobbes seeks to drive this fact home to us so that we may revise our politics accordingly. Like the Spartans we are to spend our lives hearing footsteps and arranging our affairs so as to outpace them.

Another way of putting it is that Hobbes's presentation of the state of nature is parallel not just to Thucydides' presentation of the Spartan regime, preoccupied with the threat of the Helots, but to his presentation of *stasis* (3.80-83), an equally grave threat besetting every human regime as such. True, in many of Thucydides' cities such *stasis* is endemic and far more open than that between the Spartans and the Helots, with an endless struggle for the upper hand punctuated by bloody reprisals and banishments. Sparta had avoided such *stasis* among its own citizens for hundreds of years prior to Thucydides and continued to do so during the present conflict which so disastrously intensified it in so many other cities, including Athens itself. We may therefore understand Hobbes's focus on it as the sole and definitive political problem as further attesting the "Spartan" basis of his nascent liberalism.

But then why ascribe to Hobbes (as I have done) not the promotion of a quasi-Spartan orientation but a synthesis of the Spartan way with the Athenian one? We can see that Hobbes synthesizes Sparta and Athens because, far from eschewing the rationalism and individualism that are the hallmarks of Thucydides' Athens, he promotes them vigorously. He develops, however, not their hopeful or ebullient side, but their skeptical or inhibiting one. In this he resembles above all Diodotus, the character in the work whose understanding appears to be closest to that of Thucydides himself (cf.

3.39 with 4.108. 2). Like Diodotus, Hobbes grants, as we have seen, the truth of the Athenian thesis, but like him again, he construes it not as a justification of the ambition to rule but as a critique of it. He follows Diodotus in approaching the daring typical of Thucydides' Athenians not to eulogize it *à la* Pericles but to deplore it. Indeed Diodotus even anticipates Hobbes by reinterpreting the Athenian thesis as a general theory of human irrationality and its fatal perils. Hobbes's theory thus surpasses Spartan practice, with its focus on the particular peril facing Sparta, by reformulating it on the plane of Athenian generality, thus at the same time internalizing the danger as the combustibility of our natures. Not the helots or any other particular foe, domestic or foreign, but we ourselves, human beings qua human beings, constitute in our frailness and ferocity the greatest of threats both to others and to ourselves. It is the overriding purpose of all government to avert this threat, to keep the genie clamped firmly in the bottle. We can't repeat too often that not self-fulfillment but self-repression is the principal goal of liberalism (especially during the early modern period). Such positive formulations of the liberal project as "life, liberty, and the pursuit of happiness" merely seek to put a happier face on the liberal coin than the dour image of Hobbes.

A more thorough account of the liberal democratic tradition would describe in greater detail how it has both inherited and modified Hobbes's negative or "Spartan" orientation supported by "Athenian" rationalism. Insofar as the focus of incipient liberalism remained on avoiding those evils averted by the Spartans but courted by the Athenians (notably faction and a vacillation between ochlocracy and tyranny), it continued to reflect Hobbes's distinctive reconfiguration of Thucydides. The "Athenian" appeal to rationalism and individualism to support a "Spartan" politics of aversion has proved the hallmark of successful liberal regimes.[9] It is usually where modern

[9] On the negative orientation characteristic of modern thought generally and of liberalism specifically, see Leo Strauss, *National Right and History, 7th ed.* (Chicago: University of Chicago Press, 1971), 165-251; Judith N. Shklar, "The liberalism of fear," in Shklar, *Political Thought and Political Thinkers,* ed. Stanley Hoffman (Chicago: University of Chicago Press, 1998), 3-20; Jacob T. Levy, *The Multiculturalism of Fear* (New York: Oxford University Press, 2000) and most recently Ioannis D. Evrigenis, *Fear of Enemies and Collective Action* (New York: Cambridge University Press, 2008). On Shklar's treatment of Montaigne, one of the thinkers of greatest importance to her, see Alan Levine, "Cruelty, humanity, and the liberalism of fear: Judith Shklar's Montaigne," *Montaigne Studies* 20.1-2 (2008), 157-170.

regimes have aimed much higher, at the creation of a higher human type—in this resembling the Athenians as celebrated (and incited) by Pericles—that they have repeatedly come to grief. I have in mind, of course, both fascism and communism.

Also worth mentioning, however, is the attempt of Locke and his successors (like Adam Smith) to repurpose Athenian dynamism by depoliticizing it through channeling it into the economic, religious and scientific realms as endless but peaceful competition. We can even say that they follow Hobbes by seeking to depoliticize politics itself, which becomes merely one career among others, enlisting motives that fall far short of an Alcibiadean ambition to rule. Rule must be suppressed so that the evils of subjection may be avoided. Employing a distinction foreign to Thucydides, we might say of liberal democracy that it aspires to be Spartan in its politics but Athenian in its economics and "culture." This rift has not been free of tensions.

There is one further point that must be made or conceded of liberal democracy and the theoretical framework supporting it that concerns its peculiar nobility. As Timothy Burns has persuasively argued,[10] Hobbes's brilliant but tendentious reading of Thucydides implies a misreading or critique of him above all on the subjects of piety and nobility and their roles in political life. Burns contends that all post-Hobbesian (i.e. modern liberal) politics presupposes this critique.

I agree with Burns. Yet it seems to me that this is only part of the story. Already in Hobbes we find the germ of a new notion of nobility distinctive to modern liberalism without which it would not be what it is. Whatever Hobbes's deepest thoughts, his rhetoric is that of a moralist, and in every moralism there lurks some notion of the noble. In the case of Hobbes's moralism, it is above all the nobility of candor toward both oneself and others, which requires forgoing spurious claims of fundamental superiority to them. Few would question that Kant's morality of equal dignity aspired to nobility, but paradoxically the seeds of that dignity had first sprouted in Hobbes's debunking moralism.

Generally, we may say of liberal democracy that it cultivates notions of honor or dignity peculiar to itself. Yet these were not simply absent from democracy as Thucydides depicts it. The Athenians, as eulogized by Pericles, practice a version of equal treatment among themselves, granting each the dignity of leading his private life as he chooses (2.37). The Athenians

[10] See above, note 4.

even recognize the equal dignity of their subject allies, and imply that equal treatment is the appropriate standard for Athens as their hegemon to meet in her dealings with them (1.76-77).

Lastly, there were reasons why Pericles' Funeral Oration seemed a beacon during the heyday of liberal self-confidence in the fifties and early sixties. Liberals saw it as articulating the high side of the democracy to which they aspired, and to which the emergence of mass higher education so powerfully attested. Consider the great books movement spearheaded by Stringfellow Barr, Robert Maynard Hutchins, and Mortimer Adler. It promoted the benefits of liberal education for all. This echoed the Periclean vision of democracy as aristocracy for all, of a society that would nurture the higher capacities of every citizen. Reinterpreted as peaceful rather than warlike, the virtues of the democratic citizen would draw on the best of every earlier epoch as preserved in a liberal education. Liberals were confident that a liberal education in the old sense would support liberalism in their sense: that the reading of Sophocles and Shakespeare could be relied upon to foster voters for Adlai Stevenson or John F. Kennedy. While this vision eventually foundered on the rocks of the sixties, it had inspired many youth including the present author. One doesn't understand liberal democracy if one thinks of it as Hobbesian only.

So much for the buried Thucydidean basis of modern liberal democracy. What might Thucydides himself have made of it all? Would he have approved of this strange new assemblage of pieces familiar to him? Obviously this question is highly speculative. He was no particular friend of democracy as such, although neither was he a partisan of its perennial rival, oligarchy. He is equally concerned to debunk the so often bloody pretensions of both (3.81-83).[11] Yet the democracy that he criticized was vastly different from liberal democracy. What infused it instead, however, was something with which liberal democrats have become only too familiar, namely populism.

Thucydides presents populism as a possibility coeval with democracy. Indeed he suggests that populism will be the rule for democracy, its avoidance the rare exception. Of the regimes of most concern to him, Sparta, Corinth, Thebes, and several others were largely free of populism, but only because they were equally free of democracy. It is not surprising that Hobbes should have presented aversion to demagogy (tendentiously reinterpreted as

[11] This expresses what Devin Stauffer describes in his contribution to this volume as the greater optimism of Hobbes and the liberal tradition.

affirmation of monarchy) as the most obvious lesson to be learned from Thucydides.

Thucydides does offer one great example of a nonpopulistic democracy: that of Athens under Pericles. We might say of it, however, that it is the exception that proves the rule. Pericles excelled in many things, but above all in maintaining the people's confidence. His hold on the people was so secure that he did not have to pander, and as for his opponents, what they said hardly mattered. Thucydides conveys this by reproducing the speeches of Pericles but not those of any of his opponents. Only after Pericles' death does Thucydides begin to present speeches at Athens in opposing pairs.

After Pericles, the primary question of Athenian democratic politics remained one of trust, but no politician any longer succeeded at monopolizing it. Instead each was reduced to stopping at nothing to foment such distrust of his opponent as to deny him a hearing. Consider the Mytilenian Debate (3.36-49), the greatest of all of Thucydides' pairs of opposing speeches. It pits the bloody minded demagogue Cleon against the seemingly high minded Diodotus. Cleon appeals to the vindictiveness of the Athenians in arguing that all the defeated Mytilenians should be slaughtered, Diodotus appeals to their better selves in contending that most of the Mytilenians should be spared. Cleon slanders Diodotus and anyone else who would defend the Mytilenians, while Diodotus protests such slander as depriving the city of advice by intimidating citizens from speaking.

At first glance, Cleon practices populism at its lowest while the high minded Diodotus explicitly eschews it. In fact, however, this move of Diodotus is just one aspect of what proves a highly devious strategy. He turns out to agree with Cleon that what matters in democracy is not whether your arguments are good but whether the people trust you, and that there need be little connection between the two. Thucydides shows us that even in the ancient city, where the people met frequently and their leaders debated before them in person, democratic politics was image politics. On reflection even Diodotus emerges not as less unwilling to play this game than Cleon, but as cleverer at it. He too garners trust for himself primarily by sowing mistrust of his opponent.[12]

[12] For a detailed analysis of this passage see Clifford Orwin, "Democracy and Distrust: a Lesson from Thucydides," *The American Scholar*, Summer 1984, 313-325; reprinted in Lowell S. Gustafson, ed., *Thucydides' Theory of International Relations. A Lasting Possession* (Baton Rouge: Louisiana State University Press, 2000), 98-114.

Thucydides is sympathetic to populism inasmuch as he agrees with peoples that leaders (or as we say today, elites) are rarely to be trusted. He distrusts populism in that he doubts that peoples are skilled at distinguishing the trustworthy sowers of mistrust like Diodotus from the untrustworthy ones like Cleon. While Diodotus may have prevailed on the occasion of the Mytilenian Debate, the people would continue to support Cleon right up to his death in the battle of Amphipolis. They did so not because they admired him—indeed Thucydides records their having both mocked him as a politician (4.28) and complained of his incompetence as a general (5.7)—but because he was theirs. There was no contradiction here. Had they admired Cleon more, they would have been less confident he was in their pocket. His baseness, which was apparent to all, reassured them he would remain their creature.

After Cleon's death the struggles among those who sought to succeed him in the people's favor continued to poison Athenian politics. In Thucydides' view this explained why Athens had lost a very winnable war. In retrospect it was less the wisdom of Pericles' policies (about which Thucydides had his doubts) than his unequaled ability to maintain the people's trust that distinguished him from his successors (2.65.8-13).

Among the regimes at Athens on which Thucydides comments, one is of particular relevance to our theme. It was not simply democratic, and therefore not simply populist. Neither, however, was it simply oligarchic. This was the regime of Athens as it was not under Pericles nor again under Cleon and other demagogic successors, but some 20 years after Pericles' death. By this point the city had suffered many reverses both abroad and at home, including the Sicilian disaster (8.1), and its democratic regime had been subverted and supplanted by an oligarchic conspiracy (8.47-70). In the year 411, however, it finds a brief hiatus from its troubles. Some of the oligarchic leaders, having fallen to quarreling among themselves, conspire with the exiled Alcibiades and democratic elements in the Athenian fleet at Samos to overturn the oligarchy. They do not, however, quite restore the democracy. Instead they propose a regime called the Five Thousand. In so doing they invoke a slogan that had originally served as a pretext for the oligarchic coup of the Four Hundred (8.65-66) and later as a code word for the restoration of democracy (8.92). What the number denoted, however, was the city's contingent of hoplites or heavy infantrymen, membership in which attested to a certain independence of means. [13]

The Five Thousand thus presented itself as a novelty in Athenians politics, a regime promising a middle way between democracy and oligarchy. While not excluding the rich (for they too met the stated property qualification) it conferred predominance in power on what we would call the middle class. It thus anticipated the regime that Aristotle would call polity and praise as the best of the generally practicable regimes. And Thucydides' praise of it similarly anticipates Aristotle's praise of polity.[14]

> Indeed for the first time in my life the Athenians appear to have enjoyed a good regime. For there was a measured blending together of the few and the many, and this it was that began lifting the city out of its troubles.

For Thucydides, as for Aristotle, it is not the vesting of authority in a (politically unavailable) class of superior men but the judicious blending of two usual and defective ones that represents the best we can do. Or to speak more precisely, the best that the Athenians had done in Thucydides' lifetime. We will return in a moment to the significance of these qualifications.)

By presenting the regime of the Five Thousand as the best Athens had known in his lifetime, Thucydides implies its superiority to Periclean rule-by-the-first-citizen (2.65.9). No Pericles arose under it, but it did recall the banished Alcibiades, the conspirators having so promised to secure the support of the people (before whom they had also dangled an imagined subsidy from the Persian King). The reconciliation between Alcibiades and the people would not last, and the regime that had achieved it would prove more ephemeral still. Indeed the very restoration of Alcibiades made the Five Thousand untenable, for he always insisted on being first, while the oligarchic aspects of the regime were incompatible with any one man being first. The regime delayed, but could not prevent, the city's drift back into *stasis* and eventual defeat. Yet for as long as it lasted the Five Thousand did offer a respite from chaos, and contributed to the Athenians' notable victory at Cynossema, which restored their fortunes in the war (8.104-106).

In any case Thucydides' praise of even this regime is qualified. Whatever its virtues, it was still only the best regime that the Athenians enjoyed in

---

[13] Hoplites were required to supply their own somewhat expensive set of armor. The wealthy were required to serve as cavalry, providing their own horses, and to defray the costs of the city's triremes, on which the poorer citizens served as rowers.

[14] Cf. Bernard Dobski's contribution to this volume.

his lifetime. While impressive praise as far as it goes, it leaves open the possibility that they might have (but had not) enjoyed a still better regime in his day, that they might enjoy a better one in the future, and that they might have done so in the past. Perhaps most important of all, the restriction of his praise of this regime to its Athenian context leaves it compatible with the judgment that the Spartan regime was superior to this as to all other Athenian regimes. Here the narrative frame is significant, for Thucydides has only just stressed the inferiority of the Spartans to the Athenians at making war, which inferiority had prevented them from seizing the opportunity to defeat Athens presented by its domestic disarray (8.96). This emphatic rebuke of the Spartans notwithstanding, the reader knows only too well by now that persistent civil discord would cost Athens the war, while Sparta would prevail under the same regime that had sustained her freedom for 400 years (1.6.4-5, 1.18.1, 1.84.1).

Given this crucial consideration of context, could we argue that the Athenians' very adoption of the expedient of the Five Thousand implied the superiority of the Spartan regime? What were they attempting but a greatly simplified version of that mixed regime—neither democratic nor oligarchic, but judiciously blending elements of both—that Sparta had enjoyed for centuries?

Lastly we must consider the brevity of this uniquely measured Athenian regime. The Five Thousand emerged because certain Athenians, from motivations themselves primarily factional, had resolved to suppress faction in the city to the extent required to persist in the war. They envisioned the regime as short lived, a stalking horse for the restoration of the deposed democracy (as so indeed it proved). Unlike the Spartan regime, which had withstood numerous Helot revolts and the machinations of the treacherous King Pausanias, the regime of the Five Thousand was designed to fail. As such its moderation was largely spurious.

Yet whatever the limits of the Five Thousand and of Thucydides' praise of it, that praise remains significant for our purposes. By pointing to the measured blending of the few and the many as emphatically superior to the exclusive rule of either, Thucydides already endorses a fundamental plank of liberal democracy. That is democracy, as in the rule of the many, and liberal as in the protection of the rights of the few, including of course the wealthy few. It is moreover strongly implicit in Thucydides' presentation that the accomplishments of the Five Thousand were less resplendent for what they achieved than what they avoided, namely an imbalance that by favoring either the few or the many would have supported its predictable oppression of its rival (cf. 3.83). Given that Thucydides discusses only actual regimes, and that this one proved so ephemeral, his emphatic praise of it is only the more remarkable. It evidently implies an even stronger endorsement of any regime that could establish a salutary blend of the few and the many and sustain it through decades or centuries. Insofar as liberal democracy and liberal democracy alone among modern regimes has achieved this, there is strong *prima facie* reason to suppose that it alone among them would have commanded Thucydides' admiration.

Thucydides long enjoyed a reputation as the most "realist" of classical writers. There was some truth to that judgment, although we must beware of confusing Thucydides' realism with more recent and dogmatic versions. We must also recognize that such other ancient writers as Herodotus, Plato, Xenophon, and Aristotle were more "realistic" than they have generally received credit for being. Yet it is probably true that Thucydides comes closer than any of the others to the tenet of Hobbes and all thoughtful advocates of liberalism that a policy of avoiding the worst should trump aspirations to realize the best. Precisely insofar as post-Kantian liberals so often slight this prescription, it is useful to invoke Thucydides' preliberal (and therefore transliberal) perspective. Liberal democracy is the worst regime except all the others that have been tried: such is Thucydides' hypothetical verdict no less than Churchill's actual one. That of which Athenian practice in his lifetime offered no more than the brief whiff of a suggestion, liberal democracy has institutionalized with unprecedented success.

The regime of the Five Thousand, however it anticipated liberal democracy in blending the powers of the few and the many, lacked the complex web of political, social, and economic institutions that modern liberalism has brought to that task. It also lacked, of course, the overarching worldview that has supported it. While ancient democrats and oligarchs might stumble upon arrangements such as those of 411 that incidentally anticipated liberal ones, stumble was as much as they could do. Nor can we know whether many—or any—Athenians shared the view of the by then exiled Thucydides that the regime of the 5 Five Thousand 000 was the best Athens had known in his lifetime. Liberalism required the Enlightenment, which is to say modernity (and before it Christianity): it required the thought of Hobbes and Hobbes's successors.

All this should go without saying, so we claim no credit for saying it. Nor can we describe our own putatively Thucydidean perspective on liberal democracy as itself a liberal democratic one. On the contrary it is alien to liberal democracy and not just because the latter has both required and fostered so much unknown to the former. Additionally, the Hobbesian synthesis of Athenian daring and rationality with Spartan sobriety is, from Thucydides' point of view, an impossibility. Rather, any stable politics depends on the traditional piety that Sparta had cultivated but the status of which at Athens was shaky. And any true ascent to self-knowledge such as was possible for the best of the Athenians required that one think through the issues of justice and piety rather than resort to a Hobbesian strategy of cutting these off at the knees. The problem was that any such thinking through (as accomplished by Thucydides himself and such of his characters as Diodotus and Hermocrates) was simultaneously the shining crown of politics, the one thing most needful for it, and potentially lethal to it. All these aspects are on display in Thucydides' work.

A challenge of ours that would not have surprised Thucydides is populism,[15] which, as previously mentioned, he understood as the rule for democracy rather than the exception. Because the liberalism of our regimes qualifies their democracy, so it has qualified their populism. Populism, in its turn, mistrusts liberalism, for it bridles at its restraints on the execution of the will of the people. The liberal democracies of North America and Northern Europe enjoyed remarkable success in suppressing populism for five decades following the Second World War. Is that success now coming to an end? In France and Southern Europe the presence of large Communist parties perpetually excluded from government both absorbed populist resentment and served to quarantine it. The decline of those parties has freed populism for capture by such movements as the *Front National* and *Cinque Stelle*. As for Eastern and Central Europe, there are only too many reasons for the alarming rise of a populism that while not fascistic comes too close for comfort.[16]

---

[15] On the upsurge of populism and a strategy for addressing it see William A. Galston, *Antipluralism: The Populist Threat to Liberal Democracy* (New Haven: Yale University Press, 2018).

[16] See Ivan Krastev, "Eastern Europe's illiberal revolution: the long road to democratic decline, " *Foreign Affairs* 97:3 (May-June 2018). On the recent upsurge of populism especially in Northern Europe see Rogers Brubaker, "Between nationalism and civilizationism: the European populist movement in comparative perspective," *Ethnic and Racial Studies* 40:8 (2017), 1191-1226. Brubaker argues that in positioning themselves against Islamic immigration Northern European populists have been driven to espouse "progressive" liberal secularist values which might not otherwise have rolled so smoothly from their tongues.

Thucydides presents two great non-populistic democracies: Periclean Athens and "Hermocratean" Syracuse. (The latter proves relatively ephemeral, as Hermocrates never achieves the degree of predominance that Pericles had enjoyed at Athens and by the end of the book has been exiled.) Common to both is that they feature great endeavors, which as such enlist the ambitions not only of ordinary citizens but of the most gifted. The cooperation of these two groups cannot remain on the level of the Hobbesian concern with mere life. Pericles (like Themistocles before him) demanded an Athens that was worthy of him and sought to foster one. (In his own more boisterous way, Alcibiades would follow them.) So too Hermocrates aspired to a new resplendent–and imperial--Syracuse. As with the United States and Canada, which found greatness thrust upon them by the World Wars, noble deeds must be sustained by ambitions that lead beyond the everyday. Even if, as with the League of Nations or the United Nations, or earlier the American Civil War as conceived by Lincoln, the new world for which sacrifice was required was merely one where liberal goods would be available to all, and the glory of the struggle lay in contributing to the emergence of that world.

Liberal democracy is weaker today, and the ambitions of its citizens smaller, for want of any plausible such vision. Our societies abound in the zealous pursuit of all manner of worthy goals, political, social, humanitarian, scientific and artistic. Hope still beats strongly in liberal democratic hearts. Yet the project as a whole is floundering, without clear purpose. A worthy Thucydidean goal would be its reanimation. Gaia won't suffice for this task, nor will reducing income inequality. As for "inclusiveness," it raises the questions of "inclusion in what?" and "at what cost to liberty?"

Politically speaking, Thucydides saw it as a problem with Athens that it aspired to the loftiest political goals, ampler and riskier than those of Sparta. Humanly speaking he did not. The best Athenians, compelled by the contradictions of this perspective to think through the political problem in its fullness, achieved heights of self-awareness unknown in Sparta. Insofar as the liberal project of grafting "Sparta" onto "Athens" has required the truncation of both, it has discouraged comprehensive reflection about itself. As our liberal worldview was born of Hobbesian abstraction, so it has remained abstract. Thucydides' greatest gift to us might well be his exemplary concreteness.

POLITICAL SCIENCE AND POLITICAL MEDICINE: THUCYDIDES, THE *FEDERALIST PAPERS*, AND THE NEW WORLD DISORDER

Karl Walling, United States Naval War College[1]

This essay constructs a dialogue on political science and political medicine. The interlocutors are Thucydides, the authors of the *Federalist Papers*, and contemporary scholars of international relations and American foreign policy. Thucydides pioneered a form of political science that was also a sort of political medicine, though human nature made him skeptical there would ever be a cure for the maladies he discovered. In contrast, the authors of the *Federalist Papers*, conservative as they might seem to us today, had a decidedly Whiggish faith that political science (political learning) could not only diagnose and explain the causes of political illness, but also offer prescriptions to extend the life of the patient, republican government. Many of the pathologies Thucydides diagnosed originally play a significant role early in the *Federalist Papers* in Part 1 (essays 2–14) on the "importance of Union to [American] political safety and happiness" (F 15: 89). The rest of *The Federalist* merits analysis as an effort to refine the diagnoses of these pathologies, understand the causes, sharpen the prognoses, and elaborate on the prescriptions of the Federal Convention in establishing the Constitution of 1787. So the bulk of this essay will focus on Part 1 of *The Federalist* in a manner that anticipates the remainder of the work. Finally, the generation of Americans who helped found the liberal world order after the Second World War was even more optimistic about the medicinal potential of their political science, which might unite the strength of many for the common defense and other objectives while enabling each of the parts to remain self-governing. For reasons both Thucydides and the authors of the *Federalist* could well understand, the liberal world order that Americans especially took the lead in building after 1945 is now under severe pressure, indeed attack, from both internal and external adversaries. The jury is still out on whether history is cyclical or progressive, but preventing the diseases Thucydides first identified

1. Nothing in this essay reflects the views of the United States government, the Department of Defense, the United States Navy, or the United States Naval War College. The views expressed are the author's alone.

and the authors of the *Federalist Papers* sought to treat from undermining the liberal world order may be the most important political project of our time.

******

Thucydides was a pathologist, a student of disease, especially political disease. This is most obvious in his account of the plague in Athens, which may have killed as much as a third of its population in the first years of the Peloponnesian War. Setting aside speculation as to its causes, Thucydides sought "simply to set down its nature, and explain the symptoms, by which it may be recognized by the student, if it should ever break out again" (2.48).[2] Since he himself caught and survived the disease, he had no trouble explaining its physical symptoms. It began like a severe cold or flu with sneezing, coughing, diarrhea, and nausea, but quickly led to a pox and severe inflammation of the bowels, eyes, and body parts in an "awful spectacle of men dying like sheep," usually within a week of catching the disease. No remedy was found, so the people of Athens had to let the disease run its course through the city, with those who nursed the sick being most likely to catch it themselves. No less important to Thucydides were the political symptoms of the disease. People "became utterly careless of everything, whether sacred or profane." With some throwing corpses onto the funeral pyres of others just to get them off their hands, "[a]ll the burial rites before in use were thoroughly upset," and the social order collapsed. "Fear of gods or law of man there was none to restrain them," and unbridled hedonism, "lawless extravagance," was common. With the good suffering as much as the bad, it appeared the gods were indifferent to human behavior. Since the authorities could offer no greater terror than the plague itself, it seemed only fair to enjoy life a little when all appeared sentenced to a certain and agonizing death. In times like these, it was only natural for some to swing to the opposite extreme of religious fanaticism. Many resorted to oracles, whose old sayings could be interpreted to mean a plague would result from the war, so the chief political leader in Athens, Pericles, was blamed not merely for the coming of the war, but like Oedipus of old in Thebes, for the plague too (2.48-52).

2. Unless otherwise noted, all citations from Thucydides will be from the *Landmark Thucydides*, ed. Robert B. Strassler, trans. Richard Crawley (New York: Free Press, 1996) and listed as 1.5, 1.88, etc., where the first number refers to the book and the second to the paragraph.

The plague was not the only occasion in which Thucydides investigated political pathology. The revolution or civil war in Corcyra between its oligarchic and democratic factions appeared to him to be a microcosm of revolution in general, especially since it spread like a plague from Corcyra to just about every Greek city, except Sparta but including, tragically, Athens itself. In this case, Thucydides combined diagnosis (what the malady was) with prognosis (where the malady went, and would perhaps inevitably go) if it followed its natural course. "[A]s usually happens at such times, there was no length to which violence did not go; sons were killed by their fathers, and suppliants dragged from the altar or slain upon it, while some were even walled up in the temple of Dionysus and died there." Not least among the extremes to which the belligerents were willing to go was calling in outside powers, like Corinth, Sparta, and Athens, to hurt their enemies and gain an advantage, however temporary, for their party. "The sufferings which revolution entailed upon the cities were many and terrible, such as have occurred and always will occur as long as the nature of mankind remains the same: though in severer or milder form, and varying in their symptoms, according to the variety of particular cases" (3.81-82).

In the case of Corcyra, this meant the extermination of the oligarchic faction with the tacit support of the Athenians. Although the Corcyraeans allied with Athens to preserve their independence immediately prior to the war, their internal dissensions weakened Corcyra so much that it became a satellite of Athens until the end. The only beneficiaries of these suicidal civil wars appeared to be outside powers. If the Peloponnesian War itself is understood as a quarrel between the oligarchic and democratic cities of ancient Greece, the handwriting appears to have been on the wall for them. Through their internal dissensions, the Greeks would become so weak that only outside powers, like Persia or Macedon, would benefit. If so, the Peloponnesian War was at least as mad as the civil war in Corcyra. It was at least as much pathology as fathers killing sons in Corcyra and the lawless extravagance during the plague in Athens.

Thucydides was equivocal regarding the causes of the pathological behavior in Corcyra and other Greek cities to which the civil war spread. Initially, the pathology appears to have arisen from necessity. "In peace and prosperity states and individuals have better sentiments, because they do not find themselves suddenly confronted with imperious necessities; but war takes away the easy supply of daily wants," security especially, "and so proves a rough master that brings most men's characters to a level with their fortunes" (3.82). From this point of view, what we call principles, like justice and freedom, are luxuries. However reluctantly, we dispense with them whenever they conflict with the perceived necessities of war. As civil war spread from city to city, the cunning of the belligerents and the atrocities of their reprisals, what we might call terrorism today, were consistently carried to ever "greater excess of refinement," especially in how belligerents justified their conduct to others and themselves. "Words had to change their ordinary meaning and to take that which was now given them." As it turns out, the principles were not luxuries at all. The factions did not dispense with them; instead, the nature of this pathology was that the factions transformed their meaning to gain advantage over their adversaries. Reckless audacity came to be considered the courage of a loyal supporter; caution was treated as cowardice; moderation was viewed as unmanly; the ability to see all sides of a question appeared to be indecision. The advocate of extreme measures was always trustworthy, his opponent was a man to be suspected, and the moderates were among the first to die. In due course, necessity drove this descent into Hades far less than something else: vengeance, which was "held of more account than self-preservation." With vengeance as their highest priority, the belligerents could not limit themselves to what "justice or the good of the state demanded," but had to invoke "fair phrases," like political equality, a moderate aristocracy, democracy, the good of the people, and the like to arrive at their "guilty ends." Passion, especially the "lust for power arising from greed and ambition" turned the moral world upside down and made it impossible to calculate the best interest of individuals and their communities by turning words into weapons. Thucydides called this pathology, *alogos,* against reason. In the course of the war, the citizens of ancient Greece lost their minds (3.82).

That was the great tragedy of the Peloponnesian War (and perhaps of all wars): it was not just any words, but fundamental principles, of justice especially, that began to change their meaning to suit the objectives of the belligerents, so that the very standards of civilization became instruments to destroy it. Among many other things, Thucydides' account of the Peloponnesian War is the story of the pathological breakdown of moral, political, and strategic judgment among all the belligerents, Athens especially, because of the "weaponization" of principles as the belligerents understood them at the time. The disease reveals itself most dramatically in the speeches, which anticipate "Newspeak" and "doublethink" in George Orwell's *1984* by 2500 years. This is most evident in Book III, with the trial of the Plataeans in the

Spartan kangaroo court and in the great debate over the revolt in Mytilene during which Cleon, "the most violent man in Athens," argued that mass murder is justice (3.36).[3] But the breakdown of moral, political, and strategic reason is also anticipated in the three speeches of Pericles in Book I and Book II. Pericles sold the coming war between the Athenians, with the largest navy in Greece, and the Peloponnesians as a defensive struggle to preserve the Athenian empire, though a strong case can be made that the alliance Athens made under his leadership with Corcyra, the third strongest naval power in Greece, was a diplomatic effort on his part to gain the fruits of war through diplomatic means. It was an effort to alter the strategic balance of power in all of Greece in Athens' favor (and gain a staging area to move on Sicily) without having to fight a war. Knowing full well that the alliance was technically within the letter of the Thirty Year Peace with Sparta, he had good reason to think that if the dispute with the Peloponnesians were settled, as required by the treaty, through arbitration, that Athens would probably win. He thus "took advantage of the arbitration clause to disguise an Athenian bid for domination."[4] And when the chips were down for Athens, both after the initial combat losses, which occasioned his famous Funeral Oration, and during the plague in his final speech to the Athenians, he dangled the possibility of turning the entire Mediterranean world into an Athenian lake. He got the Athenians drunk on power and fame to sustain their morale, but this all went to their heads, not merely after their great victory at Pylos, when they kept "grasping for more," but also at Melos and when Alcibiades egged them on to go to Sicily (1.140-144; 2.41; 2.62; 3.36-40; 3.53-68; 4.41).

In the Melian Dialogue, Thucydides left it to his readers to diagnose hubris in Athens; the Sicilian expedition was an example of his prognosis for that disease. The causes lay in human nature, hope and ambition especially. But Thucydides offered no prescriptions. Why he offered none is not clear.

---

3. For superb discussions of these speeches, and the tension between justice and necessity within them especially, see Leo Strauss, *The City and Man* (Chicago: University Press, 1964), 139-242; and Clifford Orwin, *The Humanity of Thucydides* (Princeton: University Press, 1994).

4. Lawrence A. Trittle, *A New History of the Peloponnesian War* (West Sussex, UK: Wiley-Blackwell, 2010), 39. See also Karl Walling, "Thucydides on Policy, Strategy, and War Termination," *United States Naval War College Review*, Autumn, 2013, Vol 66. No. 4.47-85. For the more conventional view, that Athens under Pericles had become a "sated power" with no desire for further expansion, see Donald Kagan, *Outbreak of the Peloponnesian War* (Ithaca, NY: Cornell University Press, 1969).

Perhaps he followed his contemporary, Hippocrates, and believed that above all a physician should do no harm. Perhaps too he feared that offering prescriptions would be to engage in the sort of "romance" he disdained in Homer and Herodotus. His work was meant to be "useful for those inquirers who desire an exact knowledge of the past [diagnosis] as an aid in understanding the future [prognosis], which in the course of human things must resemble if it does not reflect it." (1.22) His work was a possession for all time because it would help us understand how and why things fall apart; Thucydides said nothing about how to put them back together again. Given our nature as human beings, history is and must be cyclical. We will do the same stupid, crazy things again and again.

****

The authors of *The Federalist Papers* (Alexander Hamilton, James Madison, and John Jay) were also political pathologists, students of political disease. In *Federalist* 10, for example, the most famous essay of this work calling on Americans to ratify the Constitution of 1787, James Madison addressed the problem of faction, saying that the "instability, injustice, and confusion, introduced into the public councils" by faction "have, in truth, been the *mortal diseases* under which popular governments have *everywhere perished*" (F 10: 56-57, italics added).[5] In *Federalist* 9, Alexander Hamilton had set the stage for Madison, claiming it "was impossible to read the histories of the petty republics of Greece and Italy, without feeling sensations of horror and disgust at the distractions with which they were continually agitated, and at the rapid succession of revolutions, by which they were kept perpetually vibrating between the extremes of anarchy and tyranny" (F 9: 50). Hamilton was perhaps the most pessimistic of the authors of *The Federalist*, especially about the odds of making republican government succeed in America, but he, like his co-authors, still had a "Whiggish," cautiously progressive tone resting on the premise that history supplies empirical evidence upon which modern political physicians might reduce politics to a science. With that science, they might not merely diagnose pathology, or explain its causes, and offer prognoses, but also, and most importantly, offer prescrip-

5. Alexander Hamilton, James Madison, and John Jay, *The Federalist*, ed. Jacob E. Cooke (Middletown, Connecticut: Wesleyan University Press, 1961). All references to *The Federalist* will be from the Cooke edition and cited as F 10: 52; F11; 66, etc., where the first number indicates the essay and the second the page.

tions for curing political diseases, whether by treating the causes, or the effects, or both. As Hamilton said, "the science of politics . . . , like most sciences, has received great improvement. The efficacy of various principles is now well understood, which were either not known at all, or imperfectly known to the ancients." Representation, the separation of powers, an independent judiciary, and much else in the improved science of politics were either "wholly new discoveries" or had made their "principal progress toward perfection in modern times" (F 9: 51). So there was a chance, maybe even a probability, that the United States, if it remained united, might avoid the fatal diseases from which all other republics had perished previously. The "honor of the human race," its capacity for self-government, was about to be tested in a noble experiment to determine whether "societies of men are really capable or not, of establishing [and maintaining] good government from reflection and choice, or whether they are forever destined to depend for their political constitutions, on accident and force" (F 1: 3; F 11: 72).

This was an early, and admirable, version of what we today call "American exceptionalism." No, Hamilton was not claiming God's grace favored the American people. Nor was he saying that their exceptional character exempted them from all the vices of humankind. He knew that Americans, like all peoples at all times, were "yet remote from the happy empire of perfect wisdom and perfect virtue" (F 6: 35). Instead, he was saying something almost as audacious: with the new science of politics Americans might actually escape the cycle of history that had led previous republics to self-destruct—they might prove Thucydides and other ancient students of free government *wrong* by showing that the same pathologies that had destroyed Greek and Roman liberty were not "destined" to destroy free government in the United States (F 1: 3). And Madison agreed. Paradoxically, by building on the experience of the ages, America would succeed by defying, heroically, the accepted wisdom of the past in developing an extended federal republic. "Is it not the glory of the people of America, that while they have paid a decent regard to the opinions of former times and former nations, they have not suffered a blind veneration for antiquity, for custom, or for names, to over-rule the suggestions of their own good sense, the knowledge of their own situation, and the lessons of their own experience?" To this "manly spirit," willing to defy the wisdom of the ages and go where no republic had gone before, "posterity will be indebted for the possession and the world for the example" of a successful extended republic "in favor of private rights and the public happiness" (F 14: 88).

From the standpoint of Whiggish "medical political science," the first step in overcoming the pathologies that had destroyed the free governments of the past, whether democratic or republican, was to diagnose the pathologies that might kill the patient, political liberty, in the United States. Fortunately for Americans, in Publius, they had not one but three doctors, each focusing on a different but related pathology. The first diagnosis came from an almost forgotten author of *The Federalist*, John Jay, the most experienced American diplomat of the time, and a lawyer as well.

Jay's diagnosis might be seen as a commentary on something the Athenians said at Melos, that, as the world goes, justice (*dike*) is "taken into consideration only between equals in power;" otherwise, "the strong do what they can and the weak suffer what they must" (5: 89). One might see the Athenian claim as the quintessential expression of "classical realism" in international politics, but a case could be made that Thucydides believed it was a symptom of their disease. It describes the behavior of ancient Greeks perfectly. It is also a good rule of thumb for the behavior of states at most times and most places. And it is particularly descriptive when states go to war. Nonetheless, the strong do not always have to do what they can; self-restraint is possible at some times and some places, and Thucydides is highly critical of the Athenians for their lack of self-restraint after their victory at Pylos (4.41). In other words, the normal in international politics is not necessarily normative. And the weak do not necessarily have to suffer. They might become strong too, thus forcing other strong powers to pay more attention to justice, at least with regard to the weak (because they are no longer weak).

Unlike contemporary political scientists, who generally eschew "normative questions," both Thucydides and Jay put the relation between justice and power, or more broadly, necessity, at the center of their political science. Most speeches in Thucydides' account play on the tension between justice and power, and the dependence of justice on power. Melos is exhibit A in the plight of powerless justice; Athens at Melos exhibit B in the hubris of justiceless power. Or as Pascal put the problem famously, "Justice without power is impotent; force without justice is tyrannical. Justice without force is impossible, because there are always evil-doers; force without justice stands accused. It is therefore necessary to put together justice and force; and for that to ensure that what is just is strong, or that what is strong is just."[6] In

6. Blaise Pascal, cited in Pierre Oster, *Dictionaries de citations francaise* (Paris: Dictionnaires Le Robert, 1993) 153.

introducing the theme of power and justice, Jay did something highly unusual, however. Just as Pericles had warned the Athenians that they might be their own worst enemies during the Peloponnesian War (1.144), Jay warned that American injustice, rooted in American disunity, might at times pose the greatest danger to American national security and liberty. That warning continues throughout *The Federalist* and is essential to its new and improved science of political medicine.

The first big theme of *The Federalist* is safety, a term allowing many different meanings, so Jay focused on the "preservation of peace and tranquility" both against "*foreign arms and influence*" (italics in the original) and against dangers arising from "domestic causes" (F 3: 14). As Thucydides had explained in discussing the efforts of Athens and Sparta to manipulate democratic and oligarchic factions in their rival alliances, the Delian and the Peloponnesian Leagues, the foreign and the domestic are often intimately connected and ultimately inseparable. But Jay again limited his focus to causes, "whether *real* or *pretended*, which [might] *provoke* or *invite*" war by foreign powers against the United States (italics in original). The issue was whether a united America was more or less likely to give other powers "*just* causes of war" against itself (italics in original). As befits a diplomat, Jay eschewed all forms of national self-righteousness. He was deeply concerned that, because of their own injustice, Americans would provoke wars themselves, either from "violations of treaties" or from "direct violence" against others (F 3: 14). Justice, understood as diplomats are wont to do, as abiding by treaty commitments and restraining Americans from attacking other peoples, was essential to safety, especially while the United States was a new and weak power in the world.

Doctor Jay combined two medical approaches, prognosis and prescription. His prognosis was that a weak Union, or worse, an America divided into multiple competing states or coalitions of states, was highly likely to give other countries just causes to go to war against Americans. After all, in 1787, the so far United States of America already had treaties with six European powers, all but one of which (Prussia) were maritime powers able to annoy Americans through direct assault or, far more likely, by attacking American shipping at sea. Jay did not say so, but he knew the United States was already in direct violation of the Treaty of Paris ending the American War of Independence. The treaty required the United States not to disenfranchise Loyalists who had sided with Great Britain and to return all property confiscated from them during the war (F 3: 16). None of the states had much enthusiasm for magnanimity at the end of the war, however, so few complied; indeed in New York City and Charleston, South Carolina, where Loyalists had sheltered under British protection during the war, it is estimated that at least 100,000 refugees, fearing retribution from Patriot vigilantes, voted with their feet and emigrated to Canada and the West Indies.[7] These breaches of the treaty, giving the British a more than just cause to renew the war against the Americans at a time and place of their own choosing, sustain Jay's most important point. If the interpretation and execution of treaties with foreign powers were left to the states, as they were under the Articles of Confederation, there inevitably would be thirteen distinct self-serving interpretations of American treaty obligations and thirteen distinct ways of executing them—or not executing them at all. Whatever Americans in the states thought of such legal anarchy, foreign powers would see it as bad faith, and have more than just a pretext to go to war against an errant state, or the entire Union, when necessity required or opportunity allowed (F 3: 15).

And then there were the Native Americans, the Melians of North America. Said Doctor Jay, "[n]ot a single Indian war has yet been produced by the aggressions of the present federal government, feeble as it is; but there are several instances of Indian hostilities having been provoked by the improper conduct of individual states, who either unwilling or unable to restrain or punish individual offenses, have given occasion to the slaughter of many innocent inhabitants" (F 3: 16-17). In this respect, Jay anticipated Madison's famous argument in *Federalist* 10: the smaller the republic, the greater the likelihood that a factious majority, oblivious to the common good of the Union or bent on violating the rights of a vulnerable minority, might put the welfare of all Americans at risk by provoking a war that was unlikely to remain limited. After all, the natural tendency of the weak is to seek allies. Britain lay to the North in Canada; Spain to the south and West in Louisiana. Neither wished to see the Union expand. Each would find natural allies among the Indians. So a small war in a small place might well escalate to a much bigger war, just as the war between Corcyra and Epidamnus escalated into the great war among larger powers, Corinth, Athens, Sparta, and their allies. And both Britain and Spain had sound strategic reasons to wish to

7. Frederick Marks, *Independence on Trial* (Wilmington, Delaware: Scholarly Resources, 1984), pp. 3-51; and Alexander Hamilton, "Second Letter of Phocion," in *Selected Writings and Speeches of Alexander Hamilton*, ed. Morton J. Frisch (Washington, D.C.: American Enterprise Institute, 1979), pp. 66-88.

divide Americans, to attempt to pit factions within states and states within the Union, against each other, just as Athens and Sparta did before and during the Peloponnesian War.

Doctor Jay's prescription was a well-constructed Union. While recognizing that all states err, that virtue and wisdom are always in short supply, and that the United States, like all other countries, would wage unjust wars from time to time, his question was whether a well-constructed Union was less likely to provoke wars through its own injustice. Anticipating later essays in *The Federalist* on the judiciary, the future Chief Justice of the Supreme Court noted that if the Constitution and the laws, including treaties made pursuant to it, were the Supreme Law of the Land, and the Supreme Court had jurisdiction to interpret them, then such treaties would be interpreted in a uniform manner and often be executed uniformly, thus diminishing the likelihood that legal anarchy would lead other powers to assume bad faith on the part of the United States (F 3: 15; F 80: 534-541). Not only his prognosis, but also his prescription anticipated Madison's argument in *Federalist* 10. Whereas almost any mediocrity might get elected to a state legislature, the states were more likely to send their best to serve in Congress, especially if it were granted authority to govern effectively. And representatives from the majority of states in a Union as diverse as America's, being less moved by the interests, passions, or prejudices of individual states, or factions within them, would be less likely to "swerve from good faith and justice" (F 3: 15-16). One or two states, or factions within them, might be tempted to violate treaties or commit direct acts of violence against other countries or their subjects, but an efficient national government could create a different situation. As Hamilton would later make clear, it could hold individual violators to account in court, thus deterring violations (F 15: 72). No less important, Doctor Jay prognosticated that when such violations occurred, a presumably more "temperate and cool" national government could consider all means, including apologies and compensation, to "extricate themselves from the difficulties which threaten them" (F 3: 17). It is always humiliating to back down, but Jay noted that it is sometimes necessary, with a strong national government better able to do so than an errant state (perhaps by blaming particular states or factions within them for starting the mess in the first place and claiming that it would not allow the injustice of some to threaten the safety of all).

While taking justice seriously, Doctor Jay was also a man of the world. He concluded *Federalist* 3, his first of three essays on justice, safety, and power, by noting, almost as an aside, that "it is well known that acknowledgments, explanations, and compensations," the standard stuff of quiet diplomacy, "are often accepted from a strong united nation, which would be rejected as unsatisfactory if offered by a state or confederacy of little consideration of power." His last paragraph told the story of the state of Genoa in 1685, which had offended Louis XIV in France, the most populous country in Europe at the time. Tiny Genoa endeavored to "appease him." The Sun King demanded that they send their *doge*, or chief executive, accompanied by four of their senators, to France, to "ask his pardon. And receive his terms. They were obliged to submit to it for the sake of peace." Doctor Jay asked "Would he [Louis XIV] on any occasion either have demanded or have received the like humiliation from Spain, or Britain, or any other *powerful* nation?" (F 3:17-18 italics in original).

The moral of Jay's discussion of power and justice is thus far more worldly than first appears to be the case. Justice, however valuable it may be for its own sake, is no less desirable for the sake of safety. Safety requires all powers, especially weak ones, like the United States in 1787, to refrain from injustice, so far as states are able to do so. But all states give offense, whether real or pretended, to some states sometimes. Whether their cause is just or unjust, not merely their pride, but also their safety is most likely to be protected when they are powerful. In 1787, the United States was neither Genoa nor Melos, but it could have become like them, especially if the Union collapsed or lacked authority to prevent its collapse. The United States, through its disunion, could have become a powerless pawn in the games of kings. If it did not wish that to happen, it had to become strong. That was Doctor Jay's prescription: not mere union, but an energetic Union able to draw on all the resources of the country to deter attack whenever possible and to defend against it whenever necessary (F 3: 18; see also Hamilton, F 23: 146-151). Jay came close to saying that an energetic Union was the best cure for Americans' strategic problems because, when Americans did wrong in foreign affairs, as all nations will, such a Union would enable them to get away with their injustice. While minimizing the likelihood of Americans committing injustices toward foreign powers, a strong Union would also increase the probability that, whether they had committed an injustice or an injustice was contemplated against them, other powers would find it in their interest to settle such conflicts with the Americans peacefully.

The Federalist may well be the greatest work ever written on the problems (diagnoses) free governments face in international politics and the sorts of strategies (prescriptions) necessary for them to succeed. As it turns out, the only American Founder mentioned in *Makers of Modern Strategy*, the semi-classic history of strategy from Machiavelli to the nuclear age, is Alexander Hamilton, who was a nineteen-year-old captain of New York Artillery at the beginning of the War of Independence, and because of his youthful precocity, had served on General George Washington's staff throughout most of the war. In *Makers of Modern Strategy*, Edward Meade Earle, who had also edited *The Federalist*, compared Adam Smith, Hamilton, and Friedrich List on the economic foundations of strategy, which is fine as far as it goes, but it just does not go very far.[8] The state papers of the first Secretary of the Treasury are part of a larger whole, a vision for national greatness. Hamilton sought to avoid the fundamental problems (tyranny at the head or anarchy in the parts of federations) that had characterized the Athenian-led Delian League (and most other federations too) while capitalizing on the advantages of Union for an ambitious maritime strategy that anticipated the Monroe Doctrine, and through it, almost all other grand strategic thinking by Americans.

Although Hamilton first proposed writing *The Federalist*, enlisted his coauthors, wrote almost two-thirds of the essays, including all the essays on the executive and the judiciary, and introduced the eighty-five essay project in *Federalist* 1, he disappeared from *The Federalist* while Doctor Jay discussed the dangers of war and foreign powers, justice, and power. This does not mean he disagreed with Jay, whose political prestige far surpassed Hamilton's at the time; instead, there was a division of labor. Despite their *nom de plume* of Publius, the identities of the authors of the *Federalist* were common knowledge among elites. Jay capitalized on his diplomatic prestige to gain a favorable reception for the project and focus on the dangers of war with foreign powers; Hamilton, who was less established in his political career, focused on the dangers of war among the states (which foreign powers might aid and abet). So Hamilton reentered from stage right with a discussion of civil war, which he considered almost inevitable without a much stronger Union. In *Federalist* 6, Doctor Hamilton criticized the opponents of the Constitution for misunderstanding the causes of war. Because their diagno-

8. Edward Meade Earle, "Adam Smith, Alexander Hamilton, and Friedrich List: The Economic Foundations of Military Power," *Makers of Modern Strategy: from Machiavelli to the Nuclear Age*, ed. Peter Paret (New Jersey: Princeton UP, 1986), 217-261.

sis was inaccurate, so too was their prescription: a mainly commercial Union much weaker than the one envisioned in the Constitution.[9]

What causes war? Thucydides supplied a wealth of answers, perhaps almost too many answers: the stated causes or accusations (mainly about injustice) among the belligerents (Corcyra, Corinth, Sparta, Athens, Megara) before the Peloponnesian War began; the immediate causes in the spiral of escalation in which small powers (Corcyra) drew in big powers to help them and big powers (Sparta and Corinth) used small powers (Potidaea) as proxies against their rivals; and the "truest cause," Sparta's long-standing fear of the growing power of Athens, with the crises immediately prior to the war serving as catalysts to ignite this combustible kindling (1.23-1.88). Perhaps most fundamental was human nature. Sparta feared the growth of the Athenian empire, but what produced the empire and led it to expand, seemingly, to the Spartans and their allies, without restraint? As the Athenians explained in Sparta before the war began, three passions in human nature: fear, the ambition for honor, and the desire for gain, compelled them to establish, maintain, and expand their empire, "for it has always been the law that the weaker should be subject to the stronger"(1.75-76). Whether such passions are necessarily as compulsive as the Athenians claimed might well be disputed, but in many ways Hamilton sounds a great deal like Thucydides' Athenians regarding the causes of war.

According to Doctor Hamilton, some causes have a "general and almost constant operation upon collective bodies of society." These are rooted in human nature: "the love of power, or the desire of pre-eminence and dominion...the jealousy of power, or the desire of equality and safety"—exactly what Thucydides meant when he spoke of the "truest cause" of the Peloponnesian War (F 6: 28-29; Thucydides 1.23; 1.88). But, Hamilton observed, there are other causes which have a "more circumscribed, though an equally operative influence, within their spheres." In particular, he meant competitions within particular international systems, like wars among commercial nations, especially in the age of mercantilist empires. And finally, there are causes rooted entirely in "private passions; in the attachments, enmities, interests, hopes, and fears, of leading individuals." (F 6: 29) Hamilton employed an early version of what some political scientists call the "levels of analysis" approach to thinking about the origins of war. Sometimes the ori-

9. For the Anti-Federalists preference for a weaker, mainly commercial Union, see Herbert J. Storing, *What the Anti-Federalists Were For: Political Thought of the Opponents of the Constitution* (Chicago: University Press, 1981) 15-37.

gins are rooted in human nature; sometimes in the international system and the kind of political-economic order it produces; sometimes in the character and judgments of statesmen and their states. True wisdom is to know which causes are most important at any moment in time.[10]

Intriguingly, after setting up this level of analysis approach, Hamilton immediately mentioned Pericles as an example of a statesman led by "private passions" to go to war, thus sacrificing the interests of Athens to his own good, and causing the Peloponnesian War, "which terminated in the ruin of the Athenian commonwealth" (F 6: 29). Hamilton's source, however, was not Thucydides, but Plutarch, and a fairly twisted version of Plutarch as well.[11] Sadly, we do not know for certain whether Hamilton or any of the authors of *The Federalist* ever read Thucydides, though it seems unlikely that they had not. The point of this comparison of Thucydides and "Publius" is not to demonstrate any direct debt by the latter to the former (though the author suspects Thomas Hobbes, Thucydides' greatest translator, and the many followers of Hobbes's own new science of politics, are important suspects in that detective story).[12] Instead, the object is to compare how they practiced political medicine. If war is a disease, rather than the natural state of mankind, or even if it is the natural state, there is little daylight between Hamilton and Thucydides regarding its causes, no matter what level of analysis one employs.

But why was Hamilton discussing the causes of war? Among the opponents of the Constitution, he claimed, were "certain visionary or designing men" who were politico-medical quacks advocating "the paradox of perpetual peace between the states, though dismembered and alienated from each other.... The genius of republics, say they, is pacific; the spirit of commerce has a tendency to soften the manners of men, and to extinguish those inflammable humors which so often have kindled into wars." It therefore followed that "[c]ommercial republics, like ours, will never be disposed to waste themselves in ruinous contentions with each other" (F 6: 31).

10. J. David Singer, "The Levels of Analysis Problem in International Relations," *World Politics* 14, no. 1 (October 1961) 77-92.

11. Plutarch, "Pericles," *Lives of the Noble Grecians and Romans*, trans. John Dryden (New York: Modern Library, 1992) 201-234.

12. See Thomas Hobbes, *Thucydides: The Peloponnesian War: the Complete Hobbes Translation* (Chicago: University Press, 1989); Paul Rahe, *Republics, Ancient and Modern*, Volume II: *New Modes and Orders in Early Modern Thought* (Chapel Hill: University of North Carolina Press, 1994).

Doctor Hamilton smelled snake oil. If peace is the interest of all states, why do so many states go to war? Don't "the momentary passions, and immediate interests, have a more active and imperious control over human conduct, than general or remote considerations of policy, utility, or justice?" Is it really true that republics are less prone to war, especially with each other, than other types of regimes? And has commerce done anything more than "change the objects" of war? Much of the new science of politics was based on experience. Hamilton insisted that it would be unwise to gamble the future of the American republics on a new, largely untested hypothesis, when there was much historical and recent evidence to disprove it. In antiquity, Sparta, Athens, Rome, and Carthage were all republics, and two, Athens and Carthage, were of the "commercial kind." But in fact, they were as often engaged in wars, offensive and defensive, both against each other and against non-republican regimes, as their neighboring monarchies. Indeed, "Sparta was little better than an armed camp; and Rome was never sated of conquest." He did not say so, but the reader could infer it in the same way as Machiavelli: republican Rome was an almost perfect engine of war; far from being pacific, it seems that the most famous and enduring republic of antiquity was also the most warlike.[13] Its primary rival was the commercial republic, Carthage, which was almost as militaristic, but proved, ultimately, a tad less suited for war than Rome. In more modern times, Venice and Holland, both commercial republics (with an oligarchic cast) had furious contests to dominate the Mediterranean Sea and the Atlantic Ocean. And in Britain (which Montesquieu termed a republic disguised as a monarchy) commerce had been for ages the "dominant pursuit" of the country, with at least one hundred years of violent contests with monarchical, but nonetheless mercantilist France.[14] And then the former artillery captain fired his last barrage: there have been "almost as many popular as royal wars. The cries of the nation and the importunities of their representatives have, upon various occasions, dragged their monarchs into war, or continued them in it, contrary to their inclinations, and sometimes contrary to the real interests of the state" (F 6: 33).

13. Niccolo Machiavelli, *Discourses on Livy*, trans. Harvey C. Mansfield and Nathan Tarcov (Chicago: University Press, 1996) 20-22.

14. Baron de Montesquieu, *Spirit of the Laws*, ed. Anne Cohler, Basia Miller, and Harold Stone (Cambridge: University Press, 1997) 5: 19.

One might thus conclude that Hamilton was an arch-realist debunking what some call "democratic peace theory" today.[15] Certainly his critique overlaps with the views of ancient and modern realists, but in fairness to his opponents and to the truth, he was overstating his case. Hamilton never denied that increasing commercial ties among the states might strengthen the Union; indeed, his later funding and assumption plans as Secretary of the Treasury were meant to strengthen such ties as much as possible, and thereby preserve peace within the Union, his fondest hope.[16] His target was neither the commercial republican theory of his age nor the democratic peace theory of our own, but the assumption that there could be durable peace, even among the thirteen American republics, rather than a Thucydidean "treacherous armistice" (5: 26) without a more energetic Union. Such a Union had to vest Congress with the authority to regulate commerce, not to mention to tax, borrow, and spend without relying on the states. Without the authority to regulate commerce, which the Articles of Confederation lacked, his prognosis was that different states would erect trade barriers, leading to trade wars with each other and foreign powers. Trade wars would then lead to shooting wars, as they have from time immemorial, and invite foreign intervention (F 7: 39-41; F 23: 146-147). Thus, one might say Hamilton was calling for establishing the political conditions that would give commercial republican peace a chance to succeed within the American Union. Only if Congress had the authority to regulate commerce would there be free trade among the states and therefore no trade wars among them. But government without revenue is a sophism as too is law without a sanction to enforce it. His prescription, a well-constructed Union, demanded the authority, through the medium of the federal courts, to apply laws, including those regulating commerce, directly to individuals, who, unlike the states, would be unable to resist federal authority directly (F 16: 102; F 23: 146-147). Otherwise, as was true in the Delian League, if federal authority had to be applied directly against the states, one of two things was likely to happen: the federal government would have to wage war against rebellious

15. For the tip of this enormous iceberg of academic debate, see Immanuel Kant, "Perpetual Peace," *Perpetual Peace and Other Essays on Politics, History, and Morals*, ed. Ted Humphrey (Indianapolis: Hackett, 1983) 107-46; Michael Doyle, "Kant, Liberal Legacies and Foreign Affairs," *Philosophy and Public Affairs* 12 (1983): 205-235 and 323-353; and Christopher Layne, "Kant or Cant: The Myth of Democratic Peace," *International Security* 19, no. 2 (1994): 5-49.

16. Stanley Elkins and Eric McKitrick, *Age of Federalism* (Oxford: University Press, 1993) 77-132.

states, which Hamilton termed the "violent death" of the Union as it descended into civil war or transformed itself into an empire, or it would wither away into impotence, which he considered its most "natural death" (F 16: 101). To avoid tyranny at the head or anarchy in the parts of the Union, the Constitution and all laws made according to it had to be the Supreme Law of the Land.

Hamilton's prognosis was emphatic: the death of the Union would mean war, and all the evils that come with it. Not least of these evils in Hamilton's prognosis would be the rise of standing armies, the militarization of the different American republics, and the consequent loss of public and private liberty. Those, like the Anti-Federalists, who feared standing armies as a deadly disease within a republic needed to understand the causes that gave rise to them. In a country, or thirteen different countries, or three or four different confederations of countries, "where the perpetual menacings of danger oblige the government to be always prepared to repel it, her armies must be numerous enough for instant defense." This enhances the status of the soldier and degrades that of the civilian. "The military state becomes elevated above the civil.... By degrees, the people are brought to consider the soldiery not only as their protectors, but as their superiors" (F 8: 48).

Hamilton is often accused of wishing to model the United States on Great Britain, that is, of wishing to monarchize the republic. There is a little truth in that, in so far as he doubted the republic could succeed without an energetic national government headed by an energetic executive (F 70-73: 471-499), but this is usually a red herring designed to distract from his argument by questioning his loyalty to republican government. In truth, his larger strategic vision did not merely build on the British model; it also republicanized it in a manner offering hope of transforming the relation between justice and power, so that the United States might exceed not merely the power but also the justice of empires like those of Athens and Great Britain. How did Britain manage to combine power and liberty, freedom and public strength? A necessary part of the answer, one that made other answers possible, was the Union of England, Scotland, and Wales. This turned the United Kingdom into an island, invulnerable to attack by land, and thus with neither a need nor a pretext for a large standing army in time of peace, and usually not even in time of war. Civil authority thus remained superior to the military's and "the citizens, not habituated to look up to the military power for protection...neither love nor fear the soldiery." Instead, they looked at the military in a spirit of "jealous acquiescence in a necessary evil, and stand ready to resist a power which they suppose may be exerted to the prejudice of their rights." (F 8: 47-49) With all due respect to Thomas Jefferson, who feared Hamilton embraced power too much, this was Hamilton's model of a healthy relationship between citizens and the military, one in which citizens were masters rather than slaves. Civic health depended above all on making the "reflection and choice" of citizens (and their political leaders) superior to the "force" of the military, and the best way to ensure that was to make it unnecessary to have large standing armies, that is, to follow the British example of Union. It was the alternative, a weak Union, unable to preserve itself, that would lead to standing armies, and thus to "the same engines of despotism, which have been the scourge of the old world" (F 1: 3; F 8: 46).

In some respects, Doctor Hamilton's prescription for a well-constructed Union is analogous to that of Themistocles and Pericles. The foundation of Athens' strategic success was its long walls, which rendered Athens like an island, invulnerable to attack by land from Sparta and other Greek land powers, and no less important, free to establish a maritime empire (1.93; 1.107). And Athens, which could not feed itself, was immensely vulnerable to attack on its sea lines of communications to the grain producing regions of the Mediterranean: the Caucasus, Egypt, and Sicily. To survive and prosper, it had no choice but to be able to control the sea when and wherever necessary. In like manner, Hamilton understood that if the United States wanted to remain free at home, safe from the militaristic engines of despotism produced by conflict among land powers in continental Europe, Union and the quasi-wall, or moat, provided by the Atlantic Ocean, would be insufficient.

It was not enough to eliminate the dangers of land war among the states; Americans had to be prepared for maritime conflicts too, first because they were a commercial people who depended on imports and exports, and second, because the Atlantic Ocean was not merely a moat. It was also a highway that enabled foreign powers, the British especially, to project land forces to America. From bitter experience in the battle to save New York City in 1776, Hamilton knew that the British had sent the largest maritime expedition in history (ten ships of the line, thirty frigates, and over a hundred troop transports—with almost a thousand supply ships strung out across the Atlantic) to capture the city and crush George Washington's embryonic Continental Army. Hamilton knew that the Army had been routed on Manhattan Island, and that Washington was able to save only three out of ten thousand of his soldiers through an American version of Dunkirk, an evacuation from the city to New Jersey, with Hamilton's artillery battery covering the humiliating retreat (and earning him the respect of George Washington as a result).[17] To avoid such dismal defeats in the future, the United States had to become a maritime power with an ocean-going blue water navy to keep other naval powers at a distance.

He raised the issue implicitly in *Federalist* 8 and explicitly in *Federalist* 11 in the context of discussing the importance of the Union for commercial purposes. The "adventurous spirit" of American commerce had already "excited uneasy sensations" among the maritime powers of Europe (Great Britain, France, Spain, Portugal, and the Netherlands). They were worried that an American merchant marine might supplant their own, which supported not only their trade, but also their navies. And they were fearful that a united America might, in time, be strong enough to take away their colonies. So their natural strategy would be to "foster divisions among us" and do all they could to prevent the growth of an American merchant marine, which would answer the "threefold purpose" of protecting their own merchant shipping, monopolizing the profits of American trade, and "clipping the wings by which we might soar to dangerous greatness" (F 11: 66). Just as fear of the rising power of Athens led Sparta to go to war with Athens, so too might fear of the rising power of America lead one or more European states to go to war with America, what scholars of America and China today justly call the "Thucydides' Trap."[18]

After this diagnosis of the strategic situation (professional strategists today call it a "net assessment"), Doctor Hamilton offered a strategic prescription. A united America might use tariffs to compel the Europeans to bid against each other for access to American markets. No, he was not talking about starting a trade war. And Hamilton's funding scheme as Secretary of the Treasury depended on a steady stream of tariff revenue, especially from America's largest trading partner, Britain, so he would later prove reluctant to use the trade card to play for the highest stakes against Britain

17. Ron Chernow, *Alexander Hamilton* (New York: Penguin, 2004), 76-82; David Hackett Fisher, *Washington's Crossing* (Oxford: University Press, 2004), 81-114.

18. Graham Allison, "The Thucydides Trap: Are the United States and China Headed for War," *Atlantic Monthly*, September 24, 2015; and Graham Alison, *Destined for War: Can China America and China Escape the Thucydides' Trap* (New York, Houghton, Mifflin, and Harcourt, 2017).

especially.[19] Instead, he saw tariffs as a way to compel the Europeans, one by one, but beginning with Britain, to open their markets to American goods in American "bottoms," a term for the cargo hulls of ships at the time. To be sure, Hamilton was a bit too sanguine about the efficacy of tariffs to persuade the Europeans to open their markets to American goods carried in American ships. With the outbreak of the French Revolution and the Napoleonic Wars, the British, during the administrations of Washington, Adams, Jefferson, and Madison, followed Adam Smith's observation that "defense is more important than opulence."[20] They had to protect their navy (and thus their merchant marine as a nursery of seamen) at all costs, even the exclusion of American commerce in American ships, and they had to cut France off from trade with the United States. So Doctor Hamilton's early version of what Jefferson and Madison later called "peaceable coercion" was often a dead letter as the United States found itself caught between Britain and France in a titanic world war in which each side practiced economic warfare against the other and neither was much disposed to make commercial concessions to a distant, undeveloped, and weak country like the United States.

And there is the rub. Tariffs were necessary but not sufficient for Doctor Hamilton's prescription to be efficacious, and in certain contexts, like the world war from 1790 to 1815, they could have pernicious effects, even be a cure worse than the disease. He had in mind a "further resource," a supplemental medication, or maybe even the primary medication, the establishment of a "federal navy." Prognosis applies to health as well as sickness. If Americans remained united under an efficient national government, they would be in the catbird's seat in North America, indeed the entire Western Hemisphere. A well-constructed Union would "put it in our power, at a period not very distant, to create a navy, which, if it could not vie with those of the great maritime powers, would [like Corcyra's navy in the Peloponnesian War] at least be a respectable weight, if thrown into the scale of either of two contending powers." And in geopolitics as in real estate, little matters more than location, location, location! The weight of a small but formidable American navy would be greatest in "operations in the West Indies. A few ships of the line, sent opportunely to the reinforcement of either side, would often be sufficient to decide the fate of a campaign." If one added the utility of supplies, bases, and ports in the United States to this geopolitical algebra the American position would be a "very commanding one" and enhance the

19. Elkins and McKitrick, *Age of Federalism*, 375-450.
20. Adam Smith, *Wealth of Nations* (New York: Random House, 1965), 431.

bargaining leverage of tariffs for commercial agreements. "A price would be set not only upon our friendship, but upon our neutrality. By a steady adherence to the Union, we may hope, ere long, to become the arbiter of Europe in America; and to be able to incline the balance of European competitions in this part of the world, as our interest may dictate." But, Hamilton warned, disease was also possible. Absent these preventive measures, a navy especially, American commerce would be "prey to the wanton intermeddlings of nations at war with each other; who, having nothing to fear from us, would, with little scruple or remorse, supply their wants by depredations on our property," which is exactly what happened in the late 1790s and the early 1800s through the humiliating War of 1812. Almost as if he were thinking of the fate of Melos, Hamilton added that the "rights of neutrality will only be respected, when they are defended by an adequate power. A nation, despicable by its weakness, forfeits even the privilege of being neutral" (F 11: 68-69).

But Hamilton, like Themistocles, the founder of Athens' maritime strategy (1.89-93), always thought on a grand scale. Supposing the Americans did develop a navy able to tip the balance of power in the West Indies, what might happen next? He tried to be discreet: "There are other points of view, in which this subject might be placed, of a striking and animating kind. But they would lead us too far into regions of futurity." And they would almost have to be classified as TOP SECRET, meaning they would involve "topics not proper for newspaper discussion." Discretion, however, was never Hamilton's virtue, so he could not help letting the cat out of the bag. America's "situation invites, and our interests prompt us, to aim at an ascendant in the system of American affairs." One might think he was talking about the original thirteen American colonies, but evidently not. He was talking about the *world* and the kind of new world order, a *novus ordo seclorem*, which might develop over time. The globe, he said, could be divided, geographically as well as politically, into four parts, each having a distinct set of interests. Unhappily for the other three, in the age of European empires, Europe, by arms and by negotiations, by force and by fraud, had extended her dominion over them all. "Africa, Asia, and America, have successfully felt her domination. The superiority she has long maintained, has tempted her to plume herself the mistress of the world, and to consider the rest of mankind as created for her benefit" (F 11: 72).

At this point Hamilton did something, if not unique, then at least rare among grand strategists today. He linked his grand strategy for Union and national independence to something even grander, the "honor of the human race." America had a role in the world, "to teach that assuming brother [Europe] moderation." What would such moderation mean? That the human race was not created for the benefit of Europe, that the first principles of the Declaration of Independence applied to all humanity. "Union will enable us to do it. Disunion will add another victim to his triumphs." So in this peculiar case, the honor (or what we call dignity today) of America and the honor of the human race were linked. As a particular nation founded on universal principles, the United States, "bound together in a strict and indissoluble Union," might erect "one great American system, superior to the control of all transatlantic force or influence, and able to dictate the terms of the connection between the old and the new world!" But what was the Old World? It was a world of empires, in principle no different from the Athenian empire, based on exploiting other regions "by force" and "by fraud." And what was the New World, or rather, what might the New World become? The world that in 1776 rejected this imperial principle of governance in favor of societies governing themselves through on the basis of consent, the "reflection and choice" of the people (F 1: 3; F 11: 72-73).

This is breathtaking. Not only did Hamilton anticipate the Monroe Doctrine of the two hemispheres. Not only did he develop a maritime strategy to make that doctrine practical, over time. But he also transformed the tension between the Old and the New World into the opposition of the Free to a Non-Free world, one acting like Athens in running its empire, the other committed to becoming the anti-Athens, though with the recognition that if it did not wish to be Melos, it had to become very, very strong through Union, commerce, and naval power. The paradox, of course, is that in developing the strength to resist the empires of the Old World, the United States might itself succumb to the imperial temptation. In search of monsters to destroy, the United States might become an imperial monster itself, but that is another story for another place. Obviously, the cure for one disease can help cause another, but one problem at a time: when you are like Melos, the problem is less self-restraint than effective resistance.

Put somewhat differently, the problem with power is that it corrupts, sometimes absolutely, so some discussion of James Madison's contribution in *Federalist* 10 now seems in order. So much has been written about this essay, and its companion piece, *Federalist* 51, that it is not easy to think of anything new, or useful, to add. Thucydides, Doctor Jay, and Doctor Hamilton may come to the rescue, however. All three were acutely aware of the dangers of what Madison called faction, and for the purposes of this essay especially, of partisans at home calling in the aid of foreign powers and of foreign powers attempting to manipulate diverse domestic partisans of allies, adversaries, and neutrals to obtain their objectives. Madison defined faction as "a number of citizens, whether amounting to a majority or minority of the whole, who are united and actuated by some common impulse or passion, or of interest, adverse to the rights of other citizens, or to the permanent and aggregate interests of the community." Doctor Madison may have gone too far in saying that the instability, injustice, and confusion produced by factions have been the "*mortal diseases*" under which popular governments have "*everywhere* perished" (F 10: 56-57, italics added). After all, some, like Melos, are so weak militarily that they get conquered, sometimes easily; but Thucydides would certainly agree that it was faction and factious leaders that led to the defeat of Athens and the overthrow of its democracy in the Peloponnesian War.

At the outbreak of the Peloponnesian War, democratic Athens had been governed for fifteen years by its deeply flawed, but nonetheless most able leader, Pericles, one of those "enlightened statesmen" Madison warned would "not always be at the helm." Indeed, under "Boss Pericles," who won votes to sit on the Athenian Council of Ten Generals by funding massive public works like the Parthenon, or what we today call infrastructure projects, Athens was "nominally a democracy" but becoming in his hands "government by the first citizen." After his death from the plague in the second year of the twenty-seven-year-long Peloponnesian War, his successors were more on an equal level with each other. As each grasped for "supremacy, they wound up committing even the conduct of affairs to the whims of the multitude." This led to a host of strategic blunders, not least of all the Sicilian Expedition, which failed in Thucydides' view primarily because of "private squabbles" among the leaders of different factions "for the leadership of The People, by which they not only paralyzed operations in the field, but also first introduced civil discord," that is, inquisitions, revolution, and counter-revolution "at home." Although the Athenians struggled valiantly, and often effectively, after throwing away half of their army and navy in Sicily, they never recovered fully. All it took was one major defeat of their navy for them to lose control of the sea and become unable to feed themselves. (2.65) With the support of Persia, Sparta built up the kind of navy, and found the right admiral, Lysander, to inflict such a defeat on the Athenians at Aegospotami, which resulted in the starvation of the Athenians and their capitulation to Sparta.[21]

That being the case, it seems proper to think about the relation between faction and foreign policy and strategy, and especially about the danger of foreign powers manipulating, and being manipulated by, domestic factions. After all, such intervention by Corinth, which inserted a fifth column in Corcyra, was the catalyst for the civil war in which the democratic faction exterminated the oligarchic one, but with this great irony. Corcyra, which had attempted an independent, "isolationist" foreign policy prior to the Peloponnesian War, allied with Athens to preserve its independence from Corinth. The democrats needed foreign aid to wipe out the oligarchic faction. The Athenian navy docked in port, thus providing security against foreign attack, while the democrats did their dirty deeds. Although Corcyra began the war with the third largest navy in Greece, one never hears about Corcyra's navy after the conclusion of the revolution. One suspects there was a quid pro quo. The Athenians took it and made Corcyra their satellite. Through the most violent kind of faction imaginable, and through the intervention of both Corinth and Athens, Corcyra lost the cherished independence that led it into war in the first place. This is where the disease of faction, whether from a minority (the oligarchs) or a majority (the people), naturally goes: the destruction not merely of the rights of the parts of a community, but ultimately, if left unchecked, of the community itself, and, when factions call in outside powers to aid them, of the independence of the political community as well (3.70-86; 4.46-48).

Doctor Madison is famous for telling us there are two methods for addressing factions. One can focus on a faction's causes or its effects, the disease or its symptoms. And he is no less famous for saying there are but two methods for treating the causes of faction: "The one, by destroying the liberty which is essential to its existence; the other, by giving to every citizen the same opinions, the same passions, and the same interests." The problem with the first method of addressing the causes is that it is "worse than the disease." For republicans, devoted to both public and private liberty, it has to be ruled out on principle. The problem with the second method is that it is as "impracticable [in a free government], as the first would be unwise." We are all fallible. So long as we are free to exercise our fallible reason, different

21. Plutarch, "Lysander," *Lives*, 584-606; Xenophon, *Landmark Xenophon's Hellenika*, ed. Robert B. Strassler, trans. John Marincola (New York: Pantheon Books, 2009) 2.1.1-2.1.27.

opinions will be formed. And as long as we are proud and vain, we will be stubborn in defending our opinions. And some of us are better at making money than others, while the first duty of government is to supply equal protection to the unequal faculties of humankind, including the faculty of making money. So long as government protects the unequal faculties of making a living, some will be wealthier than others, with the influence of different degrees and kinds of wealth on the sentiments of diverse members of society ensuring a division of society into diverse interests and parties. The "latent causes of faction are thus sown into the nature of man," and they are actuated by free government (F 10: 58).

By process of elimination, we are compelled to investigate the possibility of treating the effects of faction, the symptoms of the disease. The good news is that if a faction is a minority, there is a decent chance that the majority, if well led and organized, can defeat it through the forms of republican government, majority rule especially. So the big problem to be solved, Madison argued, is treating the effects of majority faction. How? Doctor Madison loved to divide issues into two parts: "Either the existence of the same passion or interest in a majority, at the same time, must be prevented; or the majority, having such co-existent passion or interest, must be rendered, by their number and local situation, unable to concert and carry into effect schemes of oppression." Hence, Madison concluded, a pure democracy, somewhat like ancient Athens, "consisting of a small number of citizens, who assemble and administer the government in person, can admit no cure for the mischiefs of faction" (F 10: 61-62). Both the means and the motive of faction would coincide. Perhaps this is another reason why Thucydides offered almost no political prescriptions: Democratic Athens was an incurable case; the seeds of its self-destruction were planted from the founding of the democracy; it was only a matter of time before factions, and the demagogues who led them, destroyed Athens from within.

Although the patient seemed hopeless, Doctor Madison believed he had found the ingredients of a cure for the effects of faction in republican government. This form of government differed from democracies like Athens because it is based on representation. The two great points of difference in a republic, "which help us comprehend both the nature of the *cure* and the efficacy that it must derive from the union" are, first, the delegation of the government to representatives, and second, "the greater number of citizens, and greater sphere of country" over which a republic might extend. It was possible that representation might "refine and enlarge the public views, by passing them through the medium of a chosen body of citizens, whose wisdom may best discern the true interest of their country, and whose patriotism and love of justice, will be least likely to sacrifice it to temporary and partial considerations" (F 10: 62, italics added). In such cases, the republic might get the government it needs to serve both justice and the public good. But there was no guarantee, and that is an important thing to remember about Doctor Madison's political science, as well as that of his colleagues, Doctor Jay and Doctor Hamilton. Politics is not physics. There are few if any firm laws in political science, which is not rocket science, or brain surgery, because it is harder. There are just too many variables to consider, few of which can be controlled; its hypotheses, including its prognoses and prescriptions, are in truth rarely more than probability statements, based for Doctors Madison, Hamilton, and Jay on something intangible but real: human nature. So eschewing all thought of giving us a statistical probability regarding the likely wisdom and virtue of representatives, Madison assumed the worst case: "men of factious tempers, of local prejudices, or of sinister designs, may by intrigue, by corruption, or other means, first obtain the suffrages, and then betray the interests of the people." But Doctor Madison hypothesized that the sheer size of the American republic would supply Americans with a greater probability of a fit choice. There would be more fit candidates to choose from in a large than a small republic. And the more numerous the representatives' constituents, the less likely "unworthy candidates" would be able to practice the "vicious arts" of corrupting the people (by buying votes or supplying liquor for voters for example) (F 10: 63).

Maybe. Just maybe. Doctor Madison had his doubts too, which explains his extraordinarily cautious language. He relied most for controlling the effects of faction on something different: the greater number of citizens and extent of territory made possible in a republic. The smaller the society, the fewer probably will be the distinct parties and interests composing it; so it was likely that there would often be a majority of the same party able, within a small republic, to "concert and execute their plans of oppression." But in a large republic, divide and conquer, the old maxim of the emphatically non-republican Julius Caesar, might offer a solution. "Extend the sphere; and you take in a greater variety of parties and interests; you make it less probable that a majority of the whole will have a common motive to invade the rights of other citizens; or if such a motive exists; it will be more difficult for all those who feel it to discover their own strength and to act in unison with each other" (F 10: 64). Dare one say it? Madison's solution to the problem of majority faction was to use the size and diversity of America to divide its partisans into competing minority factions, which would usually lack the means, and the motive, to violate the rights of the minority or sacrifice the public good to their passions and interests.

So Doctor Madison concluded, the "extent and proper structure of the government" supplied a "*republican remedy for the diseases most incident to republican government*" (F 10: 65, italics added). And in his companion piece, *Federalist* 51, where he repeated much of the argument of *Federalist* 10, he expanded his argument to discuss not merely the extent, but also the form of the federal government, with checks built in through the structure of the national government, the competition between the national government and the states, and the diverse interests and opinions of society as a whole. If the great danger was majority faction, especially one that absorbed all power into the legislature, then divide and conquer could work again, by giving each branch of government, the executive and judiciary especially, the constitutional means and motives, to defend its office. Interest against interest; ambition against ambition would help control those who hungered for power, and it was possible, just possible, Hamilton especially would add, that the responsibilities of office and the "love of fame, the ruling passion of the noblest minds," would enlist those who might be Caesars as loyal public servants willing to defend republican liberty to the death. And since no faction could rule by itself, each would be forced to compromise to get anything done, thus increasing the probability of government serving something like the public good while diminishing the possibility that it would pose a threat to minority rights (F 51: 347-353; F 72: 488).

So the cycle of history might be broken. In curing the mischiefs of faction especially, Americans had some chance of making their republic immortal, or at least able to withstand the rough and tumble of domestic partisanship and foreign conflict for generations, maybe even centuries to come.

*****

Obviously, there is much more to this famous story, regarding both *Federalist* 10 and the *Federalist* as a whole, but with this scratch outline of Publius's science of political medicine in mind, we might reflect on an even more ambitious, far more Whiggish project inspired by the Philadelphia experiment of 1787; namely, the founding of the United Nations system in the San Francisco experiment of 1945. The Preamble of the Charter of the

United Nations begins with these three words, "We, the peoples," thus suggesting that the Philadelphia experiment and the San Francisco experiment are species of the same intellectual genus, In truth, the preamble was an afterthought, appended by Jan Smuts; the United States, a liberal regime, took the lead in founding United Nations system, but it was closer to a Westphalian order in which independent states made a concert to preserve each other's sovereignty than what many call the Liberal World Order today. Yet, if by "republican" we mean rooted in the consent of the members, accepting the rule of international law, and serving a trans-national public good (peace), the Philadelphia Experiment and the San Francisco Experiment do belong to the same intellectual genus, which some have dubbed "republican security theory" or the "Unionist paradigm." Such theory attempts to build and preserve political unions to provide for the security of each of their members, but always with the danger of tyranny at the head or anarchy in the parts of such unions.[22] The United Nations sought a solution to the tension between justice and power Thucydides captured in the Melian Dialogue, a compromise giving an equal vote to all its members in the General Assembly and a veto to the five permanent members of the Security Council (the United States, Great Britain, France, China, and the Soviet Union). The Charter also outlawed offensive war; henceforward, war would be legitimate only in self-defense or through the authority of the Security Council. In theory, the United Nations would provide collective security to all its members. Whenever one state waged aggressive war against another, the others would appeal to the Security Council for a warrant to stop the aggressive behavior; then the Security Council, based on Franklin Roosevelt's model of the "Four Policemen," would round up a posse, or coalition of the willing, in a "police action" to restore international peace and security. Alas, the United Nations was usually unable to function this way during the Cold War because of the mutual vetoes of the United States and the Soviet Union, so each side resorted to what James Madison called "auxiliary precautions" (F 51: 349). For the United States this meant leading a network of alliances, beginning with the Brussels experiment of 1949, the North Atlantic Treaty Organization (NATO), but later including Western-leaning countries like Japan, South Korea, Australia, New Zealand, and many others

22. See Daniel Deudney, *Bounding Power: Republican Security Theory from the Polis to the Global Village* (Princeton: University Press, 2007), and David Calvin Hendrickson, *Peace Pact: The Lost World of the American Founding* (Kansas: University Press of Kansas, 2003).

too. And in Europe, allies formed their own extended political community, first the European Coal and Steel Community in 1951, later the European Economic Community under the Treaty of Rome in 1957, and still later the European Union under the Maastricht Treaty in 1993. This interlocking web of cooperative institutions was meant to enable the members to gain the security from war with each other and the prosperity from free trade that had developed within the American Union. Although not all members or leaders aimed to produce a United States of Europe, they did succeed in forming a "security community" in which they were neither warring against each other nor preparing to do so, an unprecedented accomplishment for Europe. And little to none of this institution building would have occurred without American leadership, traceable through the Marshall Plan for specifically European recovery from the Second World War to the much larger, global Organization for Economic Cooperation and Development. With the end of the Cold War, one exceptionally Whiggish scholar, Francis Fukuyama, even suggested that members of this extended security community had arrived at the Hegelian end of history. Ideological quarrels, and the wars that came with them in the 20th century, had disappeared; politics would be reduced to management of economic integration. Instead of war, our greatest fear would be boredom, and Nietzsche's "last man." [23] If so, the Thucydidean cycle of history had been broken, at least among members of this community. The Whigs had won.

How might Thucydides respond? Perhaps by saying that knowledge may accumulate, progressively and Whiggishly, but wisdom does not. Thus science offers no cure from the danger of war and the danger that war poses to freedom. Each generation learns, or fails to learn wisdom, on its own. What one generation learns, another often forgets, and the same passions, fear, honor, and gain, that produced the Peloponnesian War also produce new wars varying in intensity and destructiveness according to the stakes at hand and the degree of power accumulated beforehand. That is why history is cyclical and always threatening to return to the worst cases, like the Peloponnesian War and the Second World War. From great suffering sometimes comes wisdom, however. The generation of Americans who founded the United States sought peaceful ways of settling disputes within their Un-

23. See *Security Communities*, ed. Emanuel Adler (Cambridge: University Press, 1998).Francis Fukuyama, *End of History and the Last Man* (New York: Harper, 1993); and Karl W. Deutsch, *Analysis of International Relations* (New York: Prentice Hall, 1968).

ion to save American freedom; so too did the founders of the post-World War Two order seek "win-win" solutions to secure the peace and enable the freedom of its members. The problem is that international order and domestic consensus often breaks down with the passing of generations.

Pericles was very much aware of this problem. In his Funeral Oration, he discussed three generations of Athenians: the forefathers who defeated the Persians at Marathon and Salamis; the fathers who built the Athenian empire in the Eastern Mediterranean; and the current generation of younger Athenians. To sustain their morale, he encouraged their ambition to expand; to avoid strategic overextension, he also advised them to avoid new conquests until they had finished their war with Sparta and its allies. Nicias, who belonged to Pericles' generation, agreed with Pericles' cautious side, but the much younger Alcibiades adhered to Pericles' grandest ambitions. Alcibiades was far more seductive than Nicias, however, so the younger Athenians who supported him most lost the self-restraint of Pericles and brought about their destruction in Sicily (1.104; 1: 109-110; 1.144; 2.36; 4: 21; 5.26; 6: 16-18; 7: 87).

Such loss of self-control is common as old leaders fade and new ones come to power. In 1815, for example, the Congress of Vienna established the Concert of Europe, a consensus among the great powers, including defeated France, to avoid a return to the carnage of the Napoleonic Wars by maintaining a rough balance of power in Europe. In Prussia in the 1860s, a leader of a younger generation, Otto von Bismarck, pushed that consensus to its limits. He aimed to unite all of Germany, except Austria, under Prussian control. As Prussia's Chancellor, he succeeded in a series of short wars from 1864 to 1870 against Denmark, Austria, and France, but even he understood that if he pushed too far, he might unite all of Europe against Germany. So rather than stack the deck against Germany, after 1870 he ceased trying to expand its borders and became an international peacemaker instead. But in 1890 a new king came to power, the young Kaiser Wilhelm, who fired the aging Bismarck for being too cautious, started a naval arms race with Great Britain, dreamed of Germany's place in the sun dominating the European continent and challenging England for supremacy at sea, and threw caution to the wind by dumping Germany's old ally, Russia, which sought security in the loving arms of France. By 1914, the Kaiser's younger generation in Germany found their country encircled by enemies, though in truth, under the Kaiser's leadership, Germany had encircled itself. Fearing that Germany might lose a multi-front war against France and Russia, the younger generation of political and military leaders developed an audacious solution in August 1914. They initiated a multi-front war to knock out one enemy, France, before dealing with the next, Russia. Bismarck would have known well that this was a cure far worse than the disease. It killed the patient, the Second German Empire, which collapsed in 1918. And it took the Russian, Ottoman, and Austro-Hungarian empires down with it, thus sowing war, chaos, and misery for decades.[24]

Both George Washington and Abraham Lincoln feared that, as generations passed, Americans too might lose their self-control. As Washington neared retirement in 1796, he worried that the partisan conflict between Federalists and Republicans, which had become sectional, with Federalists concentrated in New England and Republicans dominant in the South, might lead to the disintegration of the Union, even to civil war, and from thence to military despotism. With the help of Alexander Hamilton, he drafted his Farewell Address advising Americans to see their Union as the "rock" of their political salvation. "Prudence demands that we should habituate ourselves in all our words and actions to reverence the Union as the sacred and inviolable palladium of our happiness and should discountenance whatever can lead to a suspicion that it can in any event be abandoned."[25] He also advised against "permanent" alliances, like the Franco-American alliance of 1778, which had been necessary to win the American War of Independence, but had risked dragging the United States into the great war in Europe at a time when it was too weak to defend itself and partisan divisions raised the risk that the great powers would play the states against each other. This was the elder statesman's last great effort to pass on the wisdom of his generation to another, and he succeeded for quite some time. Despite great quarrels among the Founders, and among the next generation of American leaders, like Henry Clay, John C. Calhoun, Daniel Webster, and others, they found ways to compromise and preserve the Union. But, as Lincoln feared, Washington's advice did not, perhaps even could not, withstand the test of time.[26] A third generation of American leaders came to power, some

24. Henry Kissinger, *Diplomacy* (New York: Touchstone Books, 1994) 168-200.

25. Washington's Final Manuscript of the Farewell Address, *Washington's Farewell Address, In facsimile, with transliterations of all the drafts of WASHINGTON, MADISON, & HAMILTON, together with their correspondence and other supporting documents*, ed. Victor Hugo Paltsits (New York: New York Public Library, 1935) 170, 142, 146.

26. Abraham Lincoln, "Address before the Young Men's Lyceum of Springfield, Illinois," 27 January 1838, *Collected Works of Abraham Lincoln* (New Brunswick, NJ: Rutgers University Press, 1953) 108-115.

were willing to destroy the Union, if necessary, to preserve slavery; others were no less determined to prevent the expansion of slavery, even at the risk of civil war. All had access to the political science of Publius; the medicine failed, however, because the wisdom that the Union was the foundation of all other American political blessings had not passed to the next generation. And the war came.

If 1945 was for world order what 1787 was for American order, could 2018 or 2019 be for the world what 1861 was for the United States? In the United States, the last president to have lived through the Second World War, and to have helped build a new world order from its ashes, is George H.W. Bush, who is well into his nineties. When he passes away, will the wisdom of his generation pass away too? Like Washington and Lincoln, we must fear this possibility. Throughout the world, not merely in our own country, what Doctor Madison called "[m]en of factious tempers, of local prejudices, or of sinister designs" have gained an influence not seen since before the Second World War (F 10: 62). These are no friends of liberty; what they want is power for themselves and their tribes, and their secessionist tendencies risk war, either directly from their own belligerence, or indirectly, from their carelessness about preserving global order. To be blunt: shouting Britain, Poland, Hungary, or America First today makes no more sense than screaming New York or Massachusetts First would have in 1787. America Firstism today is as reckless for the international system as shouting Virginia or Mississippi First was in 1860. That way lies madness, but this time, in the age of nuclear weapons, the fate of humanity is at stake.

Like the ocean crashing against a dike, history is always threatening to make a comeback, but alas we have no Washington to sum up for our generation the lessons of constituting and preserving world order. So in the spirit of Thucydides and Publius, let this be the beginning. The diagnosis for our time is myopia, resulting in part from a new generation of leaders' ignorance of and rebellion against the wisdom of the post-World War Two generation, President Truman and his Secretary of State, Dean Acheson, especially. Too many do not understand how the international system works and the American role in stabilizing it. The prognosis is that together with America's allies, in the West especially, nothing can defeat us, but if we abandon them, or drive them to abandon us, and each other, all Hell could break loose, with Russia and China the primary beneficiaries. The prescription remains "united we stand; divided we fall" and an attack on one will be treated as an attack on all. The prescription is vigilance at home, to guard our own Constitution, and our elections especially against foreign meddling of the sort that drove Corcyra to an early grave, and *E Pluribus Unum* with our allies. This does not mean being one with them in everything, or failing to set limits to free riders and reckless drivers among our allies, i.e., those who sometimes do not contribute enough or would drag us into conflicts serving their interests more than ours. But it does mean taking a firm stance against those who scream "America First" today because, as Americans ought to have learned from now fifteen years of war in the Middle East and North Africa, even superpowers are not supermen. They need help too. As much as this goes against the grain of conventional wisdom about the Founders, which quite erroneously treats them as isolationists rather than Union builders, the practical meaning of their medical political science for our time is to remain united enough with our allies to be able to withstand any foreign power, combination of foreign powers, or terrorist organization. That way lies political health and political sanity: in an extended republican security community giving each of its member states the possibility of remaining free at home.

THE VIRTUES AND VICES OF INDIVIDUALISM

Steven Forde, University of North Texas

When contemporary Americans think of ancient Athens, especially ancient Athens as portrayed by Thucydides in his *History* of the Peloponnesian war, comparisons with the United States always seem to suggest themselves. Both were pioneering democracies in their origins, and both came to dominate their worlds, at least for a time. The dynamism that allowed them to dominate is connected with democracy and with individualism. Both nations are strong and dynamic in large part because they unleash the ambition and enterprise of individuals, and because they give individuals an unprecedented degree of freedom. Individuals develop their talents as free agents, apart from the strictures of community and tradition, in a way that would be abhorrent at Sparta, for example. In the case of Athens, though, the experiment ended rather badly.

Thucydides' presentation of Athens is in part an exploration of individualism, this most novel feature of Athenian politics and culture. He gives an account of the rise of Athenian individualism, its evolution, and its decay. Athenian individualism is an anomaly, something new under the sun. It is a break with all traditional cultures, which necessarily subordinate individuals to age-old, unquestioned practices and norms. Thucydides provides many striking depictions of Athenian individualism, the most famous of which is Pericles' Funeral Oration. In that speech, as related by Thucydides, Pericles attributes Athenian power and Athenian enlightenment largely to Athenian individualism. By Pericles' lights, this individualism stands behind all that we think of as noble and shining in ancient Athens.

Thucydides gives ample expression to the virtues of Athenian individualism, but he also illuminates its vices. Athens was defeated by the emphatically anti-individualist Sparta in the war that is the subject of his history. Thucydides connects Athens's defeat to its individualism; the same individualism that brought the Athenians to such heights ultimately laid them low. Moreover, it brought them down in a remarkably short period of time, by historical standards—within three or four generations from its first blossoming. The vices of individualism expressed themselves in two ways. One was a lack of public spirit among the Athenian citizens at large. The other was a self-serving ambition among the leaders of the city, by which they sacrificed the common good to their personal interest.[1] The result was faction, sedition, and near-civil war, attributable to what intellectuals and politicians today might call moral decay.

When Americans of the founding generation thought of ancient Athens, it was the factious Athens that was most likely in their minds. The ancient Greek cities in general were "wretched nurseries of unceasing discord," in Alexander Hamilton's memorable description.[2] Despite the kinship we today are likely to feel toward Thucydides' Athens, Athens, and the Greek cities in general, were rather a cautionary tale for the Founders. The Founders, after all, had the responsibility of putting the fledgling United States on a stable and durable footing, while we may simply admire ancient splendors from afar.

The American Founders largely took an institutional approach to solving the problem of instability. Electoral competition, checks and balances, ambition counteracting ambition—these are institutional mechanisms to contain, rather than expunge, any problems that might arise from political individualism. The Founders as a group, however, were also very concerned with moral formation or moral education. They knew that self-restraint and public spirit were necessary to the health of society, that institutional solutions could not save a people bereft of public spirit. They also knew that they were erecting an individualist regime, a regime incorporating principles from the likes of Locke and Sidney, embracing commerce and democracy (if only indirect democracy). Commerce empowers individuals as independent agents. Democracy authorizes them to think and speak freely in the public realm, as individuals largely freed from the straightjacket of social conformity. At the same time, the Founders were aware that individualism can easily shade into selfishness. It is worth our while to examine Thucydides' analysis of individualism, its vices and its virtues, to learn something about the underlying problem.

****

[1] This is my gloss on Thucydides' Book 2, chapter 65, section 7, and generally his account of the decline of Athens toward the end of the war. Thucydides, *History of the Peloponnesian War*, in four volumes (Cambridge, Mass: Harvard University Press-Loeb Classical Library, 1980). Henceforth, references to this work will be given in the text, by Book, chapter, and, where appropriate, section (*e.g.*, 2.65.7)

[2] Federalist #9 (http://oll.libertyfund.org/titles/carey-the-federalist-gideon-ed).

Athens was not always the individualist dynamo that we see through the bulk of Thucydides' history. Indeed, it is possible to identify the moment of its birth, which Thucydides traces to the experience of the Persian War of 480 BC (the Peloponnesian War began in 431). As the Persians advanced, bent on conquering Greece and Athens in particular, Themistocles persuaded the Athenians to abandon their walled city, and rely on the "wooden walls" of their navy. He reflected, Thucydides tells us, that if the Athenians "became seamen" (ναυτικοὺς γεγενημένους), it would facilitate the acquisition of power (1.93.3-4). And so it did. The Athenian navy was instrumental in turning back the Persians, and, in the ensuing fifty years, allowed Athens to become one of the foremost powers in Greece. In the process, Athens became an imperial master, and a perceived threat to the liberty of the Greeks at large.

The critical element of "becoming seamen" in Thucydides' treatment is not merely nautical power—there were other naval powers in Greece, such as Corinth and Corcyra—but the fact that the Athenians became seamen by radically uprooting themselves from the land. They abandoned their ancestral homeland, at least temporarily, abandoned their ancestral graves and their local gods. Some hint of the wrenching break that this represents is given by Thucydides later, when he describes how anguishing was the abandonment of the Attic countryside during the Peloponnesian War, allowing it to be plundered by the Spartans while the Athenians relied nearly exclusively on sea power (2.16). Such deracination, in order to stake one's all upon the sea, cuts ties to all conservative and moderating influences. Water is motion, innovation; land is roots, tradition, rest.[3] The Athenians were seafarers before the Persian War; now they become seamen in a more profound sense.

Shortly after the end of the Persian War, Thucydides says that the Spartans became apprehensive about the "daring and innovative character" the Athenians had developed during the war (τὸ τολμηρὸν καὶ τὴν νεωτεροποιίαν, 1.102.3). The Spartans' apprehension may be merely instinctive, but it proves to be prescient. Thucydides' presentation of the postwar Athenian character highlights the same traits, and the threat that they posed to the other Greeks. Daring innovation leads Athens to great power and success, but reasons for apprehension are visible from early on. In addition to tyrannizing over the Greeks, the Athenians develop an understanding of interstate politics according to which the domination of the weak by

[3] Leo Strauss *The City and Man* (Chicago: University of Chicago Press, 1964), pp. 140-41, 156, 159-60

the strong is acceptable, indeed routine. It is acceptable, moreover, because moral restrictions do not apply to the powerful.

This understanding, shocking from the point of view of traditional morality, is a prime example of the Athenians' daring innovation. Thucydides presents it as characteristic of the Athenians collectively. When the Athenians first articulate their amoralism in Thucydides, the argument is voiced by a pair of anonymous Athenian envoys to Sparta (1.72-78). Their anonymity suggests that any Athenian could make the argument they make, that any Athenian could deliver a sophisticated account of Athenian policy, that all Athenians have the power of independent thought and action.[4] The occasion of this speech is a conclave called by the Spartans as the Peloponnesian War looms, to deliberate with their allies concerning the Athenian threat. During the fifty years between the time of Themistocles and this, Athenian power had grown immensely. In their speech, the Athenians do not trace their power or their empire to anything like individualism. They do connect it to the "zeal" and "daring" that the city first evinced in the Persian Wars (προθυμία, τόλμα, 1.74). Those collective traits allowed or induced Athens after the Persian defeat to accept the leadership of those Greeks who wished to expel the Persians from the Aegean Sea and the Ionian coast (present-day Turkey). It was this alliance that grew into the Athenian empire, as the Athenians exercised ever more domineering control, eventually putting down rebellions by chafing allies-turned-subjects. The Athenians assert that any city would have behaved as they did. No city, they say, will resist the temptation to dominate where they are able, driven by the "compulsions" of fear, honor and self-interest (1.75, 76). The strong always dominate the weak (1.76.2).

Individualism, and the role that it plays in the psychology and dynamism of Athens, is a theme the Corinthians take up in a speech delivered to Sparta and her allies directly before the Athenian speech (1.68-71). The Corinthians provide one of the most vivid portrayals of the Athenian character in Thucydides. In this portrayal, the Athenians are inexhaustibly enterprising: they seize on every opportunity to advance their city. They dare beyond their strength, and succeed with remarkable regularity. When they succeed, it is only a spur to further daring; if they fail, they regard it as only a minor setback (1.70). The Athenians are innovative, ever devising new means of advancement (ibid.). They have discovered, or stumbled upon, a fundamen-

[4] See Strauss, *City and Man*, 170.

tal truth of international politics: that as in the arts, innovators prevail over traditionalists (1.71). Anticipating Machiavelli, they have discovered that daring or audacity succeeds beyond expectation, and prevails over caution.[5] The Corinthians make a point-by-point contrast with Sparta, in which the Athenians come off as far superior. You Spartans, say the Corinthians, are cautious, even timid, shrinking from action even where you would succeed (1.70.3). When you do succeed, you shrink from pressing the advantage, and thereby risk losing even the gains you have gotten (1.70.2). In the Corinthian account, the Spartans are virtually helpless before an opponent like Athens, who has now grown so powerful as to present a dire threat to Sparta and the cities in her alliance, to their liberty or even their existence (1.68.3, 1.69.1; *cf.* 1.23.6). Tacitly endorsing the Athenian position, and anticipating Machiavelli once again, they blame the Spartans for Athenian advances: imperialists are not to blame for their actions—they are simply doing what is to be expected—blame goes rather to the one who is in a position to check the imperialist and does nothing.[6]

The Corinthians make the connection that the Athenians in their speech do not, between the daring qualities of Athens and the character of her citizens individually—their individualism. This is the connection we must examine. The city of Athens is daring and innovative, in the Corinthian account, not because of its leaders, but because those traits characterize each Athenian individually (1.70.6). The city is but the individual writ large. This, however, is where our questions about individualism as a political regime assert themselves. The city of Athens, by dint of innovation and daring, has liberated itself from traditional restraints. This means, among other things, that it has shed the moral and religious restraints that make traditional cities reticent to lord it over cities weaker than they. But if Athenians individually have shed these restraints, will they not then individually violate the bonds of their moral community, and seek to dominate their fellow citizens? According to the Corinthians, the Athenians do not, and this is a key part of the remarkable (and dangerous) achievement of Athens. Athenians throw their bodies into the service of the city with abandon, they say, as if they were the bodies of others (1.70.6). Athenians are willing, almost eager, to sacrifice physically for the city, to do their duty by her (1.70.8). Their minds, however, remain utterly their own (οἰκειοτάτη, 1.70.6).

[5] See Machiavelli, *The Prince*, ch. 25.

[6] 1.69.1, 4-5; Machiavelli *The Prince*, ch. 3, *Discourses*, 1.1.4, 2.1 (trans. Mansfield and Tarcov, University of Chicago Press, 1996).

According to the Corinthians, the Athenians combine free individualism of mind (or judgment or spirit: γνώμη, 1.70.6) with utter and selfless devotion to the city. Somehow, the Athenians have combined these seeming opposites. The word the Corinthians use to describe Athenian independence of mind, which I translated as "utterly their own," could also be translated as "utterly patriotic" or communal (οἰκειοτάτη, 1.70.6). However we read their statement, the Corinthians immediately add that this trait is devoted completely to the good of the city.[7] The result is a city with as many sources of thought, imagination and initiative as it has citizens, all thrown into advancing the interests of the whole. No wonder that Athens is such a dynamo. No wonder it is such a danger to the rest of Greece. For, when the Athenians think of advancing the interests of the city, they think of advancing its power. If this Athens had its origins in the Persian Wars and the purely defensive actions taken at that time, it has transformed itself into an explosively expansionist power that threatens the independence of the Greeks. This transformation, moreover, is presented by the Athenians in their speech as a natural progression—from fear, to honor, and self-interest, from defense to imperialism. Thucydides, in his account of the rise of Athens during the fifty years prior to the Peloponnesian War, tacitly endorses this view.[8] Athenian expansionism is not based on a quasi-Machiavellian calculation that imperialism is required for defense or security; it is a natural consequence of the acquisition of power.[9] In the case of Athens, that acquisition of power is, in turn, rooted in Athenian individualism.

In their speech at Sparta, the Corinthians limit themselves to asserting that the Athenians combine individualism of mind with selfless devotion to the city. Rhetorically, they have no reason to explore how this combination works, or whether it is stable. Pericles, who guided the Athenian juggernaut in the years before the Peloponnesian War, was necessarily more concerned with these issues. In his Funeral Oration, devoted mostly to praising the regime and the practices of Athens, Pericles gives an account of Athenian individualism and its relation to Athenian patriotism. The speech is delivered over the first Athenian dead of the war, shortly after its commence-

[7] Their phrase is χρῶνται γνώμῃ οἰκειοτάτῃ ἐς τὸ πράσσειντι ὑπὲρ [τῆς πόλεως], "minds utterly their own, devoted to acting on behalf of the city," 1.70.6.

[8] This account, spanning chapters 89 to 117 of Book One, is sometimes called the "Pentecontaetia" ("fifty years").

[9] Machiavelli's "defensive" argument for empire is given in *The Prince*, Ch. 3. Note that this may not be the true or complete ground of Machiavelli's endorsement of empire.

ment. Athens is now at a peak of power, Pericles says, due to three things: the city's *practices*, its *regime*, and its *character* (ἐπιτηδεύσεως, πολιτείας καὶ τρόπων, 2.36.4). All three of these reflect or contribute to the individualist nature of Athens.

As a regime, democracy is known for its individualism, inasmuch it gives every citizen a right to speak and influence the public counsels. Pericles claims that the signature trait of Athenian democracy is that it is a meritocracy. Meritocracy is a quintessentially individualist arrangement inasmuch as it grants differential honor on the basis of individual achievement, without regard to class. Wealth and poverty are publicly irrelevant; the only consideration is the individual's ability to contribute to the city (2.37.1). Athens' justice is blind: public-spirited exertions are rewarded in the city regardless of wealth or class. This would go some way toward explaining the Corinthian claim that the Athenians are wholly devoted to serving their city. So far, however, we do not have a full explanation of Athenian individualism. After all, there were many democracies in ancient Greece, but only one Athens. Non-democracies, such as Sparta, also assigned merit on the basis of ability to serve the city, without regard to class.

What Pericles says next comes closer to explaining distinctively Athenian individualism. The freedom of the city's public life, he says, is matched by a freedom that Athenians allow each other in the affairs of daily life. Athenians do not resent their fellow citizens, do not even give them disparaging looks, when they act according to their pleasure (καθ' ἡδονήν) in their private lives (2.37.2). Athens has relaxed its general social mores to a remarkable degree. The censorious looks, the informal praise and blame that sustains public morality in ordinary communities, has been scaled back by the social tolerance of the Athenians. Though Pericles does not make the connection explicit, this is clearly part of the recipe for the Athenian dynamism identified by the Corinthians. Athens is innovative, dynamic and powerful because individual Athenians have those characteristics, and individual Athenians have those characteristics because of what Pericles calls a short while later their "unconstrained way of life" (ἀνειμένως διαιτώμενοι, 2.39.1). Athenians live free from the shackles of tradition in their private lives, which has prepared them to dare and innovate in public life. It would appear that the restrictive social codes of other cities, and the relentless public surveillance of behavior on their behalf, cramps human development. The Athenians have for the first time cut the bonds that prevent human individuality from flourishing.

But do the restrictions imposed on human nature by more traditional communities serve no purpose? Might public censure not be necessary to maintain private morality, and therefore the cohesion of the city? Pericles is aware of this problem. His statement concerning Athenian easygoingness in private morals is immediately followed by an assurance that the Athenians are not therefore lawless in public, tacitly acknowledging that public lawlessness is the result one should normally expect from such easygoingness (2.37.3). In public matters, Pericles insists, the Athenians obey legitimate authority and stay strictly within the laws, induced by fear or reverence (δέος, 2.37.3). This includes the unwritten laws—especially those that benefit victims of injustice, and bring shame upon the transgressor. But how does Athens manage to combine private laxity with adherence to the highest standard of public morality?

Pericles makes a distinction between public and private morality. In most cities, these are united in a single moral code, enforced by the laws and the ever-vigilant eye of public censure, but the Athenians have separated them. They have relaxed private morality, but this has not, in Pericles' telling, damaged public morality. With regard to law and order, and the needs of the city generally, the Athenians remain as disciplined as ever. They are disciplined not by a rigid and stultifying code of public conformity such as the Spartans impose, but by an entirely internal reverence and shame. Pericles makes a parallel case regarding Athenian courage. (2.39). While other cities—the Spartans once again come to mind—subject themselves to elaborate and rigorous training in an attempt to develop courage, the Athenians with their unconstrained way of life exhibit a native courage.[10] Pericles even suggests that the courage is directly connected to the easygoingness (ῥᾳθυμία, 2.39.4) of the Athenian way of life. Athenian courage stems more from the Athenian character, he adds, than from laws.[11] Spartans live their whole lives at war, as it were, due to the constant training and the consequently militarized way of life. The Athenians spare themselves such burdens, Pericles boasts, yet are found to be "no less daring" at the point of danger (μὴ ἀτολμότερος, 2.39.4).

We still may wonder, however, what precisely is the link between free, easygoing Athenian individualism, and Athenian law-abidingness and cour-

---

[10] 2.39.1 Pericles here uses different words for the "courage" of each side. The Athenians have native εὔψυχον, while the Spartans "attempt" to develop ἀνδρεῖα.

[11] 2.39.4 Pericles now uses ἀνδρεῖα to denote Athenian courage. His phrase is μὴ μετὰ νόμων τὸ πλέον ἢ τρόπων ἀνδρείας

age. Pericles asserts that there is a direct connection, but what is it? Athens has allowed individuals privately to live according to their own pleasure; what induces them to sacrifice their pleasure, when needed, for the public interest? Pericles alludes to two factors. First, he says that Athenians are lovers of beauty, and lovers of wisdom. These seem utterly irrelevant, but Pericles suggests precisely that love of beauty is part of the reason for Athenian public-spiritedness and courage.[12] We will have to piece together the meaning of this suggestion as we go along.[13] Pericles goes on to assert, as the Corinthians did before him, that all Athenians are engaged in the public life of their city, and all exhibit good judgment in political matters. Athenians alone, he says, regard the citizen who stays out of public life as good for nothing (2.40.2). Whereas deliberation breeds caution, even timidity, in most, the Athenians embark upon the most daring courses after full deliberation (3.40.3). This is doubtless in part what he meant when he said that the Athenians love wisdom, but without weakness. Others may be daring, but the Athenians alone combine daring and sagacity.

The Athenian reconciliation of individualism and patriotism causes the initiative and resourcefulness that Athenians develop as unfettered individuals to be channeled into the public realm. Individualism does not cause the Athenians to withdraw from politics to pursue lives of private gratification. Pericles emphasizes that even men of business devote themselves to politics in Athens. His claim is that the Athenians "alone" consider the non-engaged citizen to be a bad citizen (2.40.2). Democracy, commercialism, individual freedom: these things do not account for the distinctiveness of Athens. Coupling these things with intense public engagement is what makes Athens what it is.

The Athenians, then, exhibit both an untethered, dynamic individuality, and a complete devotion to the city. All the dynamism of Athenian individuality is channeled into efforts to benefit the city, resulting in immense, and restless, power. Pericles knows this, as do the Corinthians; both speakers identify this as a distinctive trait of Athens. They are speaking at the time of Athens' greatest power, and are rightly impressed with the way Athens has combined individualism and patriotism. We, however, know

[12] This is the force of the conjunction γὰρ, "for," in 2.40.1: φιλοκαλοῦμέν τε γὰρ, "For we are lovers of beauty...."

[13] 2.40.1 The phrase is φιλοκαλοῦμέν τε γὰρ μετ'εὐτελείας καὶ φιλοσοφοῦμεν ἄνευ μαλακίας, "we are lovers of beauty in good measure and we love wisdom ["philosophize"] without softness." This is the only appearance of "philosophy" in Thucydides.

from Thucydides that the grand Athenian experiment eventually disintegrated. We are therefore compelled to look more deeply.

Pericles, as opposed to the Corinthians, is concerned to perpetuate the distinctive Athenian combination of individualism and patriotism. His speech, after all, is a Funeral Oration delivered over soldiers fallen in war, and dedicated in part to making sure that future soldiers will also be willing to lay down their lives for the city. He is necessarily concerned about any soft spots in Athenians' dedication to their city. This is the reason for the strange, and striking, appeal Pericles makes to Athenian *eros*. Addressing the surviving Athenians of military age, Pericles declines to enumerate the personal advantages that accrue to each of them from defense of their city—he declines to appeal to their individual self-interest—but bids them instead fix their gaze on the city of Athens, or on the power of the city, and fall in love with it.[14] The word Pericles uses for love here, *eros*, is an unusual word to use in this context. *Eros*, as opposed for example to *philia*, is a much more intense, even manic, love. It is a love that can drive individuals to extremes of self-sacrifice. In Greek literature and mythology, it is also a force that drives humans to overstep, often leading them to destructive courses of action. It is likely that Pericles enlists *eros* because only *eros* is powerful enough to induce free individuals such as the Athenians to be willing to sacrifice, even die, for the city. Citizens of ordinary cities have a more pedestrian patriotism, born of a rote discipline and a conditioning that makes them citizens first and individuals only second (if at all). Athenians have a soaring, erotic love for their city and its power. Like lovers, their individual fulfillment has merged wholly with the good of their beloved, and their reward is only to have died in furtherance of Athens and its power. Pericles speaks of the glory of the fallen soldiers, but their glory is not individual. Their glory is simply participation in the glory of their beloved Athens (2.43.2-3). *Eros* seems to be the only force that can induce thorough individualists to submerge their individualism in their beloved. Inasmuch as *eros* is ineluctably tied to beauty, this exhortation echoes Pericles' earlier statement that the Athenians' love of beauty is one of the reasons for their intense engagement with politics. Whether this love (or any erotic love) can truly remain within measure, as Pericles also said, is open to question.

---

[14] 2.43. The grammatical construction is ambiguous. Pericles could either be exhorting his listeners to fall in love with Athens, or with its power. (τὴν τῆς πόλεως δύναμιν...θεωμένους καὶ ἐραστὰς γιγνομένους αὐτῆς, 2.43.1).

Eros is not a passion normally associated with patriotism, but Thucydides does vouch for the erotic character of Athens on more than one occasion. The most striking of these, and the one that most powerfully calls into question Pericles' claim to combine *eros* and moderation, is the Athenian response to the Sicilian expedition. Sixteen years after the beginning of the war (and long after Pericles' death) the Athenians undertook to conquer the island of Sicily and incorporate it into their empire. This was a massive and seemingly foolhardy undertaking, but it stoked Athenian erotic patriotism. Once the assembly voted to sail to Sicily, Thucydides says, *eros* descended upon the city (6.24.3). The Athenians were in a frenzy of desire. This moment gives a vivid sense of what it means for patriotism to become erotic: the Sicilian expedition causes such a surge of passion because it is beautiful (cf. 6.31.2), and because it is grand, even grandiose. *Eros* is enflamed by excess, and gives rise to excess in turn. This is exactly the kind of movement Pericles invited by bidding the Athenians to fall in love with the city and its power. We, however, cannot fail to notice that the grand project the Athenians have fallen in love with involves the subjugation of many thousands of their fellow Greeks. It is the boldest and most splendid manifestation yet of Athenian imperialism. After all, when Pericles spoke of the power of Athens as the object to which Athenian *eros* should become attached, the city's empire was perhaps the principal manifestation of that power (2.36.2-4, 2.40.4, 2.41.42.43.2-3).

Pericles had given a remarkably sanguine interpretation of the Athenian empire. It was a wholly glorious undertaking, the jewel in Athens's crown. Pericles even insinuated that Athens's subjects were grateful—or if resentful, only because the recipient of favors is a more grudging friend than the benefactor (2.40.4-5). Either way, the basis of the Athenian empire, in this account, is Athenian generosity. Pericles is referring to the fact that Athenian hegemony began when the city spearheaded the liberation of the Ionian Greeks from the Persians. It is more than a stretch, though, to maintain that Athens, even in the early days of the Peloponnesian War, ruled over willing, indeed grateful, allies.

Pericles starkly revises his portrait of the Athenian empire in his third and final speech in Thucydides, a revision that is connected to a new and more sober evaluation of Athenian individualism. The sobering experience that sets the stage for this reevaluation is the plague at Athens. The plague appears immediately after Pericles' Funeral Oration in Thucydides' account, as if intended to correct Pericles' portrait of Athens. If Pericles maintained that Athens had felicitously combined individualism and public spirit, Thucydides asserts that this harmony began to unravel in the plague, when "lawlessness first began in the city" (2.53.1). The horrible and random course of the disease caused people to abandon all pretense of piety and nobility, Thucydides says (2.52.3-4, 2.53). Individuals openly pursued their own pleasure, heedless of any harm to others or to the common good. Doubtless it is unfair to expect upright behavior from those under such mortal stress—the plague was beyond the strength of human nature, says Thucydides (2.50.1)—but Thucydides indicates that the Athenians' newfound immoralism only reveals a truth that had been hidden; they now do openly what they had always done or thought in secret (2.53.1). Moreover, Thucydides treats this Athenian degeneration as part of a long-term problem in Athens. We recall his statement in the eulogy of Pericles that Athens's final defeat was caused by a failure of public spirit, the city being led to policies that benefited private individuals at the expense of the common good (2.65.7). The moral breakdown of the plague is merely the first overt manifestation of Athenian decay.

The remarkable confluence of individualism and public spirit that Pericles and the Corinthians saw in Athens in its heyday, in other words, was something of an illusion. Its limitations are laid bare by the experience of the plague, and by Pericles himself, in the speech he delivers as plague and war ravage Athens. The Athenians are discouraged, naturally enough. Pericles attempts to bolster their morale and persuade them to remain with his strategy for prosecuting the war. He also revisits the theme of Athenian public spirit, this time striking a much more sober note than he had in the Funeral Oration. Rather than a soaring, all-encompassing *eros* for the city and its power, Pericles now offers the much more pedestrian reflection that each citizen's private interest is bound up with the interest of the whole. Individual citizens may be ever so prosperous, but they cannot thrive if the city goes to ruin (2.60.3). There is a distinction, in other words, even a tension, between public and private interest (*cf.* 2.61.2, 4). Pericles asserts that private citizens must support the public, even if they are tempted not to. The public good, however, is now only the accumulation of private interests, not some glorious public project. If individuals sacrifice some of their personal good for the city, it is motivated only by the reflection that the private interest of each is linked to the public interest. Pericles continues to speak of "love of the city" (φιλόπολίς 2.60.5), but this is *philia*, a much cooler passion than *eros*, and the citizen's motive for sharing it is partly personal self-interest.

As to the empire, Pericles now admits that the Athenians hold their rule "as a tyranny" (2.63.2), one that was unjust perhaps to acquire, but dangerous to give up. The pretense of benevolent rulers and grateful subjects has been dropped. Fear and self-interest are the primary motives for maintaining this empire. It is no longer a glorious project that could inspire *eros*. Indeed, to the extent that the empire was what inspired Athenian erotic passion, that passion was based on self-deception, the lie or illusion that the Athenian empire is not a tyranny but something noble. The Athenians abhorred tyranny, and were willing to turn on any leader they suspected of aspiring to tyranny.[15] Yet they tyrannized others.

For this, Athenian individualism was partly to blame. To see why, we need to explore a bit more deeply what we mean by "individualism." A key part of it, obviously, is individual freedom. The Athenians were intensely proud of their freedom, a freedom that traditional cities like Sparta could never experience, and they were intensely dedicated to it. But for the Athenians, freedom entailed empire, ruling over others. There is a sense, indeed, in which rule over others is the pinnacle or fulfillment of liberty. Is not the tyrant the freest individual? He can force others to bow to his every whim; he alone is above the law. Plato understood this logic when he described the workings of democracy in Book Eight of the *Republic*. Democracy, in this portrait, naturally develops into tyranny due to the logic of freedom. Tyranny is the excess, or the perfection, of freedom, at least a certain understanding of freedom. In Plato's portrait, the transition to tyranny is associated with democracy becoming erotic.[16] We have already seen Athenian *eros* peak in Thucydides' description of the Sicilian expedition.

Thucydides sheds further light on the connection between Athenian democracy and erotic passion in a peculiar digression he inserts into his account of the Sicilian expedition (6.54-59). The Athenians were obsessed with the danger of a home-grown tyrant, Thucydides explains, because they had suffered under the tyranny of Peisistratus and his family some one hundred years before. This tyranny was attacked by two Athenians, Harmodius and Aristogeiton, and shortly afterwards it fell from power. In Athenian lore, Harmodius and Aristogeiton were regarded as overthrowers of tyranny, indeed as virtual incarnations of Athenian freedom and democracy. Thucydides' account of the Harmodius and Aristogeiton story, however, reveals

---

[15] Themistocles and Alcibiades are the most prominent victims of this impulse in Thucydides' narrative.

[16] See especially *Republic* 563e-566d.

that, while the two did attack the Peisistratids, they killed not the tyrant but his brother. Their attack did not end the tyranny or reestablish democracy. The motive of the attack, moreover, was not the liberation of Athens, except indirectly. Indeed, their motive was not political at all, but erotic. Aristogeiton, an older man, was the lover of young Harmodius (6.54.2). Hipparchus, brother of the tyrant Hippias, also desired Harmodius, and the two lovers feared that he would use his family's power to force the matter. Jealousy thus drove them to attack the tyranny. Their attack, according to Thucydides, only had the effect of making the tyranny harsher, and it was overthrown three years later, by Spartan intervention (6.59.4).

This digression places Athenian *eros* and the Athenians' erotic attachment to democracy in a most interesting light. If, following the Athenians themselves, we take Harmodius and Aristogeiton to be the incarnation of the Athenian democratic spirit, we see that *eros* is indeed at the heart of that spirit. But it is not the fully public-spirited impulse that the Athenians believe it to be, and that Pericles believes it to be (or believes it can become). Taken as a parable, the story suggests that Athenian *eros* is essentially directed to private gratification, though it masquerades as public spirit. It may be largely aligned with the public good, as in the case of Harmodius and Aristogeiton, but it is essentially a private appetite.[17] Athens has harnessed an unprecedented source of power by igniting this private passion on behalf of the public good, but the gratification each Athenian gets from the power and success of the city is fundamentally private or individual. Athenian devotion to the public good, while genuine, is really dedication to a private good. Perhaps *eros* is always "individualist" in this sense.

The erotic character of Athenian individualism has fateful consequences. One of these is the danger that Athenian *eros* may eventually lose its public-spiritedness, and become forthrightly self-interested. Thucydides' verdict on the eventual fall of Athens suggests that this is ultimately what happened, as individual Athenians began pursuing courses that benefited them privately, at the expense of the city as a whole (2.65.7). Another danger is that that devotion, precisely when it is strongest, might become tyrannical, imperialist. When Pericles ties Athenians to their city by bidding them to fall in love with its power, he creates or inflames an expansionist patriotism. The Athenian love for the Sicilian expedition reveals the true nature of this erotic individualism. Thucydides highlights this by the jarring juxtaposition of the

[17] I develop this argument at greater length in *The Ambition to Rule: Alcibiades and the Politics of Imperialism in Thucydides* (Cornell University Press, 1987), pp. 33-40.

Sicilian expedition's launch, its brilliant appearance and its rhapsodic *eros*, with the Melian Dialogue that immediately precedes it.[18] The notorious Melian Dialogue presents Athenian imperialism in its harshest aspect. The Athenians attack the small island of Melos, to bring it within their empire. The Athenians try to persuade the Melians to surrender, using the argument that "the strong do what they can and the weak suffer what they must."[19] The Athenians have been proclaiming since before the war that power is not bound by moral restraints (v. 1.75, 76), but there is no more stark statement of the brutality of power divorced from morality than this pronouncement on Melos. The Athenians go on to tell the Melians that gods as well as human beings are subject to the same compulsion, in effect making the gods tyrants like themselves (5.105). The Athenians want to make the amoralism of power into a universal, even cosmic law. Thucydides gives some credence to this, suggesting that powerful cities do indeed slip the yoke of morality.[20] He also shows that, in slipping that yoke, they risk destroying themselves.

In the end, the true course of Athenian empire may best be encapsulated in the argument of Diodotus, a shadowy figure who appears in Book Three. The occasion is a debate at Athens concerning what to do with the city of Mytilene, which rebelled from the Athenian empire but was subdued and now is in Athens' power (3.36-48). Diodotus urges leniency, on the grounds that the Mytilenians have only succumbed to *eros*, which all too often rules human nature (3.45). *Eros*, it appears, is the impulse behind both empire and rebellions against empire. There is something tragic in the human condition, where human beings are driven by erotic longings into irresolvable conflict, to empire and rebellion against empire. If there is something grand and noble in this aspiration—both the Athenians and the Mytilenians aspire to freedom—*eros* in this telling appears as obsession or compulsion. It is dangerous, even suicidal. The Mytilenians are now in jeopardy of death—indeed, in a first meeting of the Assembly, the Athenians voted to kill all their men, and sell the women and children into slavery—and the Athenians will in due course be brought low by their imperial *eros*.

---

[18] The Melian Dialogue takes place at the end of Book Five (5.84-113), and the Sicilian expedition is undertaken at the beginning of Book Six.

[19] 5.89. The translation is that of Richard Crawley, adopted by Robert Strassler in *The Landmark Thucydides* (Free Press, 1996).

[20] This argument is too long to pursue here. See Strauss, *City and Man*, 187-193; Forde, *Ambition to Rule*, 40-57, 140-156.

As Diodotus puts it, *eros* tempts humans to foolish and destructive courses, from which nothing will deter them.

****

Athenian individualism has brought the city to great heights of glory by loosing the bonds that normally restrain individual thought and initiative. It has liberated human *eros* and put it to the service of the city. This individualism quickly becomes tyrannical, however, oppressing others in the name of its own freedom and glory. In the end, it even loses its dedication to the public good, degenerating into selfishness pure and simple. Is this a cautionary tale against individualism per se? If Thucydides is presenting Athens and Sparta as the two fundamental alternatives for political life,[21] does the demise of Athens require us to return to Sparta, to the most uncompromising anti-individualism? Spartans conform to one of the most restrictive codes of behavior ever seen. Questioning social norms is completely outside the mental horizon of the Spartan citizen. Sparta as a community displays seamless solidarity and immense tenacity; there is no question of the Spartan's willingness to sacrifice for the common good. But that same Spartan displays precious little independent thought and imagination. Sparta as a whole is a truly impressive machine, a peak of political life. Spartans individually, however, when separated from the community, are a distinctly unimpressive lot. Brasidas is the exception that proves the rule.[22]

Our original question returns: what should our attitude be toward individualism in liberal societies today? Does Athens show us the inevitable fate of any society that liberates individuals from the straightjacket of tradition? The American Founders were more likely to regard Greek history in general as a model cautionary tale rather than an object of imitation. They were likely to regard the ancient Roman republic as a model—not Sparta, perhaps, but close to Sparta. On the other hand, they created a regime based on Lockean individual rights, on freedom of conscience and commerce. These are all potent individualist elements. Are these elements destined to undermine the cohesiveness and public-spiritedness of the nation that embraces them? Arguments have certainly been made that this is exactly what has

---

[21] This is the argument of Strauss (*City and Man*, 156-8, 217).

[22] Examples of incompetent and even corrupt behavior by Spartans apart from the city include Pausanias (1.128-135) and Alcidas (3.26-33). The exploits of Brasidas are recounted in Book Four and the beginning of Book Five.

happened to the United States over the course of its history, and especially in recent generations. We are in the grip of "moral decay," we are told: American individualism has degenerated into selfishness, undermining public spirit and respect for law and morality. These are nothing more than the fruits of individualism that have been incubating from the beginning.

There is certainly merit in these arguments, but we should also be careful to diagnose our situation properly. Using the Athenian case as a foil is useful for this, for individualism is not all alike. There are some significant differences between Athenian individualism and modern, American and liberal individualism. One of the most obvious is the thoroughly political nature of the Athenians. We recall Pericles' claim in the Funeral Oration that the Athenians regard a man who is not involved in the political life of the city as a worthless citizen (2.40.2). Despite the fact that Athenians live private lives of pleasant ease, they throw themselves enthusiastically, even manically, into the service of the city (2.37; cf. 1.70). Modern, liberal individualism, by contrast, tends to the apolitical. It premises a sharp divide between public and private, with the private sphere almost monopolizing the attention and energy of the vast majority of citizens.

This is a distinction that was once widely described as the distinction between ancient and modern liberty, or between positive and negative liberty.[23] Modern, or negative, liberty is the liberty we are all familiar with. It is the liberty of liberalism, essentially the liberty to be left alone to live our lives as we please, so long as we do not harm others. This liberty is grounded in individual rights, rights that we hold against the government above all. Government does not have the power to infringe on individuals' freedom of religion, for example, or of speech, or their property (without due process of law). Ancient, or positive, liberty, by contrast, is essentially the right to be "self-governing" in the sense of participating in political life. There is no guarantee that a regime of ancient liberty will respect individual rights in the sense prized by modern liberty. There may be a "right" to participate in public life, but no right to be left alone. As Pericles said, Athenians regard it as a duty for all to contribute to the polity, and consider one who does not to be a worthless citizen. Further, citizens have no rights over against the city. If a collective decision infringes on the liberties of citizens, those citizens have no

[23] The classic statements are Benjamin Constant, "The Liberty of Ancients Compared with that of Moderns" (1819, http://www.uark.edu/depts/comminfo/cambridge/ancients.html); and Isaiah Berlin, "Two Concepts of Liberty (1958, http://www.nyu.edu/projects/nissenbaum/papers/twoconcepts.pdf).

recourse. If the Athenians decide to execute Socrates for impiety and corrupting the youth, ancient liberty affords him no protection.

Some of the pathologies of Athenian individualism can be traced to its connection to distinctively ancient liberty. That the Athenian impulse to liberty expressed itself ultimately in imperial domination reflects the fact that each Athenian was psychologically so invested in the public life of the city. The power and the glory of their beloved city was a great personal satisfaction to each citizen. This satisfaction was so intense as to be erotic, in Thucydides' telling, and helped fuel Athenian imperialism. To be sure, the Greeks' own understanding of liberty did not sanction tyranny—that is why the Athenians' imperial actions and arguments were so shocking—but Thucydides and Plato both show how this liberty leads by a natural progression to imperialism and tyranny. By contrast, citizens of modern, liberal regimes may swell with pride at the accomplishments, and even the power, of their nations, but it is difficult to imagine this becoming erotic. Modern, negative liberty is apolitical, even suspicious of politics as a possible source of oppression. Very few modern liberal citizens regard politics as central to their life; "freedom" is what they enjoy in their private lives, outside the public realm. Economics is much more likely to occupy central stage, as modern citizens overwhelmingly devote their energies to gaining economic prosperity and material comfort. Modern democracies are commercial regimes, and commercial regimes (at least since the end of colonialism) do not show much appetite for imperialism. The much-touted "democratic peace," whereby democratic states are said not to get involved in wars among themselves, is an artifact of modern liberty specifically.

There is another key reason why modern individualism can avoid the pathologies of Athenian individualism. Modern liberty is based on individual rights, and it is reciprocal. Each individual understands, in principle at least, that his liberty does not entail a right, or even a moral possibility, of lording it over others. To the contrary, each understands that his liberty is contingent upon respecting the rights of others. No one is entitled to rule without the consent of the ruled. Abuses of this principle have certainly occurred in the history of liberal politics, and individuals have certainly been seen who harbor tyrannical ambition, but liberal culture strongly militates against it, and such instances have been rare, by historical standards. Caesarism, like imperialism, is not the signature danger of the regime of modern individualism. Its signature dangers lie elsewhere.

One of those dangers is apathy and withdrawal from politics—almost the opposite danger from that found in a regime like ancient Athens. If the Athenians were so thoroughly dedicated to politics that they vested their highest hopes and their deepest impulses in the city, liberal citizens are more liable to stop being citizens at all, to lose all interest in public life, to fail to contribute to public life in even the most minimal ways. This makes grand national projects like imperialism less likely, but it is problematic to the extent that modern liberal regimes are democratic, and do require some willingness on the part of citizens to share public burdens. Alexis de Tocqueville provided the classic statement of this worry in *Democracy in America.* He goes so far as to define "individualism" as a harmful withdrawal from public life, and identifies it as a natural product of democracy and egalitarianism.[24] Democratic peoples, Tocqueville warns, are liable to lose the public-spiritedness that they need to sustain democratic health. There are devices they may use to keep the public engaged, and nurture a certain level of public virtue, but if they do not, modern democracies may succumb to "soft despotism," in which apathy and withdrawal pave the way for a paternalistic state that caters to people's material needs, but reduces them to the state of children being cared for by their parents.[25]

Thucydides attributed the decline of Athens to a failure of public spirit: Athenians led their city down paths that benefited private individuals at the expense of the public (2.65.7). But these were at least public vices, the failings of politicians and publicly-engaged men. The dangers of individualism that loom today are similar, in that they represent a moral failing, a decline of the public-spirited virtue that induces citizens to make those sacrifices necessary to uphold the common good. The difference between the two is that one is expressed on a political plane, while the other consists of a withdrawal from politics. Both, though, must be seen as unfortunate consequences of individualism.

Thucydides, chronicler of the radically politicized individualism of ancient Athens, does not give us enough information to speculate whether a regime could be devised that combined the advantages of Sparta and Athens, that unleashed some of the dynamism of individuality while retaining the stability and solidarity of Sparta. Given that he presents the two cities as opposite poles of political excellence, it would seem that they could not be

---

[24] Tocqueville, *Democracy in America* (Harvey C. Mansfield and Delba Winthrop, trans. and ed., Chicago: University of Chicago Press, 2000), Volume 2, Part 2, Chs. 2-4.

[25] *Democracy in America* 2.4.6-7.

combined in any meaningful way. The American Founders, however, were put in a position where they had to try. They knew that the newly-minted United States was going to be a commercial society. They embraced the philosophy of rights, and the tradition of individualism that had been rooted in the nation since the colonial period. At the same time, schooled by Thucydides and other classical sources, they knew some of the pitfalls associated with these. We cannot fully explore here the various devices they adopted to mitigate the vices of individualism particularly, but reflecting on those devices in light of the understanding of individualism we have gleaned from Thucydides would repay the effort. The Founders established a representative system in part because such a system lessens the burden of civic participation on the average citizen. Is this device a sage accommodation to the apoliticism of modern individualism, or does it only exacerbate the problem of civic laziness and apathy? The Founders knew that civic virtue or public-spiritedness was precarious in an individualist age, and they were concerned to create a culture of public engagement and educational systems that inculcated these virtues. Have these expedients been successful? Do they remain effective to this day?[26] The answers to questions like these are of the first importance to American politics today. They may even shed some retrospective light on ancient Athenian politics and on Thucydides as an interpreter of the human drama.

[26] These issues are explored in detail by Thomas Pangle and Lorraine Smith Pangle in *The Learning of Liberty: The Educational Ideas of the American Founders* (University Press of Kansas, 1993).

PIETY AND ATHENIAN IMPERIALISM IN THUCYDIDES' *PELOPONNESIAN WAR*

Allison Levy

Thucydides describes the Athenians' catastrophic defeat in Sicily as "the greatest event," not only in this war, but in the whole of Greek history (7.87.5): the Athenians were "defeated in all ways," having met with "utter destruction" by land and sea, and "from many few came back home" (7.87.5-6).[1] Yet, shocking as this outcome is, perhaps even more surprising is the way it comes about. For the most obvious missteps made by the Athenians, the most sophisticated people depicted in Thucydides' work, are driven in large part by their piety. First, while Athens is preparing to sail for Sicily, a number of religious statues in the city are defaced, which the Athenians interpret as a bad omen for the venture and a sign of a conspiracy against the democracy (6.27). In the hysteria that follows, the city arrests and puts to death a number of good citizens on the word of bad ones; moreover, falling prey to the manipulations of his personal enemies, she recalls the brilliant general Alcibiades from his command in Sicily for trial and execution on grounds of impiety, leaving the mission in the hands of the less capable Nicias (6.28-6.29, 6.53, 6.61-6.62, 6.101). Later, after the Athenians suffer terrible reverses in Sicily, pious concerns dictate their course of action at a critical juncture: having lost significant battles with Syracuse by sea (7.41) and land (7.44), with an army utterly discouraged and in ill health (7.47), facing an emboldened and freshly reinforced enemy (7.50), the Athenians finally decide to go home. However, when an eclipse of the moon occurs, "the many," Thucydides tells us, "take [it] to heart," and urge their leaders to wait, while the general Nicias, in turn, determines that the question of leaving cannot even be considered for twenty-seven days, per the recommendation of the soothsayers. Thus, the Athenians' escape, all reasonable hope for which depended on speed, is critically delayed because of pious fears. The importance of the Athenians' piety to their pursuit of Sicily is apparent in

---

[1] Numerals indicate book and chapter; unless otherwise indicated, all references are to Thucydides' *Peloponnesian War*. Translations of the Greek are my own, but I am greatly indebted to the translations of Charles Forster Smith (1923) and Thomas Pangle (unpublished).

other ways as well: for example, in his description of Athens' final sea battle with Syracuse, Thucydides says of those Athenians watching the chaotic scene from shore that, when it appeared to them that their side was prevailing, they "regained courage, and called on the gods not to rob them of their safe return" (7.71.3). In addition, when this great battle is lost and the army is retreating by land, Thucydides tells us that the wounded and ill, unable to follow their comrades, fall behind with "faint appeals to the gods and lamentations" (7.75.4); as to the utterly despondent men making the retreat, Nicias attempts to instill in them hope for some alleviation of their misery by encouraging them to reflect that they have been punished sufficiently for their transgressions and that they are now more worthy of the gods' pity than their jealousy (7.77.3).

While these are certainly not the first manifestations of Athenian piety we have seen in the work,[2] the frequency with which they appear and their obvious effect on foreign policy during the Sicilian expedition are remarkable given Thucydides' general portrayal of Athens to this point. After all, the spokesmen of Athens, in contrast to their enemies, hardly speak of gods or defend their city on pious grounds, in their speeches within Athens and without. As to the *demos*, Thucydides does indicate that they are more pious than at least some of their leaders: for example, and setting aside for now Nicias (whom we will discuss at greater length below), "the many" are singled out as those who "took to heart" the eclipse in Sicily and desired on that basis to delay their escape, and those who, at the start of the war, were pained by leaving their ancestral temples. In addition, Thucydides' claim that those Athenians in the grip of pious fervor after the mutilation of the Herms were manipulated by men vying for leadership of the *demos* indicates that those aspiring to leadership did not take terribly seriously that which was of great importance to those they successfully stirred up (6.28.2). Nonetheless, the fact that the Athenian people follow and revere Pericles, a man who calls publicly for stripping gold from the likeness of the goddess Athena to pad the war treasury (2.13.5),[3] who never defends any course of action, however important, on the basis of its piety (cf. the practice of Athens's en-

[2] For example, Thucydides suggests that at the beginning of the war, the many were grieved by the move, necessitated by Pericles' war strategy, within Athens's city walls, away from their ancestral temples (2.14, 2.16.2) (Bartlett, 2001, 103-104); in addition, Thucydides makes clear that the Athenians were inclined to interpret the plague as divine punishment and as the fulfillment of an ancient oracle (2.54.5, 2.59.1, 2.64.1).

[3] Bartlett, 2001, 103-104.

emies at 1.123),[4] and who praises religious sacrifice and festivals only on grounds of the "relaxation" they afford (2.38.1),[5] indicates a remarkable neglect of piety on the part of the Athenian people. Thus, it is especially striking that a surge of pious feeling derails the Sicilian expedition. This fact surely indicates that the Athenians are much more attached to piety than they often appear; it also casts doubt on the wisdom of Periclean efforts to ignore or diminish such attachment, which efforts, as some students of Thucydides have suggested, may well have produced a particularly harmful manifestation of Athenian piety.[6]

Yet, while we see that piety is clearly of tremendous importance for the Athenians, questions about how, precisely, it moves them remain. In particular, it is not clear how piety affects their imperial hopes. This consideration is of special interest because throughout Thucydides' work, the Athenians are distinguished by their apparently boundless energy, initiative, and striving, all of which is underpinned by extremely powerful, even delirious, hopes for empire, from which the Athenians expect "ageless glory" (2.43), "everlasting pay" (6.24.3), "to be opposed in nothing," and "to achieve the more impracticable things equally with the possible, whether with means great or deficient" (4.65.4), to name a few particulars. But what role does piety play in these hopes? As noted, we see the Athenians praying to the gods on the day they launch their expedition to Sicily, which clearly indicates that hopes for the gods' assistance play some role in their great hopes for conquest. However, what is the priority of these pious hopes in the Athenians' motivations? Do the examples of Athenian prayer Thucydides provides reveal the deepest source of the energy fueling their imperial pursuits? To shed light on these questions, it is helpful to consider the character of the most striking hopes Thucydides attributes to the Athenians in comparison with those of some of the most obviously pious men described in the work, the Melians, as well as the rather un-Athenian Nicias. After doing so, we will be better able to ascertain the extent to which the Athenians' hopes for empire are indeed pious hopes.

We turn first to the example of the Melians. Just prior to his account of the Sicilian expedition and in the most infamous passage of his *Peloponnesian War*, Thucydides describes the confrontation between Athens and the small

[4] Strauss, 1964, 161.

[5] Orwin, 1994, 20.

[6] For helpful discussions of this problem, see Ahrensdorf, 1997, 256; Orwin, 1994, 197-198; and Strauss 1964, 209.

island of Melos, a colony of Sparta that had previously remained independent and neutral in the war. In the sixteenth year of the conflagration, however, the Athenians sail to the island with a force that dwarfs their tiny adversary, and demand that the Melians join their alliance; when the Melians refuse, the Athenians encamp and send envoys to speak with their obstreperous would-be subjects, in order to persuade them to capitulate (5.84).

Taking their cue from the Melians' decision to bring these envoys before the rulers and the few, rather than the general populace of Melos, the Athenians open with the cordial offer not to seduce or deceive them with a long speech, proposing, instead, a conversation, in which their argument can be taken up point by point. The Melians appreciate the obvious reasonableness of such an approach, but cannot help observing that they find the presence of the Athenian army a hindrance to conversation, and venture the suspicion that the Athenians mean to press them into either war or slavery. The Athenians clarify that they have not come to argue about suspicions regarding "the future things," and say they mean, instead, to converse about the safety of Melos, in light of "the present things and what you all see" (5.87). Attaining the Melians' assent to proceed in this fashion, then, the Athenians inform them that they will dispense with the "noble names" typically bandied about in such circumstances and cut to the chase: neither do the Athenians claim to rule because they deserve to, nor are they interested in hearing that the Melians do not deserve to be conquered; rather, the Melians should consider "what is possible" in accordance with "what we each truly think," knowing, of course, that "the superior do what they are capable of, and the weak yield" (5.89).

The Melians' first response is to argue that Athens will benefit by leaving Melos free, but the Athenians are not convinced (5.90-91). The Melians then object that it would be most cowardly and base for them not to make every attempt to preserve their freedom; the Athenians pooh-pooh this assertion as well, claiming that for weaklings such as themselves the question is not one of honor or shame, but of safety (5.101). It is at this point that the discussion turns to the gods: the Melians remind the Athenians that the outcome of war does not depend merely on strength, but that the role of fortune, too, must be considered. As they see it, then, they should fight, for in fighting they are afforded some hope (5.102). However, as Thucydides' discussions of "fortune" elsewhere suggest (4.55.3-4, 4.65.4, 7.18.2), human beings tend to understand this force to be more than mere blind chance, which understanding the Athenians perceive in the Melians' comment.

Thus, they respond by reminding the Melians of the havoc that profligate hope can wreak on the weak, recommending that they not

> make [themselves] like the many, who, when it is still possible to be saved by human means, when, being hard-pressed, manifest hopes abandon them, give themselves over to those that are immanifest—to divination, oracles, and such things that bring ruin through hope (5.103).

Here the Melians confirm the Athenians' suspicions by making their hopes explicit, insisting that "we trust that in that fortune that is from the divine, we will not be at a disadvantage, being pious men who are standing against men who are not just" (5.104). The Athenians coolly rejoin that, when it comes to the gods, they themselves do not fear being at a disadvantage. As they explain, "for we believe, of the gods through opinion and of men clearly, that all through everything by a necessity of nature, they rule what they have power over" (5.105). To this the Melians make no answer, and the remaining discussion centers primarily on the question of whether the Spartans are likely to intervene on behalf of the Melians, their kinsmen, the hope for which the latter had also revealed in their remarks about fortune. The Athenians attempt and fail to convey the flimsiness, not to say insanity, of this confidence, and, in clear vexation, conclude by chastising their interlocutors because "the strongest resources you have are hoped for in the future, and what you actually possess is too slight to prevail against what is set against you" (5.111.2). Calling the Melians "unreasonable," the Athenians criticize once more their apparently unfounded hopes, and point out (finally) that they are offering relatively moderate terms—Melos will become an ally of Athens who must pay tribute but who will keep her land—before pushing them, once more, to consider clearly their situation (5.111.3-5). Once the discussion has concluded and the Melians have deliberated among themselves, they give the Athenians their answer: they will not submit, "trusting to fortune from the divine that has saved [them] to this point," and to help from the Spartans (5.112.2). The Athenians censure the Melians as the "only" men "who judge the future things as clearer than the visible things" and who "look on the immanifest, because you wish it, as already coming to be" (5.113). The conversation ends with the Athenians telling the Melians that they will come to ruin; the Athenians then besiege the city and, upon her eventual capitulation, kill all the men and make slaves of the women and children (5.114, 5.116).

Thus, in the example of the Melians, Thucydides offers, among other things, a clear illustration of an experience of pious hope: the Melians, caught in a desperate situation beyond their evident capacity to survive, are buoyed by a belief in their justice and piety, which virtues they believe will not go unrewarded by the gods; accordingly, they are confident that the gods will deliver them from a terrible peril. This confidence is likely bolstered by their sense of the Athenians' naked injustice, a sense that is surely inflamed, not only by the fact of the Athenians' attempt on them, but by the latter's insistence that justice forms no part of their designs, on Melos or any other city. It is also surely inflamed by the impiety on brazen display in much of the Athenians' speech, such as their contemptuous dismissal of "divination, oracles, and such things that bring ruin," as well as the Athenians' likening of themselves to gods.[7]

Next we turn to Nicias, in whom we find an example very similar to that of the Melians. Nicias' pious hope is seen most clearly in his reaction to the dire straits in which the Athenians find themselves in Sicily. Utterly dejected by the loss of their final sea-battle with Syracuse, the Athenians refuse to attempt a retreat by sea, finding the prospect of returning to what is left of their fleet, formerly the outstanding symbol of Athenian strength and superiority, too much to bear (7.72.4). They opt instead to attempt an escape by land, and in the miserable trek through the Syracusan countryside that follows, Nicias exhorts the Athenians not to abandon hope. He explains the ground of his confidence thus: noting that he himself, formerly renowned for "good fortune," is suffering no less (and, given the illness with which he is now afflicted, he suffers more) than "the lowest" among them, Nicias claims that he has "spent [his] life in many lawful actions to gods and many just actions to men" (7.77.1-2), on account of which his "hope for the future is still bold" (7.77.1-2). Here, then, we see the same hope expressed by the Melians: the reward of justice and piety by the gods in the form of escape from imminent destruction.

The situation here is less straightforward than that of the Melians in an important respect, for Nicias also believes the crisis facing the Athenians to be a punishment for their collective crime of invading Sicily. However here, too, we see Nicias' confidence that the gods' protection of the virtuous, or at least, those human beings whose vice is not serious enough to warrant their destruction, will assure the Athenians' safety. For Nicias also takes comfort in the very severity of the Athenians' suffering, as he goes on to say that their misfortunes will probably abate, "for fortune has sufficiently favored the en-

[7] Orwin, 1994, 105, 110.

emy, and if by making this expedition we have roused the jealousy of one of the gods we have now suffered enough retribution." He elaborates the ground of his belief that he and his fellow citizens have been "punished sufficiently" when he indicates that their transgressions have not been terribly great:

> For surely some others before now have gone against their neighbors, and after doing that which belongs to man, have suffered what can be endured. And it is reasonable for us to hope that we will now receive gentler treatment from the gods, for we are now more worthy of their pity than their jealousy...(7.77.4).

By describing the pursuit of empire as simply "that which belongs to man," Nicias flirts with the idea, which other Athenians have stated outright and discussed at length (1.75, 1.76, 5.105), that the Athenians and others who have sought rule have done so by a compulsion of human nature, which would suggest that they are not deserving of punishment at all. However, Nicias does not go this far. According to his rather muddy formulation, the disaster visited upon the Athenians is in fact punishment from the gods for imperialism, which is a transgression, but one whose criminality seems to be mitigated by the influence of nature, which, while it does not simply overpower, gives a strong kick. Hence the mitigation of the punishment as well: the Athenians and others deserve punishment, but only "what can be endured," rather than, presumably, what would destroy them. Thus, Nicias shows the paramount importance in his understanding of the gods' concern for virtue, as he expresses the expectation that his own remarkable justice and piety will guarantee the Athenians' deliverance from their current plight, as will the fact that the Athenians' crimes have not been serious enough to merit more than can be endured.

When we consider these examples of manifestly pious hope in comparison with Thucydides' most remarkable depictions of the Athenians' imperial hope—seen in their reveries about Sicily, and in the climax of Pericles' Funeral Oration—we find several key similarities, which may seem to indicate that, notwithstanding the Athenians' occasional violent eruptions of pious terror and their otherwise lax (or worse) approach to divine matters, pious hopes are present here as well. First, apparent or at least implicit in each of these cases is the hope to escape death. As Nicias and the Melians hope not to be destroyed, so too do the Athenians, a hope that is evident in Thucydides' description of the unspoken hopes the Athenians harbor for the Sicilian expedition at its conception. In his most striking formulation,

> [*E*]*ros* fell upon all alike to sail away: upon the old men, because they believed they would either subdue those things they sailed against, or that such a great power could in no way fall; upon those in the prime of life, through a longing for the sight and beholding of what was not present, and being in good hope of being saved; and as for the great multitude, the soldiers, they supposed they would get money for the present and gain power which would be a source of eternal pay (6.24.3).

The attraction to launching a force great enough that it could "in no way fall" suggests a hope for invincibility, and the pleasant contemplation of "being saved," coming as it does in a list of objects of fervent Athenian longing, suggests that this hope is not simply the precondition of attaining other goods in Sicily, but is itself a central object of desire (however complicated in the circumstances).[8] As to "eternal pay," attraction to an endless gravy train implies, of course, an expectation of being always able to ride it, and thus of always being. In other words, the Athenians don't hope merely to conquer Sicily, but with that as their obvious aim they hope for things far beyond what Sicily could offer, including immortality. Such hopes are also apparent in the funeral oration, in which Pericles promises that, for those who devote themselves to Athens, death will be "unperceived" (2.43.6) and, moreover, that such men will attain "ageless praise" (2.43).

A second important similarity between the Melians and Nicias, on the one hand, and the Athenians as a whole, on the other is the connection between their hopes and their understanding of themselves as virtuous. The Athenians' opinion of whether they are virtuous, particularly in their imperialism, is complicated to say the least, and we can only touch on it briefly here. On one hand, the Athenians understand their imperialism to be either amoral or immoral: the leading spokesman of Athenian imperialism at one point likens the city to a tyranny, albeit one kept in the ugly business of empire by the compulsion of fear (2.63). Such opinions are echoed many times by other Athenians: Pericles' demagogic successor, Cleon, plainly calls Athens a tyranny, and his opponent Diodotus apparently accepts his characterization (3.37.2, 3.44); the Athenian envoys to Melos, in a stronger statement of an earlier argument made by Athenian envoys to Sparta, maintain that justice essentially has no place in international affairs, and indicate that the powerful Athenians simply "do what they are capable of" to the weak (5.89). Thus, the Athenians speak repeatedly and openly of their injustice or absolve

[8] That is, it would clearly be safer to stay home than to embark, without apparent necessity, on a very dangerous military expedition far away and in hostile territory.

themselves of injustice only by essentially denying the very possibility of justice among cities. As we noted above, it is the sense that they are immoral (rather than the potentially exculpatory amoral) which seems eventually to overwhelm the Athenians, as they clearly come to fear that they will suffer punishment for what they believe are misdeeds, a fear that cripples their management of the Sicilian expedition; this outcome underscores the manifest dubiousness of empire, the Athenians' remarkable honesty, not least with themselves, as to this fact, and the apparent difficulty for even sophisticated human beings to neglect justice with impunity. On the other hand, the Athenians do not consistently maintain the position that their imperialism is compulsory or ugly, amoral or worse (1.74-1.75, 2.39-2.41, 2.43, 3.39.1-2, 5.107): as Orwin points out, they also understand their empire to be freely-chosen, noble, and admirably dangerous and demanding,[9] and indeed, the tremendous hopefulness we observe in the Athenians is most apparent when they have this opinion in mind (as opposed to when they have foremost in mind an opinion of their empire as compulsion or tyranny). [10] For example, on Pericles' telling, the promise of deathless glory, which he indicates to be a good surpassing all others, is clearly suggested to follow from devotion to and sacrifice for the best city that has ever existed, a city that he claims "fearlessly benefit[s]" other cities, "not so much by calculation of interest as by trust in freedom" (2.64, 2.40.5). Similarly, the considerable power of Athens is to be understood as the consequence of her virtue, including the virtue of allowing certain military advantages to her enemies, "since we trust not to practices and stratagems more than to our courage/stoutness of soul" (2.41.2, 2.39.1). As to the Sicilian expedition, the strongest statement of the Athenians' hope for it comes immediately after they hear Nicias' unwitting portrayal of the great risk, daring, and expense it will require; while the Athenians desire the expedition before his speech, it is not until Nicias clumsily at-

[9] Orwin, 1994, 15-19.

[10] See Pericles' remarks on glory in the Funeral Oration in comparison with those in his other speeches. While he speaks of glory on multiple occasions, it is in the Funeral Oration that his promises of glory are greatest, as he here tells the Athenians not only that they will be remembered, but that they will be "remembered on every opportune occasion in speech and in deed," "for of famous men the whole earth is the tomb, and their epigraph is not only shown on a gravestone in their own home, but in lands not their own there lives an unwritten memory in the mind of each..." (2.43.2-3). Thus it is in this speech, which contains the greatest demands for sacrifice and the fewest references to the notion that the Athenian empire is a mere compulsion or even a tyranny, that Pericles stokes the greatest hopes.

tempts to paint the venture as overly "burdensome" that they are said to be overcome with *eros* for it (6.19-6.24).

In this way, we see a second similarity between Thucydides' presentation of the Melians and Nicias, on one hand, and that of the Athenians generally, on the other: a sense of hope arising, in no small part, from an opinion of their virtue. For while Pericles' praise of the excellence of the city and his exhortation to the Athenians to sacrifice for her emphasizes nobility more than the justice stressed by the Melians and Nicias, Thucydides suggests that both nobility and justice are productive of hope, and that this hope is tied to a sense of sacrifice. Just as Nicias is hopeful because of the good he has done to others—just deeds to men, pious deeds to gods—so too are the Athenians hopeful because they understand themselves to sacrifice or disregard their advantage in various ways.

Consideration of this similarity between the Athenians and the manifestly pious Melians and Nicias brings us to a third, for in all the cases we have discussed, that which is hoped for is beyond the evident powers of the hopeful to attain. For the strength of the Melians alone is not sufficient to stave off the Athenians in battle, nor can Nicias and the rest of his diminished army have much hope of escaping, on their own, the Syracusans; likewise, the Athenians are not capable of ensuring that their city's glory will endure forever or that no harm will come to them in a risky military campaign or in any other circumstance. The connection in the minds of the Melians, Nicias, and the Athenians between the hope for salvation and virtues that have no manifest connection to the salvation they seek underscores this point: for the fate of the virtuous to be reasonably assured, there must exist beings who recognize the possession of virtue and who are capable of assuring those goods that self-sacrificial virtues risk or fail to guarantee.

Thus, we see that the Athenians' hopes, no less than those of the Melians or Nicias, would, if thought through, require a power amounting to that of a god for their fulfillment. It is therefore plausible that, in their extravagant hopes for empire, the Athenians, too, are animated by an expectation of support from "immanifest" beings, and thus that they are guilty of what they criticize in the Melians: while justice and traditional piety are not emphasized when the Athenians are at their most hopeful, perhaps the Athenians are nonetheless moved by the belief that their nobility, which is similarly self-sacrificial, will be rewarded by gods.[11]

[11] For a very thoughtful elaboration of this view, see Ahrensdorf, 1997, 254-265.

However, the observation that the Athenians would require gods of a certain character to make their hopes reasonable does not yet tell us whether the Athenians are reasonable in this respect, and indeed, many features of Thucydides' account suggest that they are not. We first note that Thucydides has elsewhere suggested the possibility of an attachment to nobility that does not depend on hopes for divine assistance. In his narration of the Corcyraean civil war, Thucydides claims that as civil order deteriorated, the meaning of the noble changed, but men nonetheless remained attached to nobility and took great risks on behalf of that attachment (3.82.4-7). This suggests that the hopefulness born of nobility that we have observed in other circumstances also moves the Corcyraeans; at the same time, however, Thucydides tells us that they did not "have reverence for the gods" (3.82.8), thereby indicating that the terrible daring on display in the civil war is not driven by a hope for the gods' help. Turning now to the Athenians in particular, one simple sign that their hopes may not be fundamentally pious is that, while the Melians and Nicias speak explicitly of their expectation of divine intervention, the Athenians, on the whole, do not. Gods are not mentioned at the conception of the Sicilian expedition; the "eros" that Thucydides attributes to the Athenians at the moment they are most seduced by the prospect of such a conquest follows an assembly in which neither of the speakers arguing as to the expedition's desirability refers to the gods (6.9-6.23). Nor do the gods feature in Pericles' beautiful picture of noble sacrifice and eternal glory. We have mentioned the possibility that the Athenians are implicitly or secretly hopeful in these circumstances for divine support, but in that case it is a question why, in expressing their greatest hopes, neither the Athenians nor Thucydides in his own name voice this crucial feature of them, as the Melians and Nicias do. Furthermore, if the Athenians are quietly relying on the divine in these instances, we would expect to find considerable similarity between Thucydides' descriptions of the Athenians on these occasions and on those when they explicitly call on the gods. In fact, however, his descriptions point to two rather different experiences.

This difference is suggested, first, by Pericles. While he does not lead the Athenians in prayer, his Funeral Oration does make one reference to prayer, and his lone remark implies a distinction between hopes for divine assistance and the hopes Pericles is most concerned to stoke. His reference to prayer comes immediately after he praises those Athenians who sacrificed their lives for Athens, when he tells his audience that they too must courageously face the city's foes: first acknowledging that they "must pray to be safer" than those he is eulogizing (2.43), Pericles goes on to say that his fellow citizens ought not think of their own advantage, but rather should be inspired by Athens's power, and that when they are moved by the city's greatness, they must reflect that it was won by men who knew "the terrible things" and nonetheless freely offered Athens the "noblest contribution." Everlasting glory belongs to these men who have given their lives for Athens, whom Pericles holds up as examples for the living, the latter of whom should not "not be mere onlookers to the dangers of the enemy" and should be "unsparing of their lives" (2.43). Thus, in his sole mention of prayer, Pericles ties it to the desire for safety that he urges his audience to spurn, and thereby opposes the hope to be saved by gods with the free and noble sacrifice, and resulting eternal glory, that he extols.

As to the Sicilian expedition, we recall that Thucydides shows the Athenians in prayer when they are utterly beaten and fleeing, as well as at the launch of the mission, when they are said to join together in the customary prayers. We have noted that these calls on the gods surely indicate that the Athenians' hopes, not only to escape Sicily, but also to conquer it, are to some extent hopes for divine assistance. Nonetheless, the circumstances in which the Athenians pray in fact indicate important limits to the influence of piety on their imperial hopes, and suggest that their imperialism is supported by a prior and more fundamental hope, to which hope for the gods' assistance at times offers a supplement.

We turn now to consideration of those circumstances in which the Athenians pray. Thucydides' picture of the Athenians' state of mind on the day of the expedition's launch is one of considerable complexity: the hopes they feel at this point both recall the transcendent, erotic experience of their first contemplation of the conquest of Sicily, and depart from it. The most striking difference is that, on the present occasion, the Athenians become fearful. We recall the erotic transports Thucydides ascribes to the Athenians after they first openly imagine the expedition in the much-expanded form Nicias gives it (6.24). In contrast, on the day they pray, Thucydides describes them in the following manner:

> [T]hey went at once with hope and with lamentations—hope that they would acquire, lamentations as to when they would see [their friends again], laying to heart how long the voyage was from their own land on which they were being sent. And at this critical time, when in the midst of impending dangers they were now about to leave one another, the terrible

> things came into their minds more than when they were voting for the expedition. (6.30.2).

Shortly before we see the Athenians praying, then, far from believing that they could "in no way fall," they are more aware of and disturbed by the danger confronting them than they were when they first decided to attack Sicily. Thus, in describing the conception of the expedition and its launch, Thucydides describes two rather different experiences—one purely hopeful, the other more mixed with fear—and only explicitly ties piety to the latter. The connection Thucydides draws here between piety and fear does not necessarily indicate that the Athenians are moved by piety only in fearful circumstances, but it casts substantial doubt on the notion that they somehow had the gods in mind during the happy delirium depicted at 6.24, a doubt that is consistent with the fact that gods are not mentioned there.

After speaking of the Athenians' fear, Thucydides complicates the picture, telling us that "still they regained courage (*anatharseo*) at the sight of their present strength because of the abundance that each saw before their eyes" (6.30.2). Thus, the Athenians are encouraged, but the encouragement that moves them is not simply new. For the claim that the Athenians "regained" courage indicates, of course, that they have experienced it before, namely, when they were voting for the expedition, which confident occasion Thucydides has just contrasted with the present one. Before going on, then, it is helpful briefly to sketch the broad trajectory of the Athenian hopes referred to in this passage. There seem to be three somewhat separate stages before the Athenians pray. They first openly contemplate the expedition in the massive form it comes to take on the day they vote for it, at which time they grow tremendously, erotically hopeful for it (6.24, 6.26). Then, on the day the armament sets sail, the Athenians' confidence is shaken by a sense of the danger they are in. Some form of hope endures even at this point—the Athenians are not simply full of lamentations, they also hope to "acquire"—but it now exists alongside a new awareness of obstacles to its realization. Accordingly, the hope now appears more muted: it aims merely at "acquir[ing]" rather than at invincibility, eternal pay, and the like. Finally, the Athenians' original, erotic hopefulness is partially "regained" through consideration of their massive armament; then they pray. It is reasonable to call this return to confidence merely partial because we do not now see any sort of reiteration of the tremendous expectations Thucydides so strikingly depicted when the Athenians first imagined the expedition, and because the recent awareness of danger that alarmed them seems unlikely to have been forgotten entirely.

The importance of the order Thucydides describes and of the fact that the Athenians take encouragement from their strength, that is, from manifest things, is underscored by the fact that a prayer the Athenians make later in Sicily follows the same pattern. During their final sea-battle with Syracuse, which Thucydides claims brought on "fear for the future like none [felt before]," the men watching the battle from shore whose vantage point suggested that the Athenians were prevailing "regained courage" (*anatharseo*) and then fell to praying that the gods would not "rob them" of a safe return (7.71.2-3). Here again, then, we see the Athenians becoming frightened, then witnessing a measure of earthly success, and thereby "regain[ing]," to some limited extent, an earlier courage, then praying to the gods. That Thucydides uses the same verb, *anatharseo,* to describe their return to courage—the only times in the work he uses this word in reference to the Athenians—further emphasizes the similarity between the two instances of prayer.

Thucydides suggests with this repetition that the sequence he describes may be necessary to the emergence of pious hope; at the same time, the sequence he describes suggests that the basis of the Athenians' hopes is not primarily a pious one. For on Thucydides' telling, their hopes arise first from their *eros* and their sense of strength; their pious hopes, we are explicitly told, arise only after the Athenians are encouraged by a sense of their strength. In addition, since in the case of their prayer before the Sicilian expedition a sense of their strength recalls them to their erotic hopes, we can say that the erotic hopes, too, can provide an initial basis for their pious hopes. Furthermore, the Athenians' pious hopes do not arise until their sense of their strength has been shaken. Thus, Thucydides here raises the possibility that the Athenians' pious hope functions as a support for a prior hope that has been threatened but not destroyed: when the Athenians become aware of obstacles to the fulfillment of their hope, they may become aware that it is in need of such a support. We see, then, that the two kinds of hope are related and perhaps not fully separable, as one may act as a support for the other or bleed into the other, but nonetheless, Thucydides' stresses the secondary quality of the pious hopes.[12]

[12] For a cryptic discussion of Athenian piety and the Sicilian expedition, see Strauss, 1983, 96-101. The suggestions above are consistent with Strauss's remarks on the Athenians' final sea battle and on their anger at soothsayers and diviners after the

To see further evidence of how the Athenians' hopes differ from the manifestly pious hopes of the Melians and Nicias, we will now reconsider a difference we have earlier noted, namely, the Melians and Nicias stress that they believe themselves to be just in a way the Athenians do not, and they explicitly tie this opinion to their hope for divine assistance. To repeat, Thucydides does not indicate that the Athenians are unconcerned for justice and the traditional dictates of piety—indeed, their concern is great and even of decisive importance for the outcome of the war. Still, their exculpations and praises of their empire do not focus primarily on its justice. It is true that, as we have observed, nobility and justice share crucial attributes like self-sacrifice; it is also the case that they two are not easily or cleanly separated. This is seen in the fact that, when the Athenians speak of their nobility, they tend also to claim that they are "worthy" of rule, which of course implies a notion of desert (see, for example, the Athenian envoys to Sparta [1.76.2]); similarly, it is difficult to consider an action noble when we simultaneously acknowledge it to be unjust. Nonetheless, it is surely possible to emphasize one type of virtue over another, and the emphasis of Athens's spokesmen is decidedly on the city's nobility: Athens's daring, generosity, and superiority to petty concerns of safety figure much more prominently than does her justice in the speeches of Pericles, the envoys to Sparta, the envoys to Melos, and, inadvertently, Nicias. Moreover, in his funeral oration, Pericles not only stresses the Athenians' nobility much more than their justice, but even disparages the latter by casting aspersions on the law that requires him to give the speech in the first place and by favorably contrasting the Athenians' liberality and daring with the law-bred virtue of the Spartans (2.39.4). Given the partial separability, then, and even potential opposition of nobility and justice, it is reasonable to suggest that the hopes and fears of men who are attached primarily to one are somewhat different from those of men attached primarily to the other.

One such difference is suggested when we consider the role that manifest or worldly strength plays in Thucydides' account of the hopes of the Athenians and those of the Melians and Nicias. We have noted that, in his descriptions of the Athenians at their most hopeful, Thucydides speaks frequently of their sense of their nobility and of their own strength: to repeat, at the genesis of the Sicilian expedition, the Athenians are attracted both to the tremendous risk Nicias claims it will entail and the tremendous armament he

expedition's failure, for having "confirmed them in their hope that they would conquer Sicily."

insists it will require. The relationship between strength and nobility is difficult fully to articulate, but one simple connection Thucydides brings out is that noble deeds require great strength to perform: the grandeur and scale that distinguish noble action, that is, feats that go beyond what human beings are ordinarily capable of, are only possible for those who are in possession of great means (not least ships and money) and who are aware of this possession. It is surely no coincidence, then, that Thucydides' accounts of the Funeral Oration and the conception of the Sicilian expedition, the occasions that most manifest or explicate Athenian greatness, include references to the position of unusual strength the Athenians are in at those times. For prior to the funeral oration, Thucydides notes that the Athenians are then "in the flower of their strength," having the "largest force ever assembled" and not yet having engaged in any significant battles nor lost many men (2.22-2.25, 2.30-2.31); similarly, in his account of the Sicilian expedition, Thucydides points out that the Athenians had recently recovered from the plague and that they therefore had many young men and much money to facilitate their preparations for Sicily (6.26.2). Thucydides also makes clear that a sense of strength is not only the ground, but also the consequence of the performance or imagination of noble deeds, for he suggests that the contemplation of noble acts further heightens the Athenians' sense of their strength. We see this clearly in the case of the Sicilian expedition: it is immediately after Nicias describes the undertaking as hugely expensive, demanding, and dangerous that the Athenians fall under the spell of *eros* and develop the opinion that they are invulnerable. That is, the Athenians, already in a position of strength, imagine an expedition that will require great strength and noble risk, and immediately come to believe that they are invincibly strong. It is difficult to imagine how piety would fit in to such an experience, as the Athenians' feeling of their strength would seem to be threatened by an acknowledgement that they are in need of the help of gods. The hopeful experience of the Melians and Nicias clearly does not depend on this sense of strength, as they appeal to the gods in circumstances of manifest weakness, when they are frighteningly outmatched by superior armies. Thus, the particular connection Thucydides suggests between nobility and strength suggests that nobility is at odds with piety in a way that justice does not appear to be.

Our comparison of the Athenians with the Melians and Nicias brings out an additional tension between nobility and piety when we consider the sort of ends these men seek. For the Athenians hope for much more than do the manifestly pious: while the Melians and Nicias express hopes merely to escape from a particular terrible peril—destruction by the Athenian army or destruction by the Syracusan army—in various moments of enthusiasm the Athenians express the hope for everlasting glory, for endless pay, for the "sight and beholding of what was not present" (6.24.3), to be "opposed in nothing," and to "achieve the more impracticable things equally with the possible, whether with means great or deficient" (4.65.4). Even their desire for safety takes a grander form than does that of Nicias and the Melians, as the Athenians hope for invincibility rather than a more limited desire to be saved from a specific threat. Thus, the more obviously pious Melians and Nicias have hopes more limited in scope than do the Athenians—a moderation that Nicias explicitly ties to his pious view of the world. For in trying to buck up the Athenians on their retreat through Sicily, he argues that "for fortune has sufficiently favored the enemy, and if by making this expedition we have roused the jealousy of one of the gods we have now suffered enough retribution" (7.77.3). Nicias thus articulates the view, well-known from common experience, that piety places limits on the goods we can attain. Nobility, of course, also demands that we forego certain goods, but the basis on which we are to do so differs. For in contrast to the pious notion that there is simply a cap on the goods that gods permit human beings to attain, nobility dictates that we give up certain goods because they are beneath us or petty, that is, because they are not good enough. That the Athenians are moved by this view is apparent in many of Pericles' remarks, such as his claim that the Athenians should cease to care for the loss of their private homes and fields because these are mere "ornaments" of Athenian power: their willingness to give up these goods should be rooted, on Pericles' telling, in their desire for greater things (2.62.3). While these observations capture only one aspect of nobility, it is one that is crucial and of concern to the Athenians, and it helps to account for the fact that they strive for so much more than do people like the moderate Nicias, who has no desire to conquer Sicily (6.9), and the quiet Melians, who wish simply to be left alone to mind their own business (5.94). Thus, nobility allows for the pursuit of certain goods that piety does not, which makes less likely that, in hoping for goods of this kind, the Athenians are hoping for the gods' help to attain them. This is not to say that there is no tension between nobility and pursuits like great conquest; for example, the difficulty of fully separating nobility and justice means that the noble self-understanding possessed by men who seek goods of this kind will likely be threatened by nagging doubts about their justice. For, as we mentioned earlier, it is difficult to consider noble that which is simultaneously thought to be unjust (cf., however, Pericles' claim at 2.41.4 in the midst of his praise of Athenian nobility, that the city has everywhere left eternal monuments "to bad [*kakon*] and good"). Nonetheless, when such doubts are not the focus of one's thoughts, a sense of nobility can attach to the pursuit of goods that piety cannot.

From all this we conclude that, while the Athenians' hopes resemble in important ways the manifestly pious hopes of the Melians and Nicias, Thucydides does not indicate that the former are fundamentally pious. We see this in his suggestion that when the Athenians are at their most hopeful they do not pray, that when they do clearly hope for the gods' help, they are first moved by hopes with a different basis, and that piety cuts against important features of nobility and the experience of it on which Athenian *eros* clearly depends. This is not to say that pious hopes and erotic hopes are simply separate things: indeed, given the sequence Thucydides suggests in the development of the Athenians' pious hope, it seems that pious hope can act as a support for a weakened erotic hope, that erotic hopes can come to be interpreted in a pious way, and that erotic hope provides a basis for pious hope. Still, the two remain fundamentally distinct, and in the Athenians, pious hope is not primary.

WORKS CITED

1. Ahrensdorf, Peter J. 1997. "Thucydides' Realistic Critique of Realism." *Polity* 30, 2: 231-265.
2. Bartlett, Robert C. 2001. *The Idea of Enlightenment: a Post-mortem Study*. Toronto: University of Toronto Press.
3. Orwin, Clifford. 1994. *The Humanity of Thucydides*. Princeton: Princeton University Press.
4. Strauss, Leo. 1964. *The City and Man*. Chicago: University of Chicago Press.
5. Strauss, Leo. 1983. "Preliminary Observations on the Gods in Thucydides' Work." *Studies in Platonic Political Philosophy*. Chicago: University of Chicago Press, 89-104.
6. Thucydides. 1923. *War of the Peloponnesians and Athenians*, ed. Jeffrey Henderson and trans. Charles Forster Smith. Cambridge: Harvard University Press.

LOVE, BEAUTY, AND THE PROBLEM OF POLITICS: ALCIBIADES IN THUCYDIDES AND PLATO

Ann Ward

This chapter explores Plato's *Symposium* in light of Thucydides' *Peloponnesian War* to discover the potential impact of love on politics. I begin with a brief sketch of Thucydides' account of the actions and speeches of Alcibiades with respect to Athens' Sicilian expedition in book 6 of *The Peloponnesian War*. I then turn to the *Symposium*, beginning with an analysis of the speech of Diotima, in whose voice Socrates makes his speech. Love, according to Diotima, brings knowledge of death and the attempt to overcome it through begetting, understood as the good. Achieving the highest good is facilitated by the soul's ascent up the "ladder of love," the highest rung being the idea of the beautiful. True lovers desire to give birth to virtue in the presence of the being of beauty.

The political impact of Diotima's understanding of love is twofold. First, the "ladder of love" replaces the gods with the idea of beauty as the object of one's affections. This leads to the second sense that love impacts the political, coming to light in Alcibiades' speech in the *Symposium*. Praising Socrates as the embodiment of beauty, the object of love, Alcibiades says that Socrates made him feel ashamed of himself and his political ambitions, yet nonetheless he could not give up his pursuit of political power. The *Symposium*, therefore, in the speeches of Diotima and Alcibiades, appears to teach that the philosopher, moved by love, will transcend the city in quest of the ideas which are transpolitical. Yet, it also teaches that for politicians like Alcibiades, the idea of beauty as the object of love can disenchant political life, emptying them of their love for themselves and their city, without being able to draw them toward an alternative. Love and beauty can be dangerous to democratic politics. I conclude, however, by arguing contrary to many scholars that the words of Diotima cannot simply be taken for Socrates' words.

Thucydides

In book 6 of his *Peloponnesian War* Thucydides tells us that in the seventeenth year of the war, the Athenians, on the pretext of coming to the aid of the Egestaeans and Leontines against the Selinuntines and the Syracusans, resolved to sail against Sicily (*PW* 358, 361-63).[1] To command this expedition they chose Alcibiades son of Clinias, Nicias son of Niceratus, and Lamachus son of Xenophanes (*PW* 363). Perhaps the Athenians settled on this tripartite structure because, although acknowledging him as a talented general, the people feared Alcibiades and wished to constrain him while exacting his services. According to Thucydides, "Alarmed at the greatness both of [Alcibiades'] license in his own life and habits and of the ambition which he showed in all things soever that he undertook, the mass of people set him down as a pretender to the tyranny [...] his habits gave offence to everyone, and caused them to commit affairs to other hands, and thus before long to ruin the city" (*PW* 367).

Nicias, not desirous of the command and opposed to the expedition, cautioned against it and indirectly attacked Alcibiades on account of his lifestyle, motives, and youth. In response to Nicias, most Athenians spoke in favour of the expedition. Yet, according to Thucydides, "By far the warmest advocate of the expedition was [...] Alcibiades," seeming to appeal not to his fellow citizens but beyond death to future generations, claiming, "persons [...] that have attained to any distinction, although they may be unpopular in their lifetimes in their relations with their fellow men and especially with their equals, leave to posterity the desire of claiming connection with them even without any ground, and are vaunted by the country to which they belonged [...] as fellow-countrymen and heroes" (*PW* 366). Not only does Alcibiades invoke an image of infinite expansion in time beyond death through fame, but also of infinite expansion of the Athenian empire in space. Alcibiades argues, "we cannot fix the exact point at which our empire shall stop; we have reached a position in which we must not be content with retaining but must scheme to extend it, for if we cease to rule others, we are in danger of being ruled ourselves" (*PW* 370). According to Thucydides, in the end, "All alike fell in love with the enterprise [...] those in the prime of life felt a longing for foreign sights and spectacles" (*PW* 373). Moreover, we learn that the force to set sail for Sicily was not the largest gathered by Athens or any other Hellenic city up to that time, but rather the most "splendid," the captains of the crews, "spending lavishly upon figureheads and equipments, and one and all making the utmost exertions to enable their own ships to excel in beauty" (*PW* 377). According to Thucydides, "the expedition became not

[1] Thucydides, *The Peloponnesian War*, Richard Crawley trans. (New York: Random House, 1982). All subsequent citations will be taken from this edition.

less famous for its wonderful boldness and for the splendour of its appearance, than for its overwhelming strength" (*PW* 377). It is as if the force is trying to embody the idea of beauty that Diotima, in the *Symposium*, says is grasped when one ascends to the highest rung of the "ladder of love."

Very soon before the departure of the expeditionary force to Sicily, most of the Hermae in Athens are mutilated. The Athenian people took this matter very seriously, Thucydides tells us, believing that it portended ill for the mission and was part of a conspiracy to overthrow the democracy (*PW* 374). Suspected of being involved with other young men in previous mutilations and impious mocking of the mysteries in drunken frolics, Alcibiades was named by his political opponents and suspected by the people as being behind the mutilation of the Hermae (*PW* 375). Offering to stand trial immediately and be executed if necessary, Alcibiades scares his opponents out of immediate action, fearing that the army gathered for the expedition would be with him and that the people would be angered if the Argives and Mantinaeans abandoned the expedition upon seeing their ally and protector prosecuted (*PW* 375). Alcibiades thus sets sail as one of three in command of the force. However, not letting the matter drop, after the expedition had reached Sicily, the Athenians send out the *Salaminia* to recall to Athens Alcibiades and other soldiers charged with sacrilege in the affair of the Hermae and the other mysteries. In his own ship and with his fellow accused, Alcibiades sets sail with the *Salaminia* from Sicily as if to return to Athens to answer the charges, but disappears at Thurii, and the crew of the *Salaminia* return home to Athens empty-handed. Despite this, the Athenians pass a death sentence on Alcibiades and those with him in absentia (*PW* 390, 395).

Alcibiades, we learn, travels to Sparta in the Peloponnese, there becoming a traitor to his city. Syracusan envoys with their Corinthian allies arrive in Sparta to request that the latter prosecute the war with Athens more diligently at home and send military help to Sicily. Although the Spartans resolved to send envoys to Syracuse to prevent their surrendering to the Athenians, they did not vote to send to troops. As a result, Thucydides says, "Alcibiades now came forward and inflamed and stirred the Lacedaemonians" (*PW* 412). He advises the Spartans to send troops and a Spartan commander to Sicily, to carry on the war against Athens at home more openly, and most importantly he urges them to, "fortify Decalea in Attica, the blow of which the Athenians are always the most afraid and the only one that they think they have not experienced in the present war; the surest method of harming an enemy is to find out what he most fears, and to choose this means of attacking him" (*PW* 414). Worried about what the Spartans might think of a man who "actively join[s] [his city's] worst enemies in attacking it," Alcibiades claims, "I do not consider that I am now attacking a country that is still mine; I am rather trying to recover one that is mine no longer" (*PW* 415). Listening to Alcibiades, the Spartans at once became more earnest in their intent to march against Athens and to fortify Decalea, as well as voting immediately to send assistance to the Syracusans as well as a Spartan commander, Gylippus, son of Cleandridas (*PW* 416).

Many scholars of Thucydides point to the universalism of Alcibiades' political and imperial ambitions rooted in his lack of attachment to Athenian politics and resulting in the betrayal of his city.[2] The debate among these scholars arises as to what Thucydides regards as the cause of the Alcibiades phenomenon, as it were, and the failure of the Sicilian expedition. Very generally, Palmer and Orwin argue that it was the abandoning in Athens and by Alcibiades of the traditional virtues of piety and patriotism represented by Sparta and practised by Nicias that was the cause of imperial overreach and then destruction, whereas Strauss and Riley suggest that it was precisely the piety of Nicias and the surge in frenzied piety among the Athenian people during the affair of the Hermae that caused the failure. According to Strauss, "Alcibiades [...] might have brought the Sicilian expedition to a happy issue. But Alcibiades' proved or presumed impiety made it necessary for the Athenian *demos* to entrust the expedition to [Nicias] [...] whom they could perfectly trust because he surpassed every one of them in piety" (Strauss, 1964: 209). Nichols, on the other hand, argues that, "Nicias shares the blame, but it is not his piety that is at fault, for his 'piety' masks his caution. He does not manifest genuine piety, any more than the impious Alcibiades does" (Nichols, 2015: 111). Thus, for Nichols, piety is not the issue between Alcibiades and Nicias; the cause of the problem, suggested by Thucydides in book 8 of his work, is the failure of Alcibiades to learn and exercise a Socratic "moderation" (Nichols, 2015: 162). Such moderation, Nichols argues, arising either from the examination of his own life or from a concern for how he is remembered in writing, would require Alcibiades to restrain his own personal ambitions to serve the intersts of Athens as a whole (Nichols, 2015: 162-63).

---

[2] See for instance Strauss, 1964: 228-29; Palmer, 1992: 11, 111, 113-14, 117; Orwin, 1994: 194-95, 198, 200-20, 204; Forde, 1989: 6, 7, 196-99, 208, 210; Riley, 2000: 122-23, 138-39; Nichols, 2015: 109.

Plato's Symposium

Nichols' reference to Socratic moderation brings me to Plato's *Symposium* and the philosophic consideration of Alcibiades' imperial ambitions and eventual betrayal of Athens. Did Socrates "corrupt" Alcibiades or turn him away from his city and its particular political life, as Alcibiades himself, speaking near the end of the *Symposium*, seems to imply? Allan Bloom suggests that this is indeed the case, arguing, "there is an extrapolitical immoderation in Alcibiades to which Socrates probably contributed [...] The Alcibiadean vision of politics seems like a political version of Diotima's vision of the Ideas and the beautiful" (Bloom,1993:155). Moreover, Bloom speculates that Socrates' criticism of its authoritative opinions liberated Alcibiades from loyalty to Athens and made him, "capable of arguing, when he joined the Spartans against Athens, that he loved his city and therefore was a traitor to it in order to possess it" (Bloom, 1993: 166).

Nichols disagrees with Bloom, arguing that Alcibiades misunderstood Socrates' conception of *eros* and therewith philosophy. In the *Symposium*, according to Nichols, we see Socrates characterize love and philosophy as an "in-between" state that encourages awareness of limits and thus is antithetical to imperialism (Nichols, 2007:505). Nichols argues, "Socratic philosophizing captures [...] the imperfect human condition, needy yet resourceful. In between ignorance and wisdom, Socrates is skeptical of 'universal' visions, in as much as they presume a realization of wisdom" (Nichols, 2007: 504). Rather, the philosopher, in an "in-between" state recognizes that s/he needs others and hence the equality and reciprocity of the city.

I agree with Bloom that an idea of beauty such as that invoked by Diotima likely had a crucial impact on Alcibiades' motives and actions; it disenchants political life without being able to draw Alcibiades to philosophy and hence the turn to imperial expansion and betrayal of his city. Yet, unlike Bloom and Seth Benardete, who argues, "Socrates through Diotima offers a self-portrait," I think Diotima, although she may for the most part, does not simply and absolutely speak for Socrates.[3] Like Nichols, therefore, I believe that Alcibiades did not have an adequate understanding of Socratic philosophy and thus could not be moderated by it.

---

[3] See Benardete, 1993: 193; for Diotima as a mouthpiece for Socrates see Wedgwood, 2009: 297; Pender, 1992: 73; and Warner, 1979: 334.

Diotima

Light can be shed on the relation between philosophy and politics by exploring the speeches of Diotima and Alcibiades following Socrates' refutation of Agathon in the *Symposium*. The fifth speaker after Phaedrus, Pausanius, Eryximachus and Aristophanes to eulogize love as a god, Agathon praises the divine *eros* as beautiful and good (*Sym.* 195a).[4] Socrates is supposed to speak next in praise of love as a god, but instead questions Agathon concerning the understanding of love portrayed in the latter's eulogy. By means of his questions, Socrates establishes that love is love *of* something that it does not yet possess, namely the beautiful and the good things, and thus that love itself is neither beautiful nor good and as such cannot be a god (*Sym.* 200a-201c). Agathon concludes that he must agree with Socrates, signifying his awareness that he did not know what love was when he eulogized it; he must acknowledge his ignorance.[5]

After refuting Agathon's understanding of love and thus showing what it *is not*, Socrates proceeds to recount what a woman named Diotima taught him concerning what love actually *is*. Diotima tells the story of the birth of love from the joining of his mother *penia* (poverty) and his father *poros* (plenty) (*Sym.* 203c). Due to his mother, love "is always poor [...] always dwelling with neediness," but due to his father, love, "plots to trap the beautiful and the good" (*Sym.* 203d). Diotima concludes, therefore, that "*Eros* is never without resources nor [is *eros*] wealthy" (*Sym.* 203e). Love is thus a feeling of need or lack, combined with the urge or desire to overcome this feeling of incompleteness. Love, as an awareness of incompleteness, opens up whoever experiences it to the external world, combined with the desire to join with what we lack and thus become complete or whole. Love opens one up to an object of desire, then draws one toward that object to make it one's own; to make the "other" or external to us part of us. For Diotima, therefore, *eros* is that which loves and is not the beloved object of love (*Sym.* 2014c).

In response to Socrates' question concerning love's benefit for human beings, Diotima turns to the object of love, or that which love desires. Together, Diotima and Socrates agree that one who experiences love loves the beautiful things and desires that they be his (*Sym.* 204d). Diotima then asks Socrates, "what will he have who gets the beautiful things" (*Sym.* 204d)?

[4] Plato, *Symposium*, Seth Benardete trans. (Chicago: University of Chicago Press, 1993). All subsequent citation will be taken from this edition.

[5] See Ward, 2007: 168

Socrates, however, cannot answer. Diotima then switches to the good things asking, "What if someone changed his query and used the good instead of the beautiful? Come, Socrates, the lover of the good things loves: what does he love [...] and what will he who gets the good things have" (*Sym.* 204e)? Socrates can now answer, claiming, "he will be happy" (*Sym.*204e). The benefit of love, therefore, if it can be fulfilled, is happiness. Notice, however, that at this point in the dialogue there is a certain slipping together of the beautiful and the good. Although distinct the tenor of the dialogue is to proceed on the assumption that in loving both the beautiful and the good things, the lover is loving the same or at least complimentary things.[6]

Diotima refines the object of love when she says, "This wanting and this *eros*, do you suppose [...] all want the good things to be theirs always" (*Sym.*205a)? Diotima thus indicates that there is an element of eternity in love, and love, as love, somehow expresses our desire to transcend time and live forever. Diotima thus suggests that *eros* brings awareness of death or mortality which, desiring what we do not have, it then seeks to overcome. Lovers attempt to overcome this very significant imperfection and reach toward immortality through begetting. According to Diotima, for the most earnest and intense lovers of the good, those who are pregnant or, "conceive both in terms of the body and in terms of the soul," their deed, "is bringing to birth in beauty both in terms of the body and in terms of the soul" (*Sym.* 206c). Love, for Diotima, is thus making or begetting "offspring," as it were. Moreover, a pregnant human being cannot beget in the presence of ugliness but rather only in the presence of beauty (*Sym.* 206d-e; also, for the meaning of male "pregnancy" and "offspring" here, see Pender, 1992: 72-76). The good is the object of love, which is to give birth either physically or intellectually and thereby achieve immortality; the beautiful helps love to beget and thereby achieve its object.[7]

Immediately before her more famous "ladder of love," therefore, Diotima articulates a perhaps lesser known "ladder of begetting," as it were.[8] On the bottom rung, those men "pregnant" in terms of their bodies have a bodily or sexual attraction to women and beget human children with them

[6] See for instance the exchange between Diotima and Socrates between 204d-205a, and Diotima's account of the birth of true virtue upon ascent to the idea of beauty itself at 212a-b.

[7] For the meaning of immortality through intellectual birth in this context, see White, 2004: 374-75; in contrast see Wedgwood, 2009: 312-13; and Pender, 1992: 85

[8] For "ladder of love," see Bloom, 1993: 55.

(*Sym.* 208e). The higher rungs reflect those "pregnant in terms of their soul;" those whose *eros* reflects a passion in the soul understood as higher than a longing of the body (*Sym.* 209a). According to Diotima, those pregnant in soul give birth to speeches or thought about virtue that can take three forms. First, they can be speeches about virtue, or something like philosophic conversations, with a youth beautiful in body and soul; second, they can be works of poetry such as those of Hesiod and Homer that are their "offspring," as it were; and third, they can be the laws of cities reflecting the thoughts of their founders such Lycurgus of Sparta and Solon of Athens (*Sym.* 209c-e). On the highest rung, however, Diotima turns away from speeches to deeds, claiming that, "other men [...] among Greeks and among barbarians, by their showing forth of many beautiful deeds, have engendered every kind of virtue" (*Sym.* 209e). Glorious deeds, therefore, are virtuous and engender virtue in others.

Diotima claims that a human being pregnant in either body or soul cannot engender in the presence of ugliness but rather only the presence of beauty (*Sym.* 206d-e). Hence, Diotima brings forth her "ladder of love," painting an image of an ascending order of beauty in which the lover (in soul, not body, who is now discarded) can beget in their attempt at immortality. On the bottom rung, the lover loves the beautiful body of a particular human being, causing the lover to "generate beautiful speeches" (*Sym.* 210b). On the second rung, the lover loves all beautiful bodies equally, or moves away from a particular human body to what is beautiful in all human bodies (*Sym.* 210b). On the third rung the lover loves the beautiful soul of the beloved, which is more "honourable" according to Diotima than the body, and then moves to the love all souls or what is beautiful in all souls (*Sym.* 210b). This love of the beauty of the soul then allows the lover to love the pursuits or products of beautiful souls: the laws of cities (political philosophy), comprising the fourth rung, and then the love of the sciences or all fields of study (metaphysical philosophy), comprising the fifth rung (*Sym.* 210c-d). The sixth and highest rung, comprising the highest type of beauty which is the object of a "certain philosophical science," is the idea or form of the beautiful itself, "pure, clean, unmixed, and not infected with human flesh, colors, or a lot of other mortal foolishness [...] the divine beautiful itself as being of a single shape" (*Sym.* 211a-d). In the presence of the idea of beauty itself, Diotima says that the lover will, "engender not phantom images of virtue [...] but true, because he lays hold of the true; and that once he has given birth to and cherished true virtue, it lies within him to become dear to god and [...]

to become immortal as well."[9] The soul's ascent up the ladder of love, therefore, is an ascent that begins with particularity but moves on to ever greater comprehensiveness and universality, culminating in the idea of beauty itself.

The political impact of the ladder of love is twofold. Near the beginning of her speech, Diotima says that *eros* connects human beings and gods, "interpreting and ferrying to gods things from human beings and to human beings things from gods" (*Sym.* 202e). The power of *eros*, therefore, is that it opens human beings up to and draws them towards the gods. Ascending up the ladder of love, however, *eros* is drawn not up toward the gods but to the idea of beauty. The idea of beauty, it appears, replaces the gods as the object of love.[10] Being tutored by Diotima perhaps one would no longer love nor believe in the gods of one's city. Also, perhaps in this context it may be fair to ask if the "ladder of love" encourages the lover to be abusive toward particular persons; using them—the beauty of their particular body and soul—only as "steps" or instruments to gain access to ever higher and universal manifestations of beauty beyond the persons themselves?[11]

Alcibiades

The question of whether or not the "ladder of love" treats individuals as instruments rather than ends in themselves is brought to light in the speech of Alcibiades. Bursting in on the the party very drunk and with an entourage of flute girls and raucous attendants, Alcibiades' speech is the last in the dialogue. He proceeds with a story designed to show the exceptional moderation of Socrates and thus the beauty of the latter's soul. Alcibiades says that when young he believed Socrates, "erotically inclined to the beauties" and always around him, to be his most "deserving" of lovers (*Sym.* 216d, 218c). He therewith decided to gratify what he believed was Socrates' sexual desire in exchange for "hear[ing] everything he knew" (*Sym.* 217a).

To facilitate such an exchange Alcibiades arranged to be alone with Socrates, often stripping along with him and wrestling naked together while alone, yet all to no avail. Alcibiades says he then invited Socrates to dinner, but that Socrates left him and went home after their first dinner meeting together. On the second dinner encounter he contrived to converse with Socrates long into the evening so that the latter would have to stay the night.

[9] Sym. 212a-b; for the idea of beauty as the female image of "pregnancy" and contribution to childbirth, see Pender, 1993: 84-86.

[10] But see Howland, 2007: 185.

[11] But see White, 2004: 373, 376.

Before Socrates could fall asleep, Alcibiades says he declared to him that he would gratify his sexual desire as well as make his wealth and friends available to him in return for Socrates' help in "becom[ing] the best possible" (*Sym.* 218c-d). Denying that he knew how to make others better, Socrates almost chastises Alcibiades for "intending to get the better deal" (*Sym.* 218e). Intimating that Alcibiades wishes to give his body in exchange for Socrates giving Alcibiades a virtuous soul, Socrates, according to Alcibiades, responds, "you are trying to acquire the truth of beautiful things in exchange for the seeming and opinion of beautiful things; and you really have in mind to exchange 'gold for bronze'" (*Sym.* 218e-219a).

Alcibiades, apparently not quite fathoming the depth of Socrates' rejection of his proposal, says he climbed into bed with Socrates and threw his arms around this "truly daemonic and amazing being" (*Sym.* 219c). Yet, although laying with Socrates the whole night, Alcibiades reports that nothing, "more untoward [...] happened than would have been the case if I had slept with my father or elder brother" (*Sym.* 219d). Now clearly apprehending Socrates' rejection of his proposal, Alcibiades interprets such rejection as having, "despised and laughed at my youthful beauty and [as having] committed an outrage against it" (*Sym.* 219c). Alcibiades says he was left in a quandary: "enslaved by this human being as no one has been by anyone else [...] I did not know how I could be angry at him and be deprived of his association; nor did I have any resource whereby I could attract him" (*Sym.* 219d-e).

If Socrates thought so little of Alcibiades and his physical beauty, why did Socrates spend so much time with him such that the young Alcibiades comes to mistakenly believe that Socrates is his lover? Did Socrates, as Diotima would suggest, use the attraction of Alcibiades' physical beauty as a stepping stone to begin his soul's ascent up the "ladder of love," gaining access to ever more universal manifestations of beauty while leaving the particular person of Alcibiades behind? Alcibiades suggests something like this when he concludes his speech by saying that Socrates, "committed an outrage" against him and many others, "for while deceiving them into thinking of him as their lover, [Socrates] brings it about that he is the beloved rather than the lover" (*Sym.* 222a).

Alcibiades' speech also brings to light the second sense in which the "ladder of love" impacts the political. In his speech Alcibiades praises or speaks not of *eros* directly, but rather of Socrates, and not as an image of *eros*, as Diotima does, but as the beautiful itself. According to Alcibiades, "were one willing to hear Socrates' speeches, they would at first look altogether laughable [...] but if one sees them opened up [...], one will find first, that they alone of speeches have sense inside; and, second, that they are the most divine and have the largest number of images of virtue in them; and that they apply [...] to the whole area that is proper to examine for one who is going to be beautiful and good" (*Sym.* 222a). For Alcibiades, Socrates' soul and the reasoned speeches that flow from it are the perfection of beauty, and thus, as noted above, Socrates for Alcibiades is the beloved object of love (*Sym.* 222b). Taking together what Diotima and Alcibiades say, Socrates appears as the embodiment of both lover and beloved, of *eros* and the object of *eros*.

Alcibiades indicates the affect that Socrates' speeches had on him when he says:

> whenever any one of us hears [Socrates] or another speaking [his] speeches [...] we are thunderstruck and possessed [...] Whenever I listen, my heart jumps far more than the Corybants', and tears pour out under the power of [his] speeches [...] I came to the opinion that it was not worth living in the way I am [...] For he compels me to agree that, though I am still in need of much myself, I neglect myself and handle instead the affairs of the Athenians [...] So [...] only before him do I feel shame (*Sym.* 215d-216b).

Alcibiades indicates that Socrates' speeches touched powerfully the emotional part of his soul, bringing him to tears, because they made him feel that his unexamined way of life was not worth living. By showing him something higher or beyond the city, perhaps the beautiful itself that Alcibiades could not live up to, Socrates made him ashamed of himself for his political ambitions and hence desire to win the approval of the many. The suggestion appears to be that human beings whose erotic natures reach out for their highest end will transcend their city in the quest for the highest type of beauty, either in the idea as the philosopher appears to seek or in the soul of the beloved as Alcibiades appears to seek. The problem appears to be that the idea of beauty, either as transcendent or in the soul of the beloved, separates men like Alcibiades from their city, but, while disenchanting political life for them, is not strong enough to bring them over to philosophy.

Socrates

Is Socratic philosophy, therefore, responsible for corrupting Alcibiades? I would argue that it is not, pointing to ways in which Diotima's understanding of the beautiful and the good may depart from Socrates' understanding. First, considering Diotima's understanding of the good, on her lesser known "ladder of begetting" she curiously ranks the type of philosophic conversations that Socrates engages in with his interlocutors lower than poetry and law-giving, and the highest good turns away from speech or rationality altogether toward glorious deeds.[12] Moreover, the performance of these glorious deeds, according to Diotima, is motivated by the good person's "love of honor," and "their [deeds] setting up of immortal fame for eternity" (*Sym.* 208c). Yet, does Socrates pursue this type of immortal glory as the highest good? We should notice that Alcibiades says that when he, Alcibiades, "succumb(s) to the honor I get from the many," he is ashamed to see Socrates and tries to avoid him because he knows he is not living up to the truth that he and Socrates have agreed upon (*Sym.* 216b-c). Another indication that Socrates does not care for fame or honour among the many is his refusal of the medal that Alcibiades wants to have him rewarded with for saving him in battle (*Sym.* 220e-221a). Perhaps acquiring fame through glorious deeds articulated by Diotima is actually a political or "Alcibiadean" image of the highest good, not a Socratic one. This points to the second way in which Diotima and Socrates appear to differ.

Diotima says the idea of beauty is the highest type of beauty toward which *eros* in the soul is drawn and ascends. Yet, if we turn to Plato's *Republic* where Socrates speaks in his own voice rather than in another's, Socrates says, in the context of arguing for the equality of the sexes in book 5, that, "he is empty who believes anything is ridiculous other than the bad, and who tries to produce laughter looking to any sight as ridiculous other than the sight of the foolish and the bad; or again, he who looks seriously to any standard of beauty he sets up other than the good" (*Rep.* 452d-e).[13] Socrates, therefore, seems to be arguing that the beautiful be replaced by the good. Moreover, this passage suggests, contrary to the tenor of the speeches in the *Symposium*, that one does not love the same or complimentary things when

---

[12] But see Wedgwood, 2009: 312-14; White, 2004: 369, 375; and Pender, 1992: 84.

[13] Plato, *Republic*, Allan Bloom trans. (New York: Basic Books, 1968). All subsequent citations will be taken from this edition.

one loves either the beautiful or the good. Turning to the nature of the philosopher in the same book, Socrates, like Diotima, suggests that the philosopher has an erotic and therefore open and longing soul that draws him or her to things, such as ideas or forms, outside of themselves (*Rep.* 474c-475c). Yet, when we turn to book 6, the highest idea that the philosopher's *eros* is drawn toward is not the idea of beauty, as Diotima would suggest, but the idea of the good (*Rep.* 508d-509a). I will thus conclude with a brief reflection on Socrates' understanding of the good in the *Republic.*

In book 6 of the *Republic*, as noted above, Socrates says to his main interlocutor Glaucon that the greatest study is of the idea of the good, or what Socrates simply calls "the good" (see for example *Rep.* 506b, 506d-e, and 509c). According to Socrates, every soul pursues the good but most do not know what it is; they think that the good exists but cannot comprehend correctly what it is (*Rep.*505e). The many believe the good is pleasure whereas the few believe that it is thinking and prudence, but both are wrong. In order to help his interlocutors grasp the good, Socrates first draws an image or likeness of the good, or that which he says, "looks like a child of the good," the sun (*Rep.* 506e).

Socrates begins his analogy between the sun and the good by drawing a distinction between the many particular objects in the world which are sensed, and the idea or universal characteristics that the particulars share and which group them into a class or category of things distinct from other classes or categories of things.[14] These ideas or universal characteristics that classify or categorize particulars cannot be sensed but only thought, as it were (*Rep.* 507a-b). Socrates then continues and says, "When sight is in the eyes [...] and color is present in what is to be seen, in the absence of a third class of thing [...] sight will see nothing and the colors will be unseen. [...] [The] class of thing [we] are [...] speaking of [...] [is] that which [we] call light" (*Rep.* 507d-e). The natural source of light, and that which illuminates the sensory realm, Socrates concludes, is the sun (*Rep.* 508a). Thus, in Socrates' formulation, the sun is the source of light that allows sight in the eyes to see color in the objects seen.

Socrates, turning from the sun to its analog, the good, indicates that whereas the sun illuminates the sensory realm, the good illuminates the intellectual realm. Thus, Socrates claims, "When [the soul] fixes itself on that which is illumined by truth and that which *is*, it intellects, knows, and ap-

[14] Also see Stern, 1993: 197-98; and Ward, 2009: 26.

pears to possess intelligence. [...] Therefore, [...] what provides the truth to the things known and gives the power to the one who knows, is the *idea* of the good. [...] As the cause of knowledge and truth, you can understand it to be a thing known; but, as fair as these two are—knowledge and truth—[...] it is something different from them and still fairer than they" (*Rep.* 508d-509a). In Socrates' formulation, therefore, as the sun is the source of light that allows sight in the eyes to see the objects seen, so the good is source of truth which allows mind in the soul to intellect the ideas, or that which *is*.

In this brief sketch of the good, the good appears not to be making or begetting as suggested in the *Symposium*. Rather, as that which is the source of reason's ability to classify the particular objects sensed in the world into stable categories so that we know what they are, the good appears to be that which allows us to think. Moreover, as sight in the eye can see the sun, its own cause, so reason in the soul, Socrates' suggests, can know the good (*Rep.* 508b). Perhaps if Alcibiades had grasped this good he may have acquired the Socratic moderation he lacked.

Works Cited

Benardete, Seth. "On Plato's *Symposium*." In *Plato's Symposium*, Seth Benardete trans. Chicago: University of Chicago Press, 1993. 179-99.

Bloom, Allan. "The Ladder of Love." In *Plato's Symposium*, Seth Benardete trans. Chicago: University of Chicago Press, 1993. 55-177.

Forde, Steven. *The Ambition to Rule: Alcibiades and the Politics of Imperialism in Thucydides.* Ithaca: Cornell University Press, 1989.

Howland, Jacob. "Kierkegaard's Socratic Recovery of Philosophy and Faith." In *Socrates: Reason or Unreason as the Foundation of European Identity*, Ann Ward ed. Newcastle: Cambridge Scholars Publishing, 2007. 178-89.

Nichols, Mary P. *Thucydides & the Pursuit of Freedom.* Ithaca: Cornell University Press, 2015.

_____. "Philosophy and Empire: On Socrates and Alcibiades in Plato's *Symposium*." *Polity* 30/4 (2007): 502-21.

Orwin, Clifford. *The Humanity of Thucydides.* Princeton: Princeton University Press, 1994.

Palmer, Michael. *Love of Gory and the Common Good: Aspects of the Political Thought of Thucydides.* Lanham, MD: Rowman & Littlefield, 1992.

Pender, E. E. "Spiritual Pregnancy in Plato's *Symposium*." *The Classical Quarterly*. 42/1, 1992. 72-86.

Plato, *Republic*, Allan Bloom trans. New York: Basic Books, 1968.

_____. *Symposium*, Seth Benardete trans. Chicago: University of Chicago Press, 1993.

Riley, Jack. "Freedom and Empire: The Politics of Athenian Imperialism." In *Thucydides' Theory of International Relations: A Lasting Possession.* Lowell S. Gustafson ed. Baton Rouge: Louisiana State University Press, 2000. 117-50.

Stern, Paul. *Socratic Rationalism and Political Philosophy: An Interpretation of Plato's Phaedo*. Albany: State University of New York Press, 1993.

Strauss, Leo. "On Thucydides' War of the Peloponnesians and Athenians." In *The City and Man*. Chicago: University of Chicago Press, 1964.

Thucydides, *The Peloponnesian War*, Richard Crawley trans. New York: Random House, 1982.

Ward, Ann. "The Immortality of the Soul and the Origin of the Cosmos in Plato's *Phaedo*." In *Matter and Form: From Natural Science to Political Philosophy*. Ann Ward ed. Lanham, MD: Lexington Books, 2009. 19-34.

_____. "Socratic Irony and Platonic Ideas? Kierkegaard's 'Critique' of Socrates in *The Concept of Irony*." In *Socrates: Reason or Unreason as the Foundation of European Identity*, Ann Ward ed. Newcastle: Cambridge Scholars Publishing, 2007. 164-77.

Warner, Martin. "Love, Self, and Plato's *Symposium*." *The Philosophical Quarterly* 29/117 (1979): 329-39.

Wedgwood, Ralph. "Diotima's Eudaimonism: Intrinsic Value and Rational Motivation in Plato's *Symposium*." *Phronesis* 54/4(5) (2009): 297-325.

White, F.C. "Virtue in Plato's *Symposium*." *The Classical Quarterly* 54/2 (2004): 366-78.

NIKIAS' VIRTUE

Norman Fischer

In his edition of the Hobbes translation of Thucydides' *Peloponnesian War*, David Grene points to one of Hobbes's "most inexplicable omissions," which occurs at the death of Nikias.[1] Thucydides claims that Nikias "least deserved to fall into so great a misfortune." Hobbes omits the reason given by Thucydides, which Grene supplies in his note. He least deserved to fall into such misfortune because of "having regulated all his life with what has been considered virtue". This omission is pregnant, raising many questions. Does Hobbes disagree with the attribution of virtue to Nikias? Does Thucydides think that "what has been considered" virtue is actual virtue? If not, does this modify his claim that Nikias least deserved such misfortune? Is Nikias a tragic figure, combining virtue with undeserved misfortune? And, more broadly, what is the relation between virtue and fortune as Thucydides conceives it? Consideration of these questions will involve some considerations of virtue in democracy which are relevant to not only Athenian democracy but to any democratic polity. Thus I will consider some discussions by Alexis de Tocqueville in light of Thucydides' account. Before looking at these questions in analyzing a telling episode in *The Peloponnesian War*, it will prove valuable to consider Nikias as he appears in speech and act in Plato's *Laches*. I will show there an understanding of the deficiency in Nikias' understanding of courage and virtue that manifests itself in Thucydides' account.

Nikias in Plato

In *Laches*, the relation between fortune and virtue turns out to be significant to an account of courage. Nikias reenters the conversation about courage after Socrates and Laches have reached an apparent dilemma. Laches has defined courage as a kind of persistence or endurance of the soul. Socrates' questions in response to this focused upon the relationship between courage as a virtue, and the sort of practical intelligence that is necessary in order to obtain an advantage, under the assumption that virtue is something

---

[1] Thucydides, *The Peloponnesian War: The Complete Hobbes Translation*, ed. David Grene, (Chicago: University of Chicago Press, 1987) VII, 86.

advantageous to those who possess it. Since courage is a virtue, and virtue requires prudence concerning one's good, courage must involve some kind calculation of the advantageous. Socrates then proceeds with a series of examples of acting with intelligence, from investment and business to war. The most revealing of these—and the one that seems to indicate the nature of battle—arises when Socrates asks Laches whether a soldier fighting in a more advantageous position, in supply, training and strategy, or rather "his fellow in the opposite camp," whose persistence is not supported by intelligent calculation, is the more courageous. Laches chooses the latter, and Socrates immediately points out the difficulty—that the one Laches favors is less intelligent persistence, opposing their prior agreement (192c-193d).[2] Courage, in order to be a virtue, requires calculation of advantage; but in order to remain courage, it must involve risk, thus favoring those at a calculated disadvantage. This is Laches's dilemma; to resolve it requires some conception of the "knowledge of the good" needed for virtue compatible with the presence of risk and the failure to achieve one's aims.

This emphasis upon art continues an earlier dispute between Laches and Nikias over the usefulness of the hoplite art. The dialogue had begun with two fathers, Lysimachus and Milesias, concerned with the education of their sons. They invited the two generals to watch a display of fighting in hoplite armor. They then ask the generals whether, in their opinion, this is a beneficial art for young men to learn. Nikias and Laches, noticing Socrates passing by, and knowing by reputation his concern with learning, as well as his display of sangfroid on the battlefield, engage him in the discussion. Socrates begins by deferring to the generals.

Nikias, in arguing in favor of the usefulness of the hoplite art as a beneficial practice for young men, points to the technical advantage in battle and the confidence the art brings. Nikias goes so far as to say boldly that the art makes one "undefeatable," whether in fighting alone or taking on several opponents. Laches, disagreeing with Nikias, emphasized the presumption of this in practice when exposed by the uncertainties of battle. Laches demonstrated this by reference to an example he witnessed of the ridiculous activity of an expert of hoplite armor in training. Laches does not deny that it can give one confidence, but this actually opens one up to ridicule if one cannot

---

[2] References to *Laches* use the standard Stephanus notation. I have consulted, where quotation is needed, the translation found in Plato, *Meno and Other Dialogues*, trans. Robin Waterfield, (Oxford: Oxford University Press, 2005).

deliver on the presumption of the art. Whereas Nikias is portrayed as having confidence in *techne*, art, both in hoplite armor and in the higher arts of strategy and tactics, Laches is skeptical of the value of such confidence. However, instead of pointing to a prudence that is not merely technical, he falls back on a consideration of reputation. He does not share the boldness needed to risk his reputation, which may result in being laughed at; he especially emphasizes the resentment of the *hoi polloi* of those who make a claim to artful superiority (181e-182d; 183c-184e). One is reminded of the common saying that the philosopher must not be afraid to look foolish.

The question of Laches's dilemma is whether or not the preservation of risk is compatible with the calculation of advantage necessary for virtue. Nikias reenters the conversation, putatively to help resolve this dilemma. He begins by repeating something he has overheard Socrates say: that one is good at what one knows. Hence, courage is a kind of knowledge of the threatening and reassuring. Laches, recalling the insufficiency of calculation in Socrates' examples of knowledge, ridicules Nikias, pointing out that Nikias' definition of courage seems to reduce it to a function of artful expertise. Hence, for example, the doctor would be the courageous one when he knows what is threatening or reassuring with regard to a sick patient. Likewise, each artisan in his particular sphere would be courageous due to their expertise. When Nikias denies this, pointing out that the doctor as a doctor does not "know whether it is better for a patient to recover or to die," Laches responds by pointing out that the sort of knowledge of the future necessary for Nikias' claim would be that of a prophet or even a god (195a-196b). Nikias denies that prophetic knowledge is courage, correctly pointing out that knowledge of what will happen in the future is not quite knowledge of whether what will happen is beneficial or harmful. He never quite says, however, what is needed in addition to, or instead of, prophecy. Laches, frustrated with this, accuses Nikias of sophistically evading the question at hand. Thus, Socrates is forced to take over the questioning from Laches to try to get Nikias to say directly what kind of knowledge is involved in courage. But when Socrates takes over the questioning from Laches, in an apparent non-sequitur, he returns to the question of prophecy, chiding Nikias that generals should rule prophets, since generals "have a superior knowledge of what is happening." This dramatic Platonic anachronism apparently refers to the infamous delay of Nikias before Syracuse as the result of his consultation of prophets, which in Thucydides' telling, ensures the destruction of first the Athenian army and then Nikias himself.[3]

This reference to the delay of Nikias before Syracuse occurs in the process of securing Nikias' agreement to the claim that knowing what happened in the past, present and future belongs to the same art. Eventually, this leads to Nikias inability to distinguish courage from virtue as a whole. Since Nikias had previously defined courage in relation to knowledge of only future harms and benefits, he now, in agreeing that the same art knows of past, present, and future, is forced to either define courage as the whole of "knowledge of good and evil," that is virtue, or admit his definition is merely a third of courage. This agreement regarding the knowledge present in *techne* is no less ambiguous than Nikias' original definition. It seems in one way false to say that our knowledge of the future is the same as our knowledge of what has already happened; it is patently less certain. Laches's accusation of Nikias is thus far correct; for the arts to eliminate uncertainty—to make a man, as Nikias had earlier said, undefeatable—requires their dependence upon prophecy, which in treating the future as the past seeks to eliminate such uncertainty. Thus, Nikias' preoccupation with being undefeatable by eliminating risk, implicit in his praise of the arts of war, requires his being ruled by prophets.[4] Nikias' peculiar sort of "piety" would have it be a sort of master artisanship, which would ensure the success of other artful enterprises.

Given the prophet's certainty about the future, which the artisan does not share, how are we to understand Socrates' rejoinder that it is the artisans, whether doctors or generals, who have superior knowledge? In what sense is the transcendence of temporal considerations in the arts not preposterous, if not in the sense of eliminating risk and uncertainty? Nikias' inability to answer this question is what leads to his apparent refutation. Nikias ultimately fails because he in some way understands the knowledge compatible with courage to be a kind of technical expertise. As Laches points out, Nikias' association with the speech-technician Damon has led him to be be full of

---

[3] Thucydides, *Peloponnesian War*, VII.50.

[4] I will leave to the side the thorny question of the relation of virtue as a whole to its constituent "parts" or "types". But if I am right, it seems that we can at least say that the relation present in Socrates' argument implies that a technical solution seems to obliterate any distinction between the virtues, and that it requires the subordination of all virtue to prophecy.

contempt (*kataphronesis*), instead of discovering the knowledge (*phronesis*) compatible with the risk needed for courage (199e).

Howsoever Nikias fails to say in what manner the transcendence of time is made possible by the arts, we might hazard an answer, based on Socrates' very examples of expertise. While the doctor may not know how to calculate what will heal a particular person, what remains constant over time is that he must do what he can for the patient's health and well-being, even when this means risking failure. Virtue is not mere virtuosity, and courage particularly reveals this dimension of virtue. This is not to say that it excludes such artful virtuosity; rather, we might say, the former encourages the latter. A doctor's devotion is not actual unless he takes steps to know human health and disease, both in general and in particular cases. But this devotion to knowledge is inseparable from one's opinion of the nobility of the end of his art. In an Aristotelian vein, we might call courage a confidence in the nobility for which one acts. In this sense the general "knows better what will happen" than the prophet; he will see and act for the sake of what is noble. This knowledge does not eliminate risk, but presupposes it, precisely because, in its uncertainty regarding the outcomes of action, the general's action does not possess the perfection or self-sufficiency of *to kalon*, the noble or beautiful. Failure to achieve a particular desired result, therefore, is compatible with virtue, insofar as one is intelligently devoted to a noble end or purpose. The condition for courage or virtue, therefore, is the very uncertainty about future victory or defeat, which Nikias understands the hoplite art, and its associated higher arts such as strategy and tactics, to overcome.

Socrates hints at what was at stake in the immediate aftermath of Laches' dilemma. Socrates suggests that that their words, which oppose intelligence to the persistence needed for courage, do not match their deeds. Their deeds in inquiry, particularly in deciding to continue the inquiry, combine both persistence in the face of risk and prudence. Even while they are failing to come to a precise understanding of courage, their persistence does not lack prudence. Failure to achieve a particular desired result, therefore, is compatible with virtue, insofar as one is intelligently devoted to a noble end or purpose. As Laches expresses it, the conversation has inspired in him a desire to not give up, and to see the value of being able to express his understanding adequately, something Laches undervalued prior to this conversation (188a-189c). In seeking for the definition of courage, Socrates suggests, they should endure or persist, even though their persistence, in being at a loss, is not with an art of calculation that would guarantee them success. From the point of view of artful calculation that had earlier been discussed, their persistence would be "foolish" and hence, not a virtue. But Socrates suggests that their persistence is not foolish, and hints that their acts in the remainder of their conversation may indeed manifest the nature of courage (193e-194b).[5]

Nikias, by this standard, seems to fail. Unlike Laches earlier in the dialogue, who marries the experiences of "being at a loss" and a burning desire to persist in moving forward, Nikias is unmoved by his failure. He will return to his speech technician, Damon, and resolve the issue, and then deign to return to Laches to teach him. For him, the failure is simply a problem to be technically eliminated, not a way of devoting oneself to the noble. Nikias' confidence in virtue as virtuosity has not been shaken, at least in part because none of his opinions are his own. He begins with something he overheard from Socrates—he is unwilling to risk, at first, his own understanding—and his allegiance to sophistic distinction-making in a defensive mode does not seek a positive understanding, but merely delights in not being seen to be wrong (200a-c; 197d).[6] When Socrates does finally obtain from Nikias something resembling his own opinion, it is simply this risk eliminating confidence in *techne*. The minute Socrates suggests a comprehensive art that knows all good and evil, Nikias jumps at it. That it does so at the expense of courage is not troubling to Nikias. It is for this reason, perhaps, that Nikias was from the beginning so sanguine about conversing with Socrates. He had earlier argued that "being examined by Socrates is not at all unpleasant", even in recognizing that conversation with Socrates ultimately becomes a kind of self-examination (187e-188c). Self-examination is not at all troubling to Nikias, because, being at most a technical exercise, there is no risk in it. But, because there is no risk in it, there is no courage in it, and hence, no virtue.

---

[5] Given Socrates' being the only one who persists in this manner by the end of the dialogue, I take Socrates to be the exemplar of courage needed here. The two generals fail to manifest the combination of persistence in a situation of *aporia* and risk, and the intelligent devotion of the *kalon* that Socrates does. Laches's failure differs somewhat from that of Nikias, in a way unrelated to his unwillingness to look foolish he had noted when critiquing the art of hoplite fighting. Those who take risks for the sake of the noble must be willing to open themselves to ridicule—this is another thing they must risk.

[6] It is this that Nikias shares with Laches; both are ultimately concerned with reputation.

Nikias in Thucydides

The portrayal of Nikias in Plato reveals him to be confident in the arts of war. Further, this confidence is grounded in a denial that our knowledge of the future is uncertain. As Laches points to, this ultimately involves a faith in a kind of prophecy. Implicit in this is a supposition—that ultimately, one with the art of war will be rewarded. He will be "undefeatable."

The importance of Nikias to Thucydides' purpose in the *Peloponnesian War* is beyond doubt. After the death of Pericles, no Athenian except Alcibiades is more influential. Nikias is not directly heard from until his two speeches of opposition to the expedition in Sicily.[7] In between these two speeches we hear a reply from Alcibiades to the first one. This debate is representative of Thucydides' portrayal of the limits of Nikias' virtue.

Before looking at these speeches in more depth, it will be useful to look at Thucydides' direct characterization of Nikias in light of the "peace of Nikias," which follows the death of Kleon, Nikias' earlier rival.[8] Thucydides attributes the peace to the ambition of Nikias and his counterpart in Sparta, Pleistoanax. Thucydides characterizes Nikias as "most favored by fortune." Given Thucydides' comment at Nikias' death, this characterization is striking. How can he who is most favored by fortune least deserve his misfortune? Being favored by fortune must have nothing to do with dessert. In any case, this seems to indicate a certain foolishness in relying on fortune's favor. Being most favored by fortune, Nikias does not wish to risk it, and thus favors peace, because, he supposes, "to stand out of danger is the benefit of peace." Nikias wishes his reputation to be that he "never made the commonwealth miscarry." He wishes to avoid the apparent risk of ill fortune that comes with war. This is, of course, no guarantee of good fortune. Leaders of a *demos* are subject to risks even in peace.[9] And holding the city out of war neither guarantees that war will not come to the city, nor does it guarantee the city against other "miscarriages." But it does reveal Nikias' strategy as a kind of caution for the sake of not risking defeat. Thucydides' Nikias does not seem as sanguine as that of Plato as regards the arts of war. But what they do share is an opposition to courses of action in which they would be exposed to risk. And even Plato's Nikias, as both Laches and Socrates point

[7] Leo Strauss, *The City and Man*, (Chicago, University of Chicago Press, 1964) 202.

[8] Thucydides, *Peloponnesian War*, V.16.

[9] Strauss, *City and Man*, 200.

out, is ultimately dependent upon some external factor; hence, the emphasis on prophecy. The Nikias of Plato is enthusiastic regarding the arts, the Nikias of Thucydides pessimistic; but what they both share is an aversion to risk, and a corresponding reliance on the favor of fortune.

What Thucydides says about the motives of Nikias' counterpart in the peace, Pleistoanax, act as a sort of negative image of Nikias' own motives. Pleistoanax was banished from the city for his attempt to manipulate certain prophecies in his favor. However, since his banishment, the Lacadaemonians had suffered a series of misfortunes. As a result they had called Pleistoanax back into leadership. He, like Nikias, wished to preserve his good fortune by avoiding possible misfortunes in war, the reaction to which led to his recall. They are a perfect complement to one another.

Nikias' arguments opposing the Sicilian expedition reflect his concern with the avoidance of risk and misfortune. Nikias presents his argument after the decision has already been made. Evidently, he should not have remained so long at peace. The gist of Nikias' speech is that the city should imitate him by not undertaking risky ventures, but rather by seeking to preserve what it has. Nikias presents this argument as denying his own desire for honor. As a general, were the expedition successful, it would redound to his honor. This seems, however, out of tune with his advice, which is an imitation of his own character. Were he successfully to persuade the Athenians to share his concerns, he would be honored by their imitation. The city would seek to avoid miscarrying by standing out of war and risk. Nikias also warns against the ambition of Alcibiades. The Athenians should beware a man who would expend the public stores for the sake of fulfilling his own ambition and magnificence.[10] Nikias banks on the envy of the Athenians towards Alcibiades. Given that Nikias' speech also serves his own ambition, however, the issue is not so much private ambition, but how such ambition accords with that of the public and how each of these ambitions are conceived.

It is precisely the nature of his ambition and its relation to the public ambition which Alcibiades addresses in his reply. He readily admits his personal ambition and magnificence, acknowledging the envy of his competitors and the public, but points out that such is for the glory of the city. His concern is not merely the preservation, but rather the increased magnificence of the city (6.16, 18).[11] While Nikias is concerned to not risk what fortune

---

[10] Thucydides, *Peloponnesian War*, VI.12.

[11] Thucydides, *Peloponnesian War*, VI.16,18.

has granted him, Alcibiades points to those in the past who have risked their possession for the sake of a magnificent aim. The city imitating Nikias will suffer from inactivity and torpor, whereas the city that remains active in its desire for magnificence preserves Athens. For Alcibiades, unlike for Nikias, risk is not only inevitable, but the condition for a devotion to the magnificent or noble. The torpor of the city is actually induced by Nikias' concern to "never let the city miscarry."

The Athenians are moved more by what we might call Alcibiades' love of the beautiful than by Nikias' counsel of thrift. Nikias is out of step with Athens—or so it seems. As events will soon bear out, Alcibiades is not entirely the favorite of Athens. His speech and Thucydides' own comments acknowledge the jealousy of the *hoi polloi*, and that jealousy soon manifests itself so as to divorce Alcibiades' ambitions from Athens's. The difficulty with Alcibiades' principle—action for the sake of the magnificent—is that while it may serve to distinguish Athens from her neighbors, it also distinguishes Alcibiades from his fellows, which opposes the democratic impulse. Even if Alcibiades were to be taken as truthful in wedding his own ambition to that of the city, his outstanding ability would inevitably give rise to envy. The love of the noble is an unstable political principle, especially for a democracy.

On the one hand, as Alcibiades' speech makes clear, there is no life for the city without citizens' seeing in the city the object of their ambition. One must distinguish one's city as somehow more beautiful and noble than others. This is something which his other love, Socrates, makes clear at his trial, at least in Plato's account. Socrates upbraids those who would stand before the court and beg for their lives rather than stand up and defend themselves according to the law. He compares his own activity in coming before the court and in philosophizing with his previous willingness to risk his life in war for the city. Without the willingness to risk their lives for something nobler, Socrates points out, they bring shame upon the city.[12]

On the other hand, Socrates' case also exemplifies how the love of the noble implies an inherent tendency to distinguish between the more and less worthy, the grand and the small. The love of the noble does not simply elevate one city over the other, but distinguishes between citizens as well. Insofar as democracy tends toward an egalitarian viewpoint, it will be in part opposed to this sort of distinguishing. Hence, even when Alcibiades is

[12] Plato, *Apology of Socrates*, 34b-35e, with 28c-29b.

attempting to ally his own ambition with that of the city as a whole, in supposing himself worthy of imitation rather than Nikias, he is elevating himself both above Nikias and above his fellow citizens. He is, after all, a member of an aristocratic family. While cities require the love of the noble to not fall into torpor, such a love of the noble distinguishes between men within a community, even if only by their differing devotion to the city as a whole. And this is most the case in a democracy, where there is always envy of those who are elevated—even or especially in the service of the democracy.

For these reasons even Alcibiades is forced to argue that the Sicilians and Spartans are not as formidable an obstacle as Nikias supposed. Syracuse is not that well defended, and Sicily is insufficiently unified, to be able to withstand a committed Athenian attack. Alcibiades is forced to misrepresent the ease with which the expedition will succeed. He argues, on the one hand, that the risk is great so that the victory would seem magnificent; on the other, he argues that it will not be that difficult. This foreshadows the Athenians' enthusiasm for Nikias' second speech.

Nikias' intent in giving a second speech is to dissuade the Athenians from the expedition by making them aware of its great expense. He means this as a warning, but the Athenians take it as expert advice to ensure victory.[13] While Nikias does not want to "commit himself to fortune," his audience takes Nikias as offering advice on overcoming fortune. In this, they combine Alcibiades' ambition for the magnificent with Nikias' caution, but in such a way as to make the object of ambition seem more easily attainable. In so doing, the Athenians take the risk out of ambition. The daring of Alcibiades is robbed thereby of its very greatness by the caution of Nikias. On the other hand, Nikias' caution is transformed into a kind of boldness, given artful preparation.

The Athenians would seem to mirror the portrait of Nikias himself in *Laches*. The glory-seeking of the Athenians seeks to, through expense and preparation, eliminate or greatly reduce risk. This mirrors Nikias' praise for the hoplite art as an attempt to make one undefeatable; it also mirrors Nikias' attempt in Plato to avoid risking his own in conversation with Socrates, falling back upon sophistic expertise without risking his own opinion for the sake of learning—something magnificent. This artful substitute for courage in *Laches* finds its highest manifestation in the subordination of the arts to prophecy. In saying this, it is worth recalling that virtue doesn't exclude,

[13] Thucydides, *The Peloponessian War*, VI.19-20.

but would, in fact, encourage artful preparation in its service, where possible. The danger arises when artful preparation is seen as a substitute for virtue, rather than as a mode of exhibiting it. In the former case, the risk, and so the very excess or exceeding that is part of virtue, is denied. Virtue is, after all, a sort of excellence, as Aristotle says, a "height" or "excess". Such excellence reminds us that the "exceeding" is important for virtue, because without it, it comes to be "easy" or "automatic" in being reduced to technical proficiency. In virtue being easy or automatic, it becomes a given. As such, it is indistinguishable from a gift of fortune. But since good fortune is not itself a given, it too, requires an art. Prophecy is this art.

Nikias is "most favored by fortune," and responds to this favor by trying to preserve what he has received. Since Nikias has received what is his by fortune, there is nothing which is truly his own. And, by seeking to stay out of danger, he seeks in this way to master fortune, by making the future the same as the past. Both receiving by fortune and making the future the same as the past are present in prophecy. For the prophet, there is no difference between future and past. And because all things are in a sense past for the prophet, there is nothing that a man has that is his own. This is ground of Nikias' "torpor." The desire that animates Alcibiades—magnificence—is utterly opposite to that of Nikias, which is ultimately self-effacing. As Alcibiades puts it, in the city's imitation of Nikias, it would suffer torpor or nonbeing. The irony of Nikias' own attempt to make a reputation for himself is that, in his wish to avoid "testing fortune," he is unwilling to engage in the conditions under which reputations are made—the testing of fortune through risk for the sake of the magnificent or beautiful. Of course, the unwillingness to acknowledge these conditions does not mean that Nikias can avoid acting under these conditions. He is, after all, seeking to gain a noble reputation for both himself and the city, something not simply a gift of fortune. This, we might say, is his tragedy. After all, the attempt to preserve one's fortune, even in giving oneself over to prophets, is not itself prophecy or fortune, but supposes a certain independence from fortune or prophecy. Fate is never an issue for the dumb brutes. Ultimately, it is this lack of self-knowledge regarding virtue and fortune, particularly regarding courage, that limits his virtue. His virtue is conventional, not simply in the sense of what was held to be at any particular time and place, but in the deeper sense that he does not seek to be anything other than what is already held—he does not wish to test fortune.

And America

Thucydides' critique of Nikias is also a critique of the Athenians. The Athenians are moved by the ambitions of an Alcibiades, but at the same time wish themselves to be the child of fortune Nikias is; they wish for easy ambition. We may wonder whether this is a tendency of democratic polities in general, and the American polity in particular.

Alexis de Tocqueville, in Volume Two of *Democracy in America*, appears to indicate that it is to some degree. "Democratic society", he says, "has far less to fear from boldness than from paltriness of aim" (III. 19).[14] While ambition, he says, is present in America, it tends to be dissipated among private aims and immediate desires, because of a lack of what he calls "distant goals," that is, larger and more comprehensive ambitions (II. 17).[15] He points out that traditionally, these distant goals and larger aims are present in religion in political community, since "in ages of faith, the final aim of life is placed beyond life."[16] This fixes the aim of the community on some constant and great aim, undeterred by the petty needs and ambitions which accost men on a day to day basis. The very freedom and equality of American society creates a competition that foreshortens men's ambitions, hopes and vision, making the primary task of rulers of free peoples to keep them mindful of distant goals and larger future ambitions.[17] Evidently, the sort of "torpor" that Alcibiades warns against is more of a danger in situations of freedom and equality. Recall that devotion to a nobility not easily possessed seems ill at home in Thucydides' *History* with a democratic polity. Alcibiades' fate should remind us that those rulers in any democracy or republic who hold to such ambitious goals are likely to be held in suspicion by those whose ambitions have been foreshortened; this leads to either a further foreshortening of ambitions, or, as we saw in the Athenian case, a belief that ambitions are easily accomplished if only we have the correct arts. Easily accomplished acts, or acts seen as easily accomplished, are not really objects

---

[14] Alexis de Tocqueville, *Democracy in America*, trans. George Lawrence, (New York: Harper and Row), vol II, 3.19.

[15] De Tocqueville, *Democracy*, II. 2.17.

[16] It is for this reason, it is worth noting, that I in part disagree with those commentators who attribute to Nikias an excessive piety, as if great ambition and piety are somehow exclusive of one another. Rather, insofar as Nikias is "pious," it is the character of his understanding of piety that is at stake. Piety, we might say, is not clearly always in the grasp of a kind of fear, a point Socrates appears to make in *Euthyphro* 12a-b.

[17] De Tocqueville, *Democracy*, II. 2.13, 17.

of ambition, since they do not have the appearance of excess necessary for virtue. It is for this reason that de Tocqueville argues that the worse fate for democratic peoples is the prevalence of chance in social or political promotion, for the "sudden and undeserved promotion"[18] of a person flatters the judgment and passions already typical of democracy. Democratic polities, given their suspicion regarding those who claim any sort of exceeding, will already have a tendency to see magnificence as undeserved, as a matter of chance. Thus the leaders lead by setting an example; and sudden and undeserved promotion give the idea that ambitions are easily attainable, not by effort and sacrifice. Thus it is of greater import in a democracy to make certain that only effort is rewarded, not chance.

In addition, de Tocqueville points out that the preference for the goods of the body to the goods of the soul tends towards the enervation of ambition even with regards to the goods of the body,[19] and the desire for physical pleasures so prevalent in America, because of the fleeting nature of these pleasures and their being spoiled by effort to acquire them, means that "the prevailing temper is at the same time ardent and soft, violent and enervated." In saying this, de Tocqueville does not deny American ambition; rather, he is characterizing it as rather subservient to a desire for ease. The consistent and determined effort for the sake of some "distant goal" is undermined by the desire for ease. Effort, therefore, seems to occur fitfully or "violently," and as de Tocqueville points out, for rather small and easily attainable goals. What seems to be sacrificed is the joy of a life of determined effort that is made possible by the distant and spiritual goals, precisely in their very distance and difficulty in attainment.

When de Tocqueville speaks of the enjoyment of pleasures being harmed by effort, we see him touch on the heart of the matter, speaking to an inner wish for ease and, secretly, a denigration of human effort. This may seem surprising to those of us who cherish the American valuing of industry. But perhaps de Tocqueville is reminding us that industry comes to be seen as worthless without what he refers to as distant goals; it is their very distance which makes industry worthwhile, and so sets a spur to industry. Work is seen in the absence of such as rather a necessary evil for the sake of the enjoyment of our next (and fleeting) bodily pleasure, rather than the attainment of something more substantial. Ease seems to make the assumption that we are already worthy, not requiring any strain for the noble to prove

[18] De Tocqueville, *Democracy* II. 2. 13
[19] De Tocqueville, *Democracy*, II. 2.17

our worth; but this striving is needed for industry. For such striving to occur, the aim must be seen as something currently beyond us, and hence our efforts as subject to risk. Without distant goals that transcend us, we fall into a sort of ardent softness, which is a reflection of the giving in to fortune which limits Nikias' virtue and appears to characterize the wishes of the Athenian people. The unwillingness to test fortune, to take great risks, is itself a symptom of the foreshortened ambitions that de Tocqueville warns against in Americans. When de Tocqueville speaks of the ambition of life in faith being beyond life itself, this implies the willingness to sacrifice one's life, in work and in death, to some object beyond life. That is, it implies courage for the sake of the noble in the testing of fortune.

Nikias, in having nothing that is not given to him, having nothing grand and distinct from what is immediately his, suffers from this foreshortened ambition. Likewise, the member of a democracy, when realizing how little appears open to him due to equality and freedom of competition, grasps at whatever small thing he can with some certainty acquire. Both do not see themselves as destined for, and visible in the devotion to something magnificent. For de Tocqueville, this is a danger to the body politic insofar as the public good is something of this sort; in the words of Alcibiades, without those willing to risk themselves for something greater, the city will suffer torpor and decay.

Works Cited

de Tocqueville, Alexis. *Democracy in America.* Translated by George Lawrence. New York: Harper and Row, 2006.

Plato. *Meno and Other Dialogues.* Translated by Robin Waterfield. Oxford: Oxford University Press, 2005.

Strauss, Leo. *The City and Man.* Chicago, University of Chicago Press, 1964.

Thucydides. *The Peloponnesian War: The Complete Hobbes Translation.* Edited by David Grene. Chicago: University of Chicago Press, 1987.

SEPARATION OF POWERS IN THE *HISTORY*? THUCYDIDES ON THE MEASURED VIRTUE OF THE FIVE THOUSAND

Bernard J. Dobski

In a letter dated August 11, 1777, John Adams wrote to his son, John Quincy Adams,

> My dear Son
>
> As the War in which your Country is engaged will probably hereafter attract your Attention, more than it does at this Time, and as the future Circumstances of your Country, may require other Wars, as well as Councils and Negotiations, similar to those which are now in Agitation, I wish to turn your Thoughts early to such Studies, as will afford you the most solid Instruction and Improvement for the Part which may be allotted you to act on the Stage of Life.
>
> There is no History, perhaps, better adapted to this usefull Purpose than that of Thucidides, an Author, of whom I hope you will make yourself perfect Master, in original Language, which is Greek, the most perfect of all human Languages."[1]

This advice, from one founding father and future president to another future diplomat and president, is surely sage counsel, if perhaps a bit premature. After all, Adams's son is only 10 years old. But it testifies to Thucydides' enduring significance to the concerns of practicing statesmen. Indeed, since its composition some twenty-three centuries ago, Thucydides' *History*[2] has effectively been mined for practical political wisdom by statesmen everywhere. But Thucydides' work offers much more than just practical advice for the political actor. As a work of political wisdom, the *History* also offers

---

[1] https://founders.archives.gov/documents/Adams/04-02-02-0247

[2] Thucydides' work has no official title. I follow convention in referring to it as the *History*. All references to Thucydides' *History* are in standard book, chapter, and, where relevant, sentence, form. Translations of Thucydides' Greek are from *The Landmark Thucydides: A Comprehensive Guide to The Peloponnesian War*, edited by Robert B. Strassler (Free Press: New York, 1994).

guidance for those theorists who would hope to solve the fundamental and pressing problems facing all political communities; it supplies theoretical insight into the limits to political life as such, refining our sense of what can reasonably be hoped for from any solutions we may devise. It is not unreasonable therefore to wonder what Thucydides would say to our own founding fathers, men who are justly famous for the political innovations they designed to preserve our liberty. More precisely, what would Thucydides say about one of the more famous innovations of modern political science—the separation of powers as embodied in and preserved by our own constitution?

This may seem like a strange question to ask. Thucydides never explores the systematic approach to political liberty so readily associated with the American founding. And the closest Thucydides comes to a discussion of the separation of powers is his brief mention near the end of his work about the rule of the Five Thousand in 410 BC, a regime that more accurately reflects a mixed or blended regime than one with clearly defined mechanisms for distributing political powers. That he fails to discuss the separation of powers is not simply the product of historical accident (i.e., that he was born in Greece some two thousand years before Montesquieu). It is the product of his political wisdom. And this wisdom highlights the limits to any political science that offers systematic solution to the problems we face. Studying Thucydides' view of the Five Thousand, of this apparently mixed regime, helps us get a better grasp of these limits and the wisdom that informs them.

Thucydides' statement on the Five Thousand comes near the end of Book VIII of the *History*, a book that recounts a tumultuous period in Athenian domestic history. Following her catastrophic defeat in Sicily in 413, Athens embraced a more conservative approach to political affairs, appointing a board of overseers to ensure that the city proceeded with greater moderation. By 411, this conservative momentum in Athens peaked when the city elected to replace its ancient democracy with the oligarchic regime of the Four Hundred. It was this regime, which, just a few short months after *it* was voted into power, gave way to the rule of the Five Thousand. Of this regime Thucydides says, "And now first, (at least in my life) the Athenians seem to have ordered their state aright; which consisted of a measured temper, both of the few and of the many. And this was the first thing that after so many misfortunes past made the city again to raise her head" (VIII.97.2). Though he qualifies this statement twice, those familiar with Thucydides' reticence on such matters will recognize the absolutely extraordinary nature of his comments. They thus deserve closer examination. Just what does Thucydides have in mind when he praises this regime for its measuredness?

Regarding the government itself, he mentions the criterion for membership in the government (to supply one's own arms), refers to their pay (none), and mentions elected posts. This praiseworthy government is one that mixes the few (supplying one's own arms; no pay for serving) with the many (participation for five thousand; elections).[3] Indeed, while its predecessor, the oligarchic regime of the Four Hundred, originally introduced the institution of the "five thousand" as part of its government (VIII.65, 72), it never activated this body and only intended it to serve at the will of the oligarchs and to deliberate on matters they selected (VIII.67). As far as its deeds, Thucydides only reports that it recalled the brilliant and ambitious Alcibiades and ordered the army at Samos, ostensibly under his leadership, to continue the war. The Five Thousand so lauded by Thucydides thus seems to effect a superior combination of the many, the few, and the one. But what does it mean to call such a combination measured, especially when it embraces the singularly immoderate talents of someone like Alcibiades? By what standard are we to judge this *metria*? And what would Thucydides' view of such a standard mean for our own institutional mechanics?

Given the relatively short tenure of the Five Thousand (it was in power less than a year before gradually returning to the full democracy), it is difficult to think that our author intends for us to take this regime seriously as a legitimate political alternative to be pursued. After all, it fails the most basic political litmus test: it is too unstable to preserve itself. And yet precisely because of its instability, one might think that Thucydides would welcome the mechanisms theorized originally by Montesquieu and perfected by James Madison. After all, wasn't it the stability between the Crown, the House of Lords, and the House of Commons that Montesquieu sought to effect in his own justification for the separation of powers? Would not a regime as desirable as the Five Thousand be a perfect example of those "intervals of felicity," those "momentary rays of glory," that "transient...brilliancy," whose transience founders like Hamilton lamented (*Fed.* 9) and which the American founders sought to remedy? If the measured virtue exercised by the oligarchic and democratic factions of Athens represents a kind of restraint or political moderation exercised by its various parts, then one might think that

[3] On the Five Thousand, see Bernard J. Dobski, "Athenian Democracy Re-Founded: Xenophon's Political History in the *Hellenika*," *POLIS: The Journal for Ancient Greek Political Thought*, 26:2 (2009) 316-338.

the institutional mechanics advanced by James Madison would be just the thing to preserve and perpetuate such moderation. Indeed such institutional designs are successful largely because they abstract from claims to rule based on justice, effectively reducing political conflicts to a clash of interests.

Exploring Thucydides' view of these questions depends on what our author means by measuredness here, especially since *metrios* and its cognates can also be rendered as moderate and in this way are apparently no different from another Greek term whose meaning also covers "moderation:" *sophrosune*. To see the extent to which Thucydides distinguishes *metrios* from *sophrosune*, that is, to appreciate what makes *metrios* such a distinctive virtue for Thucydides, one must reflect on the way Thucydides uses these terms in his *History*.[4]

"Measured," Not "Moderate"

Measuredness represents a term of praise that knows few equals in Thucydides' *History*. In the first place, political references to measuredness frame the entire work. The word appears near the beginning of the *History* when Thucydides locates the humble origins of Greek political life in a common garment, one that is measured, worn alike by the poor and elite of Sparta (I.6.4). And it shows up at the very end of the *History* when, as Athenian fortunes appear resurgent, Thucydides points us to the apparent peak of Greek politics (VIII.97.2). Measuredness thus appears to represent the poles between which his work unfolds, moving from the origins to the peak of the Greek story that his *History* majestically preserves. And when he praises in his own name political men and their regimes, Thucydides invokes measuredness. Thus in his famous eulogy of Pericles (II.65.2), Thucydides declares that the peace-time rule of this great statesman was "measured and safe." Twice he describes as "measured" brilliant wartime moves by the dazzling Spartan general Brasidas (IV.105, 108). And when he bestows what is arguably his greatest praise for any regime on that of The Five Thousand in

[4] According to Leo Strauss, moderation is "in a way the key term in Thucydides and takes the place of justice because unmitigated justice is impossible. Some injustice is inevitable. The criterion cannot be justice, therefore, but rather the degree of injustice, and that is moderation" (PPT, p. 97). This passage from Strauss's unpublished lecture notes on Thucydides appears in Robert Howse, *Leo Strauss Man of Peace* (New York: Cambridge University Press, 2014), 142. Howse's extensive quotations from the lectures on Thucydides indicate that Strauss was sensitive to the distinction between measuredness and moderation.

Athens, a regime he calls the best the Athenians had in his lifetime, he does so on account of it being "measured" (VIII.97.2). It is true that other actors are praised by Thucydides for their intelligence and virtue (Themistocles, I.138.3; the Pesistratid tyrants, VI.54.5). But measuredness constitutes for our author a distinct political category.

Measuredness and its cognates also appear in some of the work's most famous passages and in the mouths of some of its most famed actors; it is used by Pericles in his Funeral Oration (II.35.2), by Diodotus in the Mytilenean debate (III.46.4), by the Athenian ambassadors in the Melian dialogue (V.111.4), and multiple times by Thucydides in his report of the daring escape from the siege of Plataea (III.20.3, 4), among others. It thus appears to constitute an important component of Greek political discourse. Based on its appearance in such important passages and in our author's rare explicit political judgments, we can conclude that measuredness is a virtue important to Thucydides and to the actors in his *History*. Given the attention scholars dedicate to other terms in Thucydides, the relative paucity of work about moderation in Thucydides general, and about measuredness in particular, terms that are so important to our author's political judgments, is surprising.[5]

It is true that *metrios* and *sophrosune* share meanings such that one can legitimately render both as "moderate." But there are also important differ-

[5] One should consider, for example, the treatments of *eros* in Thucydides by Steven Forde in *Ambition to Rule: Alcibiades and the Politics of Imperialism in Thucydides* (Ithaca, NY: Cornell University Press, 1989) and by Paul Ludwig in *Eros and Polis: Desire and Community in Greek Political Theory* (New York: Cambridge University Press, 2002); on *gnome* and *tuche* in *Chance and Intelligence in Thucydides* by Lowell Edmunds (Cambridge: Harvard University Press, 1975); Martin Ostwald's treatment of *ananke* in *Ananke in Thucydides* (American Classical Studies 18 [Atlanta: Scholars Press, 1988]); *akribeia* in C.N. Cochrane's *Thucydides and the Science of History* (London: Humphrey Milford, 1929); *aitia* and *prophasis* in *The Humanity of Thucydides* by Clifford Orwin (Princeton: Princeton University Press, 1994), especially his treatment of the secondary literature on these terms throughout and in Appendix 2; *tolma* in Forde, *Ambition to Rule* and in "The Virtue of Thucydides' Brasidas" by Timothy Burns (*Journal of Politics*, vol. 73, no. 2, 2011, pp. 508-523); *arête* in "Alcibiades and the Question of Tyranny in Thucydides" by Michael Palmer (*Canadian Journal of Political Science*, No 1, 1982, pp. 103-124). On the distinction between measured and moderate, one should see Strauss, noted above and Michael Palmer, discussed below. For one of the few explicit treatments of "moderation" in Thucydides, see Noreen Humble's "*Sophrosune* and the Spartans in Xenophon" in *SPARTA: New Perspectives*, ed. Stephen Hodkinson and Anton Powell (Classical Press of Wales: Duckworth), 1999 pp. 339- 353.

ences between the two terms.[6] For instance, *sophrosune* literally means "soundness of mind." And it is a soundness of mind, as Aristotle reminds us, with respect to the particular desires of the body, such as those for food, drink and sex and the pleasures associated with these (*NE*, 1118a2-1119a20). As such it can also be rendered as "self-control." *Sophrosune* can also describe an intellectual or prudential moderation. A moderate man will know what he is capable of doing and will act in accordance with that knowledge. For this reason, "moderation" (and its cognates) can be rendered as "wise;" a moderate man is a wise man insofar as he knows the proper moral course of action. Because it partakes of "right-reason,"[7] "moderation" retains its proper sense of shame; a moderate man will possess a proper posture towards shameful actions, like those associated with the pleasures of food, drink, and sex.

In *metrios*, by contrast, Thucydides employs a term that can, but need not, invoke the moral overtones pregnant in "moderate" and typically captured by *sophrosune*. While both terms invoke a sense of restraint or of avoiding extremes, *metrios* comes closer to meaning "average," "common," "not too great," "proportionate," or "reasonable." *Metrios* can thus convey the sense of the more prudential calculation implied by "measured." On this distinction, Palmer notes that a "'measured' policy as opposed to a 'moderate' policy is merely a means to an end, which end, in itself, may be immoderate. It would be possible for a policy *not* to be 'measured' because it *was* 'moderate.'"[8] One could thus be measured in one's vices, something in which one could never be moderate. An overview of Thucydides' use of these two terms deepens our appreciation of the differences that emerge from these preliminary reflections.

"Measured" and its cognates appear 28 times in the *History*; "moderation" and its cognates, by contrast, are used almost twice as much (43 occurrences). More than half of the references to "moderation" occur in Books I (12) and III (11), but there are no appearances in Book II or in Book VII. "Measured" is also absent from Book VII, though it does show up twice in Book II. That both of these words are absent from Thucydides' account of

---

[6] For the sake of ease and readability, when I refer to *sophrosune* and *metrios* I do so as inclusive of the all the words linguistically related to them.

[7] Aristotle notes that "moderation" follows "right-reason" because it pursues "what reason tells us are the proper objects, at the right time and in the right way" (*NE*, 1119b18-20).

[8] Palmer, 'Question of Tyranny', 119, fn. 34, emphasis in the original.

Athens's disastrous campaign in Sicily, an expedition and defeat whose magnitude seemed to defy all moderation and measure, is not surprising. That "moderation" dominates Books I and III but is missing from Book II might well draw one's attention to the "measured" character of Pericles there, a statesman whom Thucydides never praises for his moral virtue. "Measured" shows up the most (8 times) in Book IV, a book that arguably reveals the peak of what some have labeled "Athenianism." In Book V, "measured" and "moderation" appear twice, each with all four occurrences appearing in the Athenian responses to the Melians.

A breakdown of the actors who use these terms is also suggestive. If Thucydides' interventions belong in their own category, then we see that the Athenians use or invoke "moderation" twelve times (addressing domestic and foreign audiences)[9] and it is used by foreigners five times before their assembly.[10] The Spartans use it before Spartan audiences only five times (Archidamus, I.80.2, 84.2, 84.3, twice; Sthenelaidas I.86.2); the Plataeans (III.58.1, 59.1), Corinthians (I.68.1, 120.3), and Thebans (III.62.3, 65.3) all invoke "moderation" before the Spartans. Aside from Thucydides, Hermocrates employs it the most.[11] Thucydides himself uses it eight times: describing Sparta or Spartans (I.79.2, VIII.24.4), oligarchic government (VIII.64.5), the Corcyrean Civil war (III.82.4, 82.8, 84.1), and Athenian actions (IV.28.5, VIII.1.3).

A first glance at these examples suggests that *sophrsune* represents a civilizing restraint on the conduct of men and states, one that stands apart from domestic laws and international treaties. As the examples of Hermocrates (see fn. 12) and Nicias (VI.11.7) indicate, it is often invoked in that spirit.[12] In the absence of political and legal conventions, moderation can be called upon to foster peace between rivals. Moderation thus appears to represent a non-conventional alternative to justice in its capacity to curb the aggression of men and cities. That it can produce a unity that preserves one's community would also appear to testify to its prudential and rational character. And as one sees in the account of the Corcyrean civil war, moderation is

[9] Kleon, III.37.3; Diodotus, III.42.5, 43.5, 44.1; Nicias, VI.11.7; Euphemus, VI.87.3, 87.4; Phrynichus, VIII.48.6, Pisander, VIII.53.3; Athenians on Melos, V.101, 111.3, Alcibiades, VI.29.2.

[10] Spartans, IV.18.4; Corinthians, I.37.2, 40.2, 42.2; Corcyreans, I.32.4.

[11] IV.60.1, IV.61.1, IV.64.4, VI.78.2, 79.2,

[12] See also the Egesteans at Athens (VI.6.2) and the call for moderation by the Syracusan general (VI.41.2).

the *sine qua non* of civilized life, such that when it goes, other civilizing restraints, like divine and filial piety, disappear (III.82). But in cases like the Spartan envoys at Athens (IV.18.4), the Athenians after Sicily (VIII.3), Diodotus in the Mytilenean debate (III.43.5, 44.1), and the Athenians at Melos (V.101, 111.3), Thucydides invites us to wonder if moderation is not merely the means by which one evades or concedes to superior force. And in the examples of the Corinthians at Sparta (I.68) and Kleon in the Mytilenean debate (III.37.3) moderation comes to sight either as an obstacle to or at the expense of (see also III.82) the free use of an individual's reason.

The example of Archidamus, the Spartan King whose first speech in the *History* (I.80-84) invokes moderation more than any other single episode in the book, is particularly illustrative of this point.[13] In the first part of his speech, Archidamus calls on his Spartans to reflect moderately on the difficulties involved in the kind of war they are to wage against Athens; because such reflection will avoid reckless behavior it is necessarily the precondition for any moral conduct. But Archidamus complicates this picture in the second part of his response (I.84), where he famously remarks that the moderation for which the Spartans are renowned might make them slow in action but also makes them orderly. This orderliness in turn makes them "good soldiers" and "good counselors." It makes them good soldiers because "shame is the greatest part of moderation, and courage is the greatest part of shame" (84.3). And such shame-induced orderliness makes them good counselors because they are not raised with so much education that they will, out of an excess of sophistication, try to "look over" the laws. Orderliness thus produces and is the beneficiary of soldiers who are attentive to shame and counselors who won't question or disobey the laws of the city. Spartan moderation makes possible an order whose goodness is identified by the moderate behavior it produces.

The speech of Archidamus makes clear that the moderation he exalts here, itself the product of painful discipline and which the Spartans embody throughout much of the *History*, comes at the expense of the free exercise of one's rational faculties. It is not simply the use of force to create Spartan moderation that should lead one to question Sparta's defining virtue; it is that Sparta's moderation serves political ends whose choiceworthiness is merely given or asserted. Spartans do not choose to be moderate nor can they critically reflect on its goodness. Thus while moderation may be criti-

[13] In the entire *History* "moderation" appears with the greatest frequency in this episode (I.79.2-86).

cally important to political obedience, one is also not surprised to see the link, intimated more than once by Thucydides, between moderation and force (or violence, most notably III.37.3, VIII.24.4, and 48.6). The preceding review of moderation in the *History* should therefore prompt us to wonder if this virtue isn't essentially driven by fear, one that inhibits fuller consideration of one's genuine good, making it difficult to see the nobility or even sensibility of this important political trait.

While *sophrosune* is well-distributed among the *History's* actors, such that Sparta can hardly lay exclusive claim to this virtue, *metrios* is an almost entirely Athenian trait. The Athenians use it amongst themselves and when addressing others[14] (7) and foreigners use it in speech directed to them (Spartan envoys, IV.19.2, 4, 20.2; Corinthians, I.38.5). Spartans never use it when they address a Spartan audience. In fact, the only other Spartan to counsel measuredness was Lichas to the Milesians (VIII.84.5). The conduct and strategy of the Spartan general Brasidas is characterized as measured no less than three times by Thucydides (IV.81.2, 105.2, 108.2), though such exceptions seem to prove the rule; Brasidas' character was more Athenian than Spartan, part of which is due to his being "measured." Including his references to Brasidas, Thucydides employs measuredness sixteen times.[15] The only other actors to invoke both moderation and measuredness are Alcibiades, the Corinthians at Athens, the Athenian ambassadors to Melos and Diodotus, and only the last three do so in the same speech. The most that these four might be said to have in common is that they all represent questionable models for political success. Of course, the same could be said of that Athenian exile Thucydides.

As we will see in the following sections, measuredness in contrast to moderation seems to lack a consistently clear moral compass by which one can measure a person, regime, or course of action. The character of the *metron*—that by which things are either measured or judged to be measured—is not implicit in the term itself and appears to vary depending on the context in which it is used. Absent a consistent moral compass, measured appears utilitarian, a kind of principle of maximum efficiency. The reduction of *metrios* to "moderate" frequently found in translations of the *History* thus conceals a distinction critical to the political judgment of Thucydides; it pre-

[14] I.76.4; I.77.2; II.35.2; III.46.4; V.111.4 (twice); VI.89.5.

[15] In some cases here, Thucydides calls measured the aim or intent of some of his actors, like Demosthenes and Kleon at Pylos or the Chians responding to Athens's siege, a judgment which may be shared by the actors themselves.

vents one from seeing when Thucydides might be pointing to a capacity or conduct whose praiseworthiness belongs to a register not found in moral virtue alone. To understand why measuredness, a virtue so clearly linked by Thucydides to his Athenians, might not be compatible with a more politically salutary virtue like moderation, one must examine Thucydides' uses of measuredness in the *History*.

Measuredness as Self-Restraint

At first glance, measuredness, like moderation, comes to sight as a limit on the self-interests of political actors. Unlike moderation, however, it does so largely as a limit that appears self-imposed. As such, measuredness is exercised almost exclusively by those who possess a surfeit of power—that is, power in excess of one's needs seems the necessary precondition for one to be measured. This is how it appears the first time we encounter it in the *History*: the Spartan great voluntarily adopt the more measured garment worn by the poor (I.6.4). They voluntarily forgo the goods (such as lavish attire) that their superior wealth and position in Spartan society affords. By doing so, they secure a common good between the powerful and the poor, a common good that would come to define Greek politics as distinct from barbarian mastery. That they do this at least partly to avoid the envy and resentment of the poor does not diminish the luster of such a measured policy. Nor does it reduce it to mere self-serving.[16] For instance, when the Athenian envoys at Sparta defend (and justify) Athenian imperialism, they do so partly on the grounds of Athenian measuredness: Athens alone of all imperial powers exercises her power less freely than she otherwise could (I.76, 77.2). By contrasting this measured self-restraint with the unrestrained rule of the Persians who preceded her or Sparta's present hegemony over the Peloponnese, the Athenian envoys advance their city's claim to her imperial domain: her measured, or self-limited, rule signifies her superior nobility, thereby making her worthier of empire than her imperial rivals. As such, this form of self-limitation appears as a crucial element legitimizing that rule.

The Corinthians resort to the same view of measuredness when they hypothesize about Corcyrean conduct before the war: if the Corcyreans had been measured in their treatment of Corinth, they contend, it would have

---

[16] On the political significance of this passage, see Bernard J. Dobski, "Thucydides' Philosophic Turn to Causes" (*Interpretation: A Journal of Political Philosophy*, Vol. 37 Issue 2, Winter 2010), 123-155.

been unjust for the Corinthians to insult them (I.38.5). Instead of being measured towards their mother-city however, the Corcyreans ruthlessly pursued their own interests at the expense of others, thereby justifying Corinth's current hostility. One might be tempted to claim on the basis of this and the preceding examples that measured conduct ennobles one, making one worthy of a form of deference on the part of others. The Spartan envoys, seeking to end the Athenian siege of Pylos and restore the 292 Spartiates trapped there, employ this view of measured behavior. If Athens offers measured conditions to the Spartans, they declare, she will do less than is generally permitted to those who have gained a decisive edge over her enemies. But she will also more quickly earn the peaceful acquiescence of the vulnerable (IV.19.2, 19.4). These envoys thus offer the striking example of Sparta deferring to Athens, of conceding to her an imperial leeway that they had originally gone to war to prevent. Athenian acceptance of such an unheard of and unexpected gift from the Spartans would be measured. Of course, since the weaker have no claims on the stronger, they cannot justly expect to be treated with a certain gentleness. But the reverse is also true; absent this gentleness one cannot expect the vulnerable and the vanquished to embrace their would-be overlords or to confirm that they rule by virtue of their superior natures (IV. 20.2, IV. 22.3, IV. 30.4 and V.111[17]).

The absence of such expectations is precisely what makes measuredness an important part of political success. A measured city (or individual) refuses what is traditionally or customarily granted to the right of the stronger. It recognizes the kind of conduct that is customarily reserved to it on account of its superior strength, but resists the temptation to take advantage of such liberties. Because they originate in extra-lawful considerations and because they defy the self-aggrandizing conduct typically associated with the rule of the stronger, the measured actions of the powerful appear to the weak and defeated as a form of graceful benevolence to which one is not otherwise entitled. It is the unexpected receipt of such beneficence that attaches the weaker to the stronger, the vanquished to the victor (IV.108). The offer that the Spartan general Brasidas extends to the defeated Amphipolitans reinforces this lesson while also hinting at the strategic and personal value of measured behavior.

Shortly after seizing Amphipolis from the Athenians, Brasidas allows the citizens to stay in their city and to retain both their property and their

[17] In these cases, measuredness appears as the equivalent of a kind of ease or gentleness, characteristics that are also attributed to Brasidas.

government; the only change that will take place is in the allegiance of their city (from Athens to Sparta). To those for whom this is unacceptable, he gives five days to pack up their belongings and leave the city (IV.105.2; cf. 105.1 and 106). As the narrative makes clear, had the Amphipolitans actually taken five days to decide to leave, Brasidas would have been likely to lose this strategically important city to Thucydides, whose ships arrived within 24 hours. Given what we know of Brasidas from his earlier exploits in the war, it is hard to think that he simply got lucky here. His offer, while no doubt generous to the vanquished, was strategically savvy. For in the very measuredness of his proposal, he was able to win to himself the support of the city before Thucydides could arrive to try to win it back. Brasidas' leniency here justly wins him the title of measured since he was able to preserve and strengthen his conquest without violence.

But it wasn't just the loyalty of the Amphipolitans that Brasidas' measuredness won for him. The citizens of Scione honored him as the liberator of Greece and an Olympic victor (IV.121). And after his death, the Amphipolitans honored him as a founder and a demigod (V.11). That the Amphipolitans bestowed on Brasidas honors traditionally reserved for the gods suggests that the measured self-restraint Brasidas displays, a restraint that saves the Amphipolitans from slavery and destruction, is a trait they associate with the divine. Like the gods who possess the power to crush men if they so choose, Brasidas holds within his hands the fate of their city. In return for his benevolent self-restraint, on which they had no just claim or expectation, the Amphipolitans offer up their gratitude by voluntarily submitting to his "rule" even after he has died.

In view of these examples one can better understand Thucydides' decision to link one of his most important political notes—the example of the Spartan elite and the origins of Greek political life (I.6.4)—with a seemingly innocuous observation about the Spartan innovation of nude wrestling, a practice eventually employed in the quadrennial games at Olympia. Perhaps the self-limitation reflected in the grapplers' decision to forgo conventional covers and constraints, a decision to stake out a kind of natural self-sufficiency, is best understood as a claim on their part to their worthiness of the victor's garland. Competing in light of one's natural virtues is thus the flip side of the Spartan elite's decision to voluntarily place themselves on an equal footing with the commons by adopting their common dress. For what better reveals one's noble superiority, and thus one's superior worthiness to rule, than the voluntary decision to forgo the material goods that attend such greatness? After all, such self-restraint signifies the capacity to use political power to serve more than one's own base interests.[18]

And this desire to reveal one's natural greatness, reflecting something of a moral obsession with justifying their superiority, seems to explain why the Athenians so often insist on employing a remarkably frank imperial rhetoric even when such frankness is at odds with their imperial interests. Thus the envoys to Sparta deliver a speech which confirms for an audience, which is already likely to be hostile them, the frenetic and reckless picture of them painted by their Corinthian predecessors (I.70); in speaking as they do, the Athenians simply prove the Corinthians right. One can understand the rhetorical choice of the Athenian ambassadors at Melos in the same way. There the Athenians insist on employing a candor at odds with their immediate objectives. For instead of concealing the darker implications of their own political and moral understanding behind disingenuous, but politically salutary, appeals to the divine (a move more consistent with the Machiavellianism typically associated with them), the Athenians attempt to force the pious Melians to accept a view of the gods and of man stripped almost entirely of ethical restraints. It is no surprise their speech failed.

Measuredness as Self-Interested

Of course, the exception to this view of *metrios*—like the exception to so many rules in the *History*—can be found in the speech of Diodotus. As with the preceding examples, he contrasts Athenian measuredness with Kleon's violently indignant response to the Mytilenians' revolt (cf. VIII.24.6). But unlike those other examples, he does not claim that the measured punishment of revolted cities ennobles Athens or makes her worthy of respect. He only claims it offers the best means to securing the obedience of her subject cities and securing Athenian imperial interests (III.46.4). The restraint of measuredness thus cannot be exclusively identified with the concern to disclose our superior nobility. As the link between the Spartan grapplers and the Spartan "great" suggested earlier, the disclosure of one's superior worthiness—whether to victory or to rule—can translate into considerations of justice, which is to say to the instrumental claims to deserve to win or to rule and the rewards that come from victory.

---

[18] See Mark Munn, *Mother of the Gods, Athens and the Tyranny of Asia: A Study in Ancient Religions* (Berkeley: 2006), p.21fn22 and pp.21-22. See also Simon Hornblower, *Thucydides and Pindar: Historical Narrative and the World of Epinikian Poetry*, (Oxford: 2004).

What Thucydides' narrative about the early Greeks leaves implicit, the speech of the Athenian envoys at Sparta seems to make explicit. Shortly after demonstrating Athens's worthiness of her empire, the envoys argue that the effort by Sparta to deprive her of that rule would be unjust.[19] Because their measured conduct makes them worthy of rule (so this logic goes), they deserve to rule as a matter of right; being measured thus constitutes a means to their rule and is not merely a good pursued for its own sake. Viewed this way, their measured conduct is instrumental to some other more desirable end (i.e., empire) and thus cannot constitute the basis of her praiseworthy or noble conduct. Athens therefore becomes unworthy of imperial rule on the very grounds the envoys advance to establish their superior claim to such rule. By contrast, the measured policy that Diodotus urges the Athenians to pursue in his speech is free from this temptation (and thus this inconsistency) because it is not grounded in the concern with the disclosure and recognition by others of one's superior nobility. Diodotus simply wants to preserve Athens's imperial interests. For him, measuredness doesn't entitle one to more goods, it is how one best acquires them. As a result, he is free to indicate, rather openly, that he must lie to his fellow citizens (III.47).

Of course, being free in the way that Diodotus here advises means that the Athenians can pursue policies that are less than noble and thus perhaps less than just. So while the refined understanding of self-interests that he promotes frees the Athenians from the kind of inconsistency pursued above, it also liberates them from having to observe any ethical restraints in their conduct. If the Athenians follow his advice, they may come to possess those goods they want, but they cannot do so thinking that they deserve them or that they are a reward for their superior goodness.

The divergence between this aspect of measuredness and nobility appears even in the hero Brasidas. After all, Brasidas does not win over all of the towns that he does through the exercise of an open-handed generosity; this measured Spartan also takes towns by lies and treason (IV.84.2). Thucydides gives us no indication that such underhanded dealings are at odds with his measuredness. And it is on the margins of justice that the Athenian ambassadors to Melos make their measured offer to their hosts: either ally with and pay tribute to Athens, preserving your lives and your government in the process, or be crushed and enslaved. In other words, both the offer

---

[19] The anger of the Athenian ambassadors at the Melians's refusal to accept surrender on the grounds of Athens's superior nobility suggests that they too translate their superior worthiness to rule others into a just claim to such a rule.

and the Athenians who extend it are examples of measuredness, while the decision to accept that offer is moderate or wise (V.111.4; see V.104, 111.).

The potential for measuredness to conflict with more traditional views of justice, propriety, or nobility comes out most clearly in the example of the Spartan Lichas. Lichas advises the Greeks of Miletus, who had revolted from the Persian satrap Tissaphernes and had desecrated a local temple in the process, to halt their rebellion and to obey (*douleuein*) Tissaphernes in all "measured things" until after the war ends (VIII.84.5). Advocating Greek *submission* to the Persian, however reasonable such advice might be, violates the basic canons of Greek statecraft. Indeed, for those Greeks who cherish their freedom the suggestion that they submit voluntarily to a barbarian master would be seen as most indecent. It would certainly not be noble. One is thus not entirely surprised to learn what Thucydides relates in the immediate sequel: years later, upon his death in Asia Minor, the people of Miletus refused Lichas burial rites.

Part of the hostility to Lichas's suggestion might stem from the fact that the measured counsel he proposes is at odds, and even undermines, the Milesians's attachment to what is "their own," in this case to Greekness as opposed to barbarianism. What Lichas advises appears ignoble to the Greeks at Miletus because it would require them to betray an element of their identity crucial to their own self-understanding. This at any rate seems to be the understanding of the challenges facing measured behavior shared by Pericles. In his famous Funeral Oration, Pericles opposes to the measured praise he wants to extend to the fallen both those excessive hopes for praise of one's own that are born from friendly fellow-feeling (*eunous*), on the one hand, and envy, itself born from an attachment to one's own, on the other hand. Pericles states that it is difficult to speak justly or measuredly about those who have died because those in the audience who knew of their sacrifice and who are partial to them will think a praise truly spoken somehow falls short of their own expectations. And those who didn't know these men or their sacrifice, men who are partial to themselves, will find unbelievable any praise that surpasses what they consider to be their own capacity for valor (II.35.2). Giving to each man his due, what Pericles understands to be measured, opposes the partial self-love of his various listeners. Pericles' ability to navigate the contentious partiality of elements within Athenian society, which Thucydides captures with amazing subtlety in Book I and throughout Book II, may explain why our author describes his rule of Athens as measured (II.65.5). But this turn to Pericles also returns us to that view of *metrios* sketched in the preceding section, one in which measuredness cannot be reduced to mere self-concern.

In light of these apparently conflicting portraits, measuredness appears, on the one hand, to make possible a generosity that cannot be reduced to cold self-interest, a capacity that allows one to give to each what he deserves, a power that secures distributive justice for some and what appears as a kind of divine grace to others. And yet it also appears to be a capacity that allows one to deviate from traditional understandings of justice and nobility in order to manage the contending forces of political life in pursuit of one's self-interests. *Metrios* thus at once appears as a kind of warm generosity and a cold *realpolitik*; it is both the end chosen for its own sake and the means needed to secure it. This is puzzling. How is one to understand Thucydides' apparently muddled presentation of a category so important to his own political judgments?

To understand how Thucydides might seriously employ a term so fraught with opposed meanings, it helps to recall that our author attributes measuredness to the peace time rule of a man who prepared his city to wage a lengthy war, a man whose fixed judgment demands that Athens embrace their kinetic navy. And he calls measured the wartime moves of a Spartan, carried out in the midst of a most unSpartan campaign, which appear at once graceful and generous, and purely self-interested. Being measured, in other words, appears consistent with the ability to embody successfully qualities that are mixed, contentious, and perhaps even mutually exclusive; it is somehow consistent with the ability to be both one thing and its opposite. In his account of the daring escape from Plataea, Thucydides shows us how a grasp of "the measure" might reconcile two things that, at first glance, appear so opposed.

Plataea, Pericles, and the Five Thousand

Thucydides' artful account of the siege of and escape from Plataea is critical to our inquiry here. *Metrios* and its cognates appear three times closely together near the story's denouement, which happens to be the only place in the *History* where Thucydides shows how one grasps that *metron*, that standard, by which anything else can be judged as measured.[20] Indeed, discovering the *metron* here is absolutely indispensable to the ability of those besieged to escape. In 429 BC, the Spartans laid siege to Plataea, an Atheni-

[20] For the other three times *metron* appears, see IV.118, VI.1, and VIII.95.

an ally. After more than a year under siege, half of those who remained in the city (including the reinforcements Athens had sent to help), judging that continued resistance was hopeless, decided to make a daring night-time escape out of the city, over the Spartan siege works, and back to Athens. As this passage artfully indicates, the successful effort to measure both the enemy counter-walls that hemmed them in and the length of the ladders necessary to scale those walls was critical to the salvation of those who would escape the siege. But as the passage also makes clear, the act of political salvation effected by the escapees, an act which this passage narrates and which in more than one way calls to mind the ascent out of the cave made famous in Plato's *Republic*,[21] depends on an act intellectual liberation too. Specifically, it depends on liberation from thinking that parts can be understood independently of the wholes to which they belong. Thus, whether one is talking about the length of scaling ladders (which the besieged will use to escape), the size of the mud bricks (that make up the layers of the counter wall that they have to count), or the functions of prisoner-citizens (each of whom plays different roles in this mini-community "on the run"), one can only hope to understand them for what they are in terms of their relation to each other, in terms set by the particular whole of which they are a part. If one is to understand "parts", like human beings, for what they are, then one must understand them in terms of the political whole to which they belong, a whole which, in this case, Thucydides details with great care.

The story of Plataea concludes with the execution by the Spartans of all those who remained behind at the urging of the Spartans' Theban allies (III.68.2). Immediately following this (III.70-85), Thucydides provides an account of the Corcyrean civil war, one whose horrifying details foreshadows the civil wars that will wrack other Greek cities and whose consequences will lead to Athens's eventual surrender to Sparta (III.82.1; II.65). As this narrative makes clear, the butchery at Corcyra was inspired and made possible in no small part by the political factions in whose name such atrocities were committed. Though the massacre at Corcyra is often understood as the product of the breakdown of language and moral restraint, it is, rather, the reduction of all moral life to a single principle, in this case, that of one's faction, that makes possible the savagery that Thucydides describes. Fighting under their partisan banners, the Corcyreans, be they defenders of "the Peo-

---

[21] On the link between this passage in the *History* and Book VII of Plato's *Republic*, see Bernard J. Dobski, "Escape from Plataea: Political and Intellectual Liberation in Thucydides' History" (*Philosophy and Literature*, vol. 42. no. 1 April 2018, pp. 201–216).

ple" or of aristocracy (VIII.82.8), abandoned all prior legal, ethical, and religious restraints in the name of the political justice that inspired them. Contrary to the popular reading of this passage then, it is the persistence, not the fragility, of our attachment to justice that Thucydides attests to here. It is the persistence of this moral attachment that seems to make possible a violence that exceeds all measure. But the Plataeans' daring escape from a doomed city, the peak of a narrative that structures Thucydides' account of the first five years of the war, represents an antidote to such moral rigidity. It offers a path by which one can avoid the annihilation to which the breakdown of political life, driven by ideological moralism, can lead. His narrative of that escape shows that such salvation depends on the ability to derive the measure from those things which are most familiar to, and thus first for, us. And the measure of these things is to be understood relationally, an understanding made possible by the apprehension of the interdependence of parts and wholes within a political context.

Grasping the relational quality of things requires that one resist the impulse to sacrifice the moral and political complexity of human life to a single unifying principle. To avoid imposing on the phenomena that we would understand categories whose well-defined contours distort reality, one must avoid the overstatement or hyperbole so often present in political speech. It is this hyperbole that Pericles resists when he attempts to offer measured praise for those first Athenians who died in the war, balanced as it was against the concerns of both those who knew and those who did not know the fallen. And it is this same dangerous partiality that Pericles must effectively navigate during the war's first years. He is thus most measured when balancing the contending forces of Athenian political life against each other in order to protect the common good from the invasions of the Spartans and the ravages of the plague.[22] It is therefore no surprise that Thucydides praises Pericles as that Athenian most capable in speech and deed (I.139.4).

A similar necessity seems to inspire the measured policy of The Five Thousand, a regime that appeared to Thucydides as the best the Athenians had during his lifetime. Faced with a dwindling treasury, enemy fortifications in Attica, the revolt of its nearest ally Euboea, and a democratic navy at deadly odds with its own oligarchic rulers, Athens deposed The Four Hun-

[22] To alleviate the tensions created by his wartime policy, Pericles dispatches Athenian ships to harass the Peloponnesian coast. These triremes, specially designed to carry horses with them, brings together the city's land and sea forces, combining its democratic and oligarchic elements, in a policy that serves the good of the city.

dred and installed a mixed-regime, one that effectively blended the rule of the one, the few, and the many. Because this regime lasted only a few months, Thucydides does not record many of its deeds. His praise of this regime as measured must therefore be due to its willingness to reserve a place within its ruling structure for those factions of the city that would, under different circumstances, try to subordinate the whole community to their rule alone, perhaps even eliminating their competitors altogether. If the narrative about the escape from Plataea shows that political salvation requires us to see parts in their relation to and interdependence on each other, then it means that parts must understand themselves in their very partiality. In the case of the factions under The Five Thousand, it means they must not confuse themselves or the just claims they make on behalf of political office with the whole of the city or the whole of justice; it means seeing the parts as parts of a greater whole. And it means recognizing that the other claims advanced by parts of the city, while no less partial, are not for that very reason less just. Forced by necessity to recognize their own limitations and the danger of overstating their claim to rule, each faction in the city must grant the legitimate claim to participate in political life advanced by their rivals. The measured rule of The Five Thousand thus consists in its ability to preserve the distinctiveness of the parts of the city within the political context supplied by Athens.

That The Five Thousand was a response to necessities does not mean that its emergence was necessary or that any regime in similar circumstances would respond the same way, as the Corcyrean civil war indicates. Thucydides' praise of The Five Thousand stems partly from his knowledge that other human beings in this situation could have (and would have) done differently. The measured character of this regime, like that of Pericles, reflects Thucydides' use of measuredness throughout his *History* insofar as the city does less in this case than it otherwise could. In this way, it recalls the gentle policies of Brasidas or the Athenians at Melos or Diodotus in the assembly. That such policies serve the interests of those proposing them doesn't make them simply self-serving; on the contrary, in their very measuredness they implicitly testify to the limits on self-seeking.

Of course, like Pericles and so many of the other measured characters in the *History*, the rule of The Five Thousand in Athens fails. If Thucydides means for his readers to take seriously measuredness as a virtue, then it seems unlikely that he wants them to view it exclusively in terms of practical politics. The narrative of the escape from Plataea shows us how to manage the costs of political failure while highlighting the necessity of remaining engaged with politics, as the exiled Thucydides surely was. If our author is somehow more measured than even the measured actors whose conduct he records and in some cases praises, it is because he observes more fully than they do—in and through his *History*—the relational character of political phenomena and thus refuses to impose on human affairs the sharp categorical distinctions that our beliefs in justice appear to demand.

If measuredness consists partly in doing and saying less than one otherwise could, that is, if measuredness requires a form of understatement, then Thucydides must also resist the temptation to insist on disclosing his greatness in the way that the Spartan grapplers did at the Olympic games. Such resistance may seem odd for a man who seems to boast of having written a work for "all time" (I.22.4). But perhaps Thucydides' presentation of the war between Athens and Sparta resembles the "flip side" of these wrestlers, namely the Spartan elite whose measured garment made possible the common good at Sparta. This practice not only allayed the concerns of those they ruled, providing the elite a form of defensive concealment, but also effectively if indirectly revealed their greatness and justified their claim to rule. The practice of measuredness is the condition of their greatness. Such attention to and respect for ordinary political opinion and custom might help us understand how Thucydides' own measured presentation of practical political life surpasses those of his hyperbolic poetic rivals.[23]

It is fair to wonder if the "great improvement" to "the science of politics" effected by our own founders and lauded by Hamilton (*Fed.* 9) would produce adverse effects for Thucydidean measuredness. These great improvements, like our separation of powers, try to solve the problem of political instability and produce civic liberty largely by treating politics as if it were merely a matter of balancing contentious powers. One sees this not only in the mechanical design of the three branches of government, but in Madison's famous approach to the problem of factions in popular regimes, an approach which, like the separation of powers, relies on pitting ambition against ambition. The proliferation of factions that is to cure the problem factionalism presents is made possible in the first place by the government fulfilling its "first object," namely protecting the "diversity in the faculties of men, from which the rights of property originate" (*Fed.* 10). Madison continues:

---

[23] For a political image of this insight, consider Demosthenes's use of "disclosive" athletic contests to conceal his "theft" of the Athenian garrison at Epidaurus (V.80.3).

> From the protection of different and unequal faculties of acquiring property, the possession of different degrees and kinds of property immediately results; and from the influence of these on the sentiments and views of the respective proprietors ensues a division of society into different interests and parties.....The regulation of these various and interfering interests forms the principal task of modern legislation (*Fed.* 10).

Thus the effective manipulation of self-interest through the promotion of commerce produces liberty while abstracting from a concern with justice. But Thucydides shows us that measuredness means coming to grips with the real and insistent moral demands that we make on others and the world when we try to make evident to others our superior worthiness to rule. It is not merely, or even, a simple case of clashing interests. Such "coming to grips" entails recognizing and embracing the limits facing such demands, a recognition achieved by understanding political and human affairs relationally in light of our nature as political beings.

The architects of the American founding do not allow us to confront these demands partly because they take for granted the continued power and influence of those social and spiritual sources of moral education that once exercised great authority in the lives of American citizens, sources like organized religion, the bonds of family life, and a sober respect for civic honor. As such, their political and social recommendations don't actively promote those conditions necessary for sustaining a decent respect for moral virtue in public life and thus an appreciation for the claims moral virtue make on us. In fact, the American founders promoted institutions and practices that would deliberately emphasize the instrumental aspects of moral and intellectual virtue, making it increasingly difficult for their citizens to cultivate a taste for the theoretical reflection that belongs to philosophy, theology, and the fine arts. As Thomas Pangle points out, early American statesmen like Thomas Jefferson, Benjamin Franklin, and Benjamin Rush, among others, designed curricula for national and state sponsored universities that directed the character and intellect of future statesmen and citizens towards the legislative and practical arts that would allow them to serve the needs of "a commercial and agricultural society."[24] The end of such education was to serve the practical requirements of liberty, stability, and individual security and not contemplation on the ends of a regime dedicated to such goods. The univer-

---

[24] Thomas Pangle, *The Spirit of Modern Republicanism: The Moral Vision of the American Founders and the Philosophy of Locke* (Chicago: University of Chicago Press, 1988) 76-77.

sities proposed by the early American founders thus sought to develop a public reason that would serve the design of our new political order without requiring one to explore the mysteries and tragedies of the human condition or the larger moral and spiritual whole of which we are a part.

What does this mean for the separation of powers? By promising to secure political liberty systematically, the modern separation of powers provides little incentive for the parts of the political community to restrain the pursuit of their self-interests or to refrain from identifying the good with one's own. To be sure, such a system of checks and balances aims to produce a government and its agents that will act moderately. But the kind of moderation intended by our founders belongs to a different register than the measuredness portrayed in Thucydides' work since what appears generous, graceful, or noble about *metrios* gets sacrificed to Madison's "enlightened, calm, and prudent pursuit of security and ease for oneself and for the the society in which one finds oneself."[25] It is true that both the measuredness praised by Thucydides and the moderation of Madison and Montesquieu share "an absence of moralism, an absence of self-righteousness or blinding pride and indignation, a capacity for amoral flexibility."[26] But the measuredness found in the pages of Thucydides' *History* ennobles its readers precisely insofar as it requires them to look beyond their self-interests and to view themselves as parts of broader whole, one in which their pursuit of self-interest properly understood requires recognizing both the legitimacy and the limits of the claims placed on them by others. Thus, while Thucydides would likely be impressed by the practical efficiency of the American founders' separation of powers, he would also understand our science of politics to narrow significantly the possibility of our becoming truly measured because it abstracts from the moral impulse behind the desire to justify one's rule. While this lesson might not be the kind of utility that his father had in mind, such an insight, I think, would nevertheless be useful for the young John Quincy Adams. Indeed, it would be useful for all of those who believe they possess a just claim to rule others.

---

[25] Pangle, *Spirit*, 92.
[26] Pangle, *Spirit*, 91.

THUCYDIDES AND THE NEW POLITICAL SCIENCE OF THE AMERICAN FOUNDING

Devin Stauffer

Despite its broad title, the aim of this essay is fairly limited. I seek to make a modest contribution to this volume—a volume dedicated to putting Thucydides in dialogue with the American Founders—by highlighting an important difference between Thucydides and the American Founders. My foray into the American Founding will be a brief, surgical strike: I will focus on a single passage from *The Federalist Papers*, albeit a passage with far-reaching implications. My discussion of Thucydides will be a bit longer and more involved; but in that case, too, my intention is merely to call attention to a few key points that are relevant to the comparison at issue.

Now, lest I give the misimpression that there is a vast gulf between Thucydides and the American Founders, let me begin by acknowledging that there is much that Thucydides and the American Founders have in common. Thucydides, like most of the Founders, was a man of both action and thought, and he, like they, is known for his gravity, humanity, and sobriety. If Thucydides were somehow to overcome the boundaries of time and place and encounter the American Founders, he would surely recognize in them kindred spirits—men who shared his belief in the dignity and importance of politics, as well as his sober realism about its problems. Despite their kinship, however, I want to suggest that there is one respect in which Thucydides was more sober, not to say more somber, than the American Founders, namely, in his estimation of whether there could be transformative change for the better in political affairs, or whether the most serious political problems could be solved. When Thucydides described his ambition to write, in his unforgettable phrase, "a possession for all time" (1.22),[1] he did not mean that he was offering human beings a guidebook for a transformation of politics that would bring about a permanent change. Rather, he meant that his aim was to write a work that would help at least some of his readers to grasp the permanent problems of political life, problems rooted in

[1] All citations of Thucydides refer to the Oxford Classical Texts edition, *Thucydidis Historiae*, edited by Henry Stuart Jones (Oxford: Oxford University Press, 1942). Translations are my own.

permanent aspects of the human condition and human nature, and, although he promised that there would be some use in knowing those problems and those aspects, he never suggests that such knowledge could pave the way for revolutionary change toward a more perfect political order. A Thucydidean statesman, that is, a statesman educated by reading Thucydides, would be equipped to act with greater prudence, not least because his hopes would have been moderated by Thucydides' text; he would not be equipped to transform the very character of political life, and, if he tried to do that, it would be a sign that he had not learned what Thucydides wanted to teach him. The same cannot be said of the American Founders, not only because they were revolutionaries themselves, but because they saw their revolution as laying the foundations of something fundamentally new.

I.

Let me turn to the passage I want to focus on in the works of the American Founders. The passage is from *Federalist* #9, written by the Publius that was Alexander Hamilton. At the beginning of *Federalist* #9, as he is introducing his case for "The Union as a Safeguard Against Domestic Faction and Insurrection," Hamilton grants that the "advocates of despotism" have a strong case to make against republican government and indeed against "the very principles of civil liberty."[2] They only need to point to the historical track record of republics. Hamilton spells out the problem himself, in this remarkable passage:

> It is impossible to read the history of the petty republics of Greece and Italy without feeling sensations of horror and disgust at the distractions with which they were continually agitated, and at the rapid succession of revolutions by which they were kept in a state of perpetual vibration between the extremes of tyranny and anarchy. If they exhibit occasional calms, these only serve as short-lived contrasts to the furious storms that are to succeed. If now and then intervals of felicity open themselves to view, we behold them with a mixture of regret, arising from the reflection that the pleasing scenes before us are soon to be overwhelmed by the tempestuous waves of sedition and party rage. If momentary rays of glory break forth from the gloom,

[2] Quotations and citations of *The Federalist Papers* are from *Federalist* #9, unless otherwise noted. I have used the Signet Classics edition, edited by Clinton Rossiter with an introduction and notes by Charles R. Kesler (New York: New American Library, 2003).

> while they dazzle us with a transient and fleeting brilliancy, they at the same time admonish us to lament that the vices of government should pervert the direction and tarnish the luster of those bright talents and exalted endowments for which the favored soils that produced them have been so justly celebrated.

Among the historians from whom Hamilton drew in forming this sweeping impression of the history of classical republicanism was surely Thucydides. But what does Hamilton conclude from the bleak portrait he paints? His conclusion is not, of course, that the cause of republican liberty is hopeless. Even if the advocates of despotism have a powerful argument in the sordid history of republics, not only does Hamilton suggest that there are counterexamples—"stupendous fabrics reared on the basis of liberty, which have flourished for ages" that have "in a few glorious instances, refuted their gloomy sophisms"—but he also thinks that the American experiment, if rightly conducted, will be the decisive example that will vindicate, once and for all, the cause of republican government and provide a model for "other edifices" of equal magnificence. Why is this development possible now, as it was not in earlier times? Because, Hamilton contends, "the science of politics...like most other sciences, has received great improvement."

To support his contention that the science of politics has progressed to the point that the prospects of republican government are now far brighter than they were in the past, Hamilton points to several innovations or principles that are "now well understood, which were either not known at all, or imperfectly known to the ancients." His list of innovations includes the division of powers into separate departments, checks and balances, an independent judiciary with lifetime appointments for judges, and a sensible scheme of representation. According to Hamilton, "these are wholly new discoveries, or have made their principal progress toward perfection in modern times." Another innovation must be added to the list, not only because Hamilton adds it, but because it is the one to which he and James Madison devote their greatest attention in the key sequence of *Federalist* #9 and #10: the enlargement of the orbit within which the other principles will operate, or, in other words, the expansion of sphere of government such that it encompasses a very large republic. The arguments in favor of expanding the sphere, just as those for the separation of powers and checks and balances that would enable ambition to counteract ambition, are well known: expanding the sphere of the government not only makes it more likely that representatives, who will be drawn from bigger pools, will be of better character and judgment, but it addresses the problem of factionalism, not by getting rid of factions, but by multiplying them and using them to check one another such that no faction will be able to carry out its schemes of oppression at the expense of the common good.[3]

This last argument is worthy of examination in detail, especially since its very familiarity often leads people to suppose that they grasp the underlying reasoning better than they do. The argument suggests that the petty rivalry of interest groups and the grinding stalemate it often causes—problems so often bemoaned today—were in some sense intended by the Founders, just as they regarded the selfish pursuit of private ambition by politicians as a price worth paying for the preservation of liberty. My aim here, however, is not to get into the weeds of the details of the arguments in *The Federalist Papers*, but to make a broader point. Hamilton and Madison—and of course, they were not alone in this[4]—thought that certain advancements in "the sci-

[3] Madison gives the fullest explanation of this last point in *Federalist* #10. Although he makes a number of arguments there about the virtues of a large republic, his most interesting and important argument is that a large republic renders factions "less to be dreaded" precisely because it encompasses more of them: "Extend the sphere and you take in a greater variety of parties and interests; you make it less probable that a majority of the whole will have a common motive to invade the rights of other citizens; or if such a common motive exists, it will be more difficult for all who feel it to discover their own strength and to act in unison with each other." This argument should be compared with Madison's more famous argument in *Federalist* #51 in favor of a scheme of checks and balances that uses ambition to counteract ambition, an argument that shares with the one from *Federalist* #10 the approach of using prudently juxtaposed private interests as "a sentinel over the public rights" (*Federalist* #51).

[4] For another expression of the same thought, see the passage of the preface of John Adams's *Defense of the Constitution of Government of the United States of America* in which Adams contrasts the stability of modern politics with the chaos of ancient politics and refers to Thucydides by name. Adams writes: "We shall learn to prize the checks and balances of a free government, and even those of modern aristocracies, if we recollect the miseries of Greece, which arose from ignorance of them....It is impossible to read in Thucydides, his account of the factions and confusions throughout all of Greece, which were introduced by this want of an equilibrium, without horror." After then quoting extensively from Thucydides' account of the terrors of the Corcyrean revolution and of *stasis* in general (a passage in Thucydides which will be discussed below), Adams quotes Thucydides' famous remark that, "Such things ever will be...so long as human nature remains the same" (Adams's translation). But then, before resuming his series of quotations, Adams adds this remark of his own: "But if this nervous historian had known a balance of three powers, he would not have pronounced the distemper so incurable, but would have added—*so long as parties in cities remain unbalanced*" (*The Works of John Adams*, vol. 4, ed. Charles Francis Adams [Boston: Little, Brown, and Co., 1865] 285). I am grateful to

ence of politics" had paved the way for something new in the world: a stable, non-oppressive, very large republic that would be, not indeed immune to factional conflict, but protected from its most extreme and dangerous forms. Factionalism—that is, divisions over economic, cultural, and religious questions—would not tear the new republic apart, because there had been discovered, as Madison put it, "a republican remedy for the diseases most incident to republican government" (*Federalist* #10).

II.

Thucydides, for his part, does not talk about "republican government"—at least not in so many words. But he was well aware of the kinds of diseases that Hamilton and Madison had in mind, and he knew of their prevalence especially in the more democratic cities of the ancient world. Some of the most striking passages in Thucydides concern precisely such diseases. For example, there is his account of the divisions that emerged in Athens, not only after the failure of the Sicilian Expedition, but almost as soon as the Peloponnesian War began; even under Pericles, Athens was never so unified a place as Pericles' presence and rhetoric made it seem, and once Pericles died the factional divisions in Athens came to the surface (see, e.g., 2.59, 2.65, 6.60). But the passage that stands out most in this regard is Thucydides' account of the Corcyrean Civil War, a stunning passage that culminates in a general statement on civil strife, or what Thucydides calls *stasis*, as a plight that struck almost every Greek city at some point during the war.

In his account of *stasis*, both of its specific horrors in Corcyra and of its general features as a phenomenon that swept through Greece, Thucydides does not spend much time discussing institutional structures or arrangements. It is true that he speaks of the breakdown of the restraints of law as they were overwhelmed by the tides of passion; but he does not suggest that specific institutional structures were the primary bulwarks against *stasis*. In fact, it is characteristic of Thucydides' work as a whole that he says surprisingly little about institutional structures. The passage that stands out as the clearest counterexample—Thucydides' discussion and praise in Book Eight of the semi-oligarchic regime of the Five Thousand in Athens (see especially

---

Timothy Burns for alerting me to this passage and its significance; see Burns, "The Problematic Character of Periclean Athens," in *On Civic Republicanism*, edited by Geoffrey C. Kellow and Neven Leddy (Toronto: University of Toronto Press, 2016) 39, n. 41.

8.97)—is the exception that proves the rule, and not just because it stands out in its difference from so many other passages in Thucydides, thereby helping us to notice what is mostly absent elsewhere in the book. By bestowing very terse praise on a short-lived arrangement of no lasting significance, Thucydides also indicates how fleeting moderate political arrangements are likely to be, especially in cities like Athens.

Of course, one of the reasons that Thucydides says comparatively little about institutional questions may be that he was a historian telling the story of a war, not a statesman arguing for the ratification of a Constitution. As a historian, he may have thought that the various institutions in the different cities were simply not the most important features of those cities or the most determinative causes of their actions. But there may be another reason as well for Thucydides' near silence about institutions, for he gives no sign in his work of thinking that different institutions would have made a decisive difference in solving the problems that he devotes his attention to illuminating. Even in the case of Sparta, the only major Greek city that avoided *stasis*, Thucydides focuses more on the spirit of Sparta—its devotion to the law, its moderation, and the effects of its long-standing Helot problem—than on the structure of Sparta or its political institutions *per se*.

Rather than discussing or proposing institutional solutions to political problems, Thucydides' main aim is to help his readers understand the roots of those problems in human nature. This is clearest in the case of his account of *stasis*, for Thucydides does not treat *stasis* as an aberration due to the flawed structures of those cities that were engulfed by it. Rather, he treats it as a permanent disease of political life—one that may go into remission for long stretches but that will always reemerge. As he puts it, "The calamities that befell the cities on account of *stasis* were many and grievous, such as have occurred and always will occur, so long as the nature of human beings remains the same, although the instances can be more severe or milder, as they take on a diversity of forms with changes in circumstances" (3.82). This statement, as others have pointed out,[5] is the clearest echo from later in Thucydides' text of his initial promise to help men understand the problems

[5] See, e.g., Clifford Orwin, *The Humanity of Thucydides* (Princeton: Princeton University Press, 1994), 176; Peter J. Ahrensdorf, "The Fear of Death and the Longing for Immortality: Hobbes and Thucydides on Human Nature and the Problem of Anarchy," *The American Political Science Review* 94 (3), September 2000: 579-93, 587. I have benefitted from both Orwin's and Ahrensdorf's illuminating discussions of Thucydides' account of *stasis*. See Orwin, 175-82; Ahrensdorf, 587-89.

that will confront them in the future, a future that, "in accordance with the human," will broadly resemble the past even if it does not perfectly replicate it (see 1.22).

Thucydides' account of revolution focuses on the passions—ambition, resentment, envy, vengefulness, greed—that mix with convictions about justice, convictions that become simplified, radicalized, and intensified as the spirit of party and an insistence on the rights of anger replace any concern with the common good. In such circumstances, moderation, civic spiritedness, piety, and respect for the law lose their standing as the conditions on which they depend are destroyed, and, in a terrible downward spiral, the loss of respect for the peaceful virtues further destroys the conditions in question. The result is the exposure of the fragility of ordinary decency and its collapse, not into pure anarchy or a Hobbesian war of all against all, but into a desperate and frenzied form of partisan strife in which moral convictions are transformed such that they fuel rather than restrain the cycle of violence.[6]

---

[6] That morality is transformed but not destroyed in times of *stasis* is indicated in Thucydides' famous statement on the changes that *stasis* caused in man's estimations of virtue and vice, and in the words used to describe various kinds of action:

> The accepted connotations of words, as they referred to deeds, were altered by the new way of judging. For irrational daring came to be regarded as the courage of a committed comrade; caution born of forethought, as a pretext for cowardice; moderation, as a façade concealing unmanliness; and an appreciation of all sides of an issue, as an inability to act on any of them. Rash hostility came be regarded as part of being a man, and calculating in safety a clever excuse for shirking from a fight. The one who spoke vehemently was always trusted; his opponent, regarded with suspicion. Whoever hatched a plot and succeeded was regarded as intelligent, and anyone who foresaw the plots of others was thought still more clever. But the one who tried to figure ought how to avoid doing either of these things was regarded as weakening his side and showing his fear of his opponents. Simply put, he who preempted impending harm was praised, as was he who exhorted those whose minds were not yet turned in that direction (3.82.4-5).

Ahrensdorf makes a similar point about the above passage as a reflection of the "new moral code" that emerged as *stasis* rampaged through many Greek cities (see "The Fear of Death and the Longing for Immortality," 587). He then goes on, however, to place great weight on Thucydides' subsequent statement at 3.82.7 that, for the antagonists in the various conflicts, "to avenge oneself against someone was valued more than never to have suffered [injustice] oneself," which he takes as a clear indication that the people Thucydides describes were inspired by a hope for divine favor and ultimately for immortality (see 588-89). According to Ahrensdorf, "By stating that people preferred to suffer injustice and then avenge it rather than not to suffer at all, Thucydides indicates that people were motivated not by a genuine anger at injustice but by an overriding desire to win divine assistance; they somehow expected to save themselves from death by clearly and emphatically suffering and punishing injustice" (589). In my view, Ahrensdorf goes

Thucydides' description of revolution reminds of his earlier account of the plague in Athens, in which a similar dynamic emerged, albeit one that did not lead to fierce partisan conflict (see especially 2.53).[7] Rather than look at Thucydides' account of the plague, however, let me highlight two other important passages in which Thucydides points to the deepest sources of the periodic upsurges of destructive immoderation in politics. I will take them out of order, since one of them comes in Book Three, but the one I will take up first comes in Book Four.

The passage in Book Four comes in the midst of Thucydides' account of the Spartan commander Brasidas' bold Thracian campaign, in which he tried to liberate a number of Greek cities that were subject to Athens' empire but reachable by land. Although Brasidas threatened some of those cities, such as Acanthus, that were reluctant to join his cause of Greek liberation, more important than the stick he carried was the carrot he dangled. Brasidas promised these weak cities a kind of secular salvation—not just freedom from Athenian domination, but a civic existence free of both external and internal oppression. It is all too understandable that weak cities, having long suffered the humiliation and deprivations of submission to an imperial power, would welcome the promises of this Spartan Che Guevara. "Indeed, it seemed to them that they had no reason to fear," Thucydides says (4.108). But then Thucydides delivers his own stern judgment on their prudence: "their self-deception in their estimate of the power of the Athenians was as great as that power later proved to be, judging as they did more by uncertain wish than by sound forethought; for human beings are wont to entrust what they yearn for to unexamined hope, and to use sovereign calculation to cast aside what they do not want to accept" (4.108).

Trusting in hope and allowing hope to distort what would otherwise be the sober counsel of reason—this, according to Thucydides, is a powerful

---

too far with this interpretation of Thucydides' remark. Although it is certainly true that Thucydides points to a surprising, if recognizable, psychological tendency—Why would one prefer getting revenge, which requires first suffering harm, over avoiding damage in the first place?—it does not follow from the apparent unreasonableness of this tendency or impulse that its deepest cause must be a longing for immortality. There are other possible explanations, such as a desire to smite one's enemies not out of mere hatred or self-interest but with a rightful wrath, which need not imply a hope for divine assistance or a concern to render oneself worthy of immortality.

[7] See Clifford Orwin, "*Stasis* and Plague: Thucydides on the Dissolution of Society," *Journal of Politics* 50 (1988): 841-46; Burns, "The Problematic Character of Periclean Athens," 23-27.

human tendency that often creates chaos and devastation, because it spurs men to strive and dare when they should not. The second passage to be considered is perhaps the most important statement on this dynamic in Thucydides' entire work. It comes from the pivotal paragraph of the greatest speech in the book: Diodotus' speech in favor of treating the rebellious Mytilenians with greater lenience than the fiery demagogue Cleon exhorted the Athenians to do. In the crucial paragraph of his speech (3.45), Diodotus, for complicated reasons that need not concern us here,[8] explains why men are led to strive for freedom and empire even when calm calculation would have advised against their pursuit. Once again, Thucydides—now through the mouth of Diodotus—points to the problem of hope. But in this case, he calls our attention to a force prior to hope: *eros*. As Diodotus puts it, "Hope and *eros* in each instance—the latter leading and the former following, *eros* hatching the plan, hope supplying a belief that fortune will be favorable—cause the greatest harm, and, although they are invisible, they overpower the visible dangers."[9] Hope and *eros*, aspects of human nature that most are inclined to see as precious gifts, are the targets of Thucydidean critique, or, if "critique" is not quite the right word, Thucydidean warning. In contrast to Barack Obama, who wrote a book entitled *The Audacity of Hope*, Thucydides teaches us about the mendacity of hope, especially when it follows the lead of *eros*. It may seem unduly pessimistic or misanthropic to emphasize the

---

[8] For helpful discussions of the reasons, see Orwin, *The Humanity of Thucydides*, 147-57; Timothy Burns, "Anger in Thucydides and Aristophanes: The Case of Cleon," in *The Political Theory of Aristophanes: Explorations in Poetic Wisdom*, ed. Jeremy J. Mhire and Bryan-Paul Frost (Albany: State University of New York Press, 2014).

[9] Because this sentence (3.45.5) is one of the most important in Thucydides' entire work, offering as it does the most direct statement by the most impressive figure in the work on the forces in the human soul that lead men to make grievous mistakes, it is especially unfortunate that the translation on which many readers today rely, Richard Crawley's translation in Robert Strassler's *Landmark Thucydides*, renders the sentence so loosely and inaccurately. Crawley translates the sentence in this way: "Hope also and greed, the one leading and the other following, the one conceiving the attempt, the other suggesting the facility of succeeding, cause the widest ruin, and, although invisible agents, are far stronger than the dangers that are seen." The two most significant problems with this translation are the translation of *eros* as "greed" and the false impression it gives that hope is "the one leading" rather than "the other following." On this last point, it is clear from the genders of the nouns and the corresponding participles in the Greek text that *eros* is the one leading, hope the one following. On Thucydides' view of the role of *eros* in leading hope, see Timothy Burns, "What War Discloses," in *Recovering Reason: Essays in Honor of Thomas L. Pangle*, ed. Timothy Burns (Lanham, MD: Lexington Books), 45.

dangers of hope and *eros*; I know of no other philosopher who speaks so harshly of these aspects of human nature. But Thucydides would defend himself by explaining that, unlike the poets, he wanted to present human nature and the problems it poses as they really are, in the reasonable expectation that some readers could benefit from knowing what moves human beings to strive beyond reason (consider 1.21-22).

III.

The *eros*-driven hopes that Thucydides warns against are most immediately those for freedom and empire when they are not available or when their pursuit is too risky. Among the many other examples of the rash pursuit of freedom and empire in Thucydides' work, the most massive is the Athenians' decision to launch the Sicilian Expedition. Thucydides stresses how little the Athenians knew of what they were getting themselves into in Sicily (see 6.1); yet he indicates that at a certain point, as they contemplated the massive armada that would be required to conquer Sicily, the Athenians fell in love with the vision of its conquest. As Thucydides puts it, describing the reaction of the Athenians to a speech of Nicias emphasizing the magnitude of the task they were about to undertake, "*eros* for the expedition descended into all of them" (6.24). It is not only, then, those weak cities that yearned for freedom from the Athenian empire that were led astray by their erotic hopes. Similar hopes—hopes that are, after all, for "freedom *and empire*" (see 3.45)—gripped mighty Athens herself, thus showing that, despite the infamous Athenian assertion that "the strong do what they can, while the weak suffer what they must" (see 5.89), the strong no more than the weak are spared from suffering the destructive consequences of irrational hopefulness.

It is important to be clear about the kinds of hopes Thucydides has in mind when he warns against them, so as not to conflate them with the kinds of hopes that I indicated one can see in Hamilton and Madison. There is a reasonable objection that could be raised to the way I have set things up so far: Thucydides warns of the dangers of passions and hopes for freedom and empire as they expressed themselves in a war between relatively small Greek cites. Is that not a far cry from the kind of assessment that Hamilton and Madison made of what could be expected from the application of a new science of politics to a large republic? Of course there is an important difference here, and my contention is not—cannot be—that Thucydides would simply argue that Hamilton and Madison are yet two more examples of political men led astray by their *eros* and their hopes. For all I know, Thucydides would even have regarded what they were arguing for—the ratification of the Constitution—as an eminently sensible proposal. My point, rather, is to emphasize that Thucydides focuses on something different from what the Founders focus on—passions and hopes, as opposed to institutional arrangements—and that that difference goes together with the fact that he does not present the science of politics as a progressive science. For the basic passions and hopes of human beings, while they can be understood more or less well, do not admit of the modification and improvement that institutional arrangements do.

What if Thucydides were presented with the innovations of the new political science that the Founders put into practice? Would he grant that the new institutional arrangements could solve a permanent problem of politics? I doubt it, and I see no signs in his text that he would. As Clifford Orwin says of Thucydides, "nothing could be more alien to him than the view that mankind poses no problems that it cannot solve."[10] But what if Thucydides were confronted by the (ongoing) results of the American experiment in large-scale, constitutionally structured republican self-government? What would he say? The only reasonable answer is that it is impossible to know. But I suspect he would say something along the following lines: It is true—and impressive—that America has survived as a free republic for as long as it has. And it is true—and very impressive—that America has never been torn apart by internal class struggles between economic factions. But it is also true—and also very important—is that America did almost come apart at the seams through a bitter conflict that the Founders' faction-checking-ambition-counteracting stability machine proved unable to prevent. Is not the American Civil War an example of the kind of *stasis* that Thucydides thought would recur so long as human nature remained the same?

To be sure, the Civil War had complicated causes, including a stark division over a profound moral question. It was not an instance of a simple struggle between an oligarchic faction and a democratic one, as most of the Greek instances of *stasis* were. Still, Thucydides would likely have been less surprised by the fracturing of our political order, and by the passions that were unleashed then, than Hamilton and Madison would have been. And he would likely point out that, even though the Founders did not place their hopes in enlightened statesmen, because "enlightened statesmen will not

[10] *The Humanity of Thucydides*, 4.

always be at the helm" (*Federalist* #10), it was very fortunate that an enlightened statesman *was* at the helm in that terrible crisis. Beyond the isolated instance of the Civil War, Thucydides might also help us to us to understand why, every time America seems to have reached a new stage in achieving the Founders' aim of "a more perfect union," our politics also show disconcerting signs of instability and internal discontent. Since we are going through one of those periods of instability and discontent right now, that is all the more reason that Thucydides' work should not be dismissed as the lamentations of an old pessimist who has been rendered obsolete by the innovations of modern political science.

A PHILOLOGIST IN THE AMERICAN CIVIL WAR

Sarah E. Gardner

In 1892, Johns Hopkins philologist and former Confederate officer, Basil L. Gildersleeve published "The Creed of the Old South" in *The Atlantic Monthly*. In it, he recounted a "lively conversation" he had overheard between two veterans of "the war between the States." The two went into "minute detail" about the "various battles in which they had faced each other more than a quarter century ago." Gildersleeve confessed that he would make a poor job of it were he pressed to give an account of his time in service. "I may as well acknowledge at the outset that I have as little aptitude for the soldier's trade as I have for the romancer's." To be sure, "single pictures" had etched themselves into his brain. But, he continued, "I have no vocation to tell how fields were lost and won." His admission hardly surprises. Indeed, Gildersleeve spilled very little ink in the battle over postwar memory that raged in the popular press during the late-nineteenth and early-twentieth centuries.[1] Though he considered his brief stint in the Confederate Army "significant," his intellectual interests rested elsewhere.[2]

Gildersleeve was a prodigious scholar, perhaps best known among classicists as the founding editor of the *American Journal of Philology* and for his syntactical commentaries on Caesar's Gallic Wars and on Pindaric odes. But he also wrote for general readers, most notably in *The Nation* and *The Atlantic Monthly*. In only one other essay, "A Southerner in the Peloponnesian War," published five years after "The Creed of the Old South," did Gildersleeve ruminate on his time in the Civil War. Yet even here, Gildersleeve was less interested in telling tales about the American Civil War than he was in positioning Thucydides for Gilded Age-Americans. And true to his earli-

[1] See David Blight, *Race and Reunion: The Civil War in American Memory* (Cambridge, Mass: Harvard University Press, 2002); Caroline E. Janney, *Remembering the Civil War: Reunion and the Limits of Reconciliation* (Chapel Hill: University of North Carolina Press, 2013); K. Stephen Prince, *Stories of the South: Race and the Reconstruction of Southern Identity, 1865-1915* (Chapel Hill: University of North Carolina Press, 2014).

[2] Basil L. Gildersleeve, "The Creed of the Old South," *The Atlantic Monthly* (January 1892): 75. On Gildersleeve's initial reticence to write this article, see Basil L. Gildersleeve to Horace E. Scudder, in *The Letters of Basil Lanneau Gildersleeve*, Ward W. Briggs, Jr., ed. (Baltimore: Johns Hopkins University Press, 1987) 184-185.

er claim in "The Creed of the Old South," Gildersleeve offered no special insight into battles won or lost, nor did he employ the literary techniques of the romantics, so popular with readers of an earlier generation.[3]

Instead, Gildersleeve strategically used the national literary marketplace to advocate the classics' relevance for an increasingly modern, mechanized, and specialized postbellum America. He had his work cut out for him, for his project was at direct odds with larger trends in the academy. As Caroline Winterer has documented, classicists, beginning in the antebellum era, promoted their discipline as the antidote to the excesses of democracy run amok. "Rather than looking to antiquity as a guide to the present," as the founding generation had, classicists "now looked to the remote past as a way to combat such cancers of modernity as materialism, civic decay, industrialization, and anti-intellectualism." Put another way, the classics were no longer posited as a guide, but as a retreat. Repurposed as "antimodern," classicism thus appeared "unsuited to a flourishing market economy with an increasingly popular ethos," a tension, Winterer has observed, that classicism's [...] focus on Greek democracy failed to resolve." Classicists continued their efforts in the postwar period and were, according to Winterer, "among the first to propose a major critique of the ideal of social utility that many scientists had offered."[4]

Gildersleeve, too, challenged the technocrats and the bureaucrats who sought order in the war's aftermath, but he did so by confronting head on the vexing questions that plagued postwar America.[5] He used Thucydides' *History* not as a means of escape but as a tool in his arsenal. What text could more clearly illustrate that at any effort to order the world was a fool's errand?

---

[3] See, for example, Coleman Hutchison, *Apples and Ashes: Literature, Nationalism, and the Confederate States of America* (Athens: University of Georgia Press, 2012).

[4] Caroline Winterer, *The Culture of Classicism: Ancient Greece and Rome in American Intellectual Life, 1780-1910* (Baltimore: Johns Hopkins University Press, 2004): 4. For a broader discussion of antimodernism in late nineteenth-century America, see Jackson Lears, *No Place of Grace: Antimodernism and the Transformation of American Culture, 1880-1920* (New York: Pantheon Books, 1981).

[5] The classic work in the field remains Robert H. Wiebe, *The Search for Order, 1877-1920* (New York: Hill and Want, 1967.) As he noted, "For lack of anything that made better sense of their world, people everywhere weighed, counted, and measured," 43. See also, Mark Wahlgren Summers, *The Gilded Age: Or, the Hazard of New Functions* (New York: Prentice Hall, 1997); Leon Fink, *The Long Gilded Age* (Philadelphia: University of Pennsylvania Press, 2015.)

Gildersleeve might seem like an unlikely candidate to buck these anti-modernist trends, for so much of the myth of the Old South rested on a nostalgia for a past that never was.[6] Yet that is precisely what he does in his 1897 essay. The way in which Gildersleeve mediated Thucydides to a reading audience, now distanced from the Civil War by more than a generation, marks his awareness of those anxieties and concerns that animated the nation as it sped toward the twentieth century. We can best understand Gildersleeve's presentation of Thucydides, then, by acknowledging his (proto) modernist sensibilities.

In 1849, Gildersleeve, at the age of eighteen, was graduated from Princeton—the "go-to" institution of higher learning for well-bred, wealthy southern men up through the late antebellum period. He then studied in Berlin and Bonn, finally earning his PhD from the University of Gottingen in 1853.[7] Some forty years later, as he tried to find his way into his essay "The Two Wars," the original title for what became "A Southerner in the Peloponnesian War," Gildersleeve recollected his time in Europe: "When I was a student abroad, American novices used to be asked in jest, 'Is this your first ruin?' 'Is this your first nightingale?' I am not certain that I can place my first ruin or my first nightingale," Gildersleeve interjected, thus disrupting what sounded like a nostalgic reverie, "but I can recall my first dead man on the battlefield."[8]

---

[6] See, for example, Blight, *Race and Reunion*; Karen L. Cox, *Dreaming of Dixie: How the South Was Created in American Popular Press*, 2011); Tara McPherson, *Reconstructing Dixie: Race, Gender, and Nostalgia in the Imagined South* (Durham, N.C.: Duke University Press, 2003); Prince, *Stories of the South*; Nina Silber, *The Romance of Reunion: Northerners and the South, 1865-1900* (Chapel Hill: University of North Carolina Press, 1993).

[7] See Basil L. Gildersleeve, "Classical Studies in America," *The Atlantic Monthly* (December 1896): 728-36 for the importance he placed on German education in the mid-nineteenth century. See also two other autobiographical writings, "College in the Forties," originally published in the *Princeton Alumni Weekly* (1916) and "A Novice of 1850," originally published in the *Johns Hopkins Alumni Magazine* (1916), both reprinted in *Soldier and Scholar: Basil Lanneau Gildersleeve and the Civil War*, Ward W. Briggs, Jr., ed. (Charlottesville, VA: University Press of Virginia): 50-76. See also, Michael O'Brien, *Conjectures of Order: Intellectual Life and the American South, 1810-1860* (Chapel Hill: University of North Carolina Press, 2004): 125-145, 327 and James Turner, *Philology: The Forgotten Origins of the Modern Humanities* (Princeton: Princeton University Press, 2014): 168-171; 178-184.

[8] Basil L. Gildersleeve, "A Southerner in the Peloponnesian War," *The Atlantic Monthly* (September 1897): 330.

Of course, it is unlikely that this conversation ever took place. It was a bit late in the game for Gildersleeve to be hanging out with Young Werther, after all. But Gildersleeve was not recording dialogue. He was documenting a moment: the demise of Romanticism. Indeed, Gildersleeve used this passage, powerful in its rhetorical effect, to set up a tension between Romanticism's emphasis on the sublime, with its deliberate evocation of Shelley and Keats, and the very real devastation wrought by the most destructive war in America's history. Note the way in which Gildersleeve ordered the questions asked of the "young American novices"—is this your first ruin, is this your first nightingale—presenting first the transitory work of man, the ruin, and then nature, the nightingale, thus implying the power of the latter to transcend the former.

But Gildersleeve immediately countered by suggesting both were abstractions, irrelevant ones at that. "To those who have seen the midday sun darkened by the burning homesteads, and wheatfields illuminated by stark forms in blue and gray," he elaborated, "war is sufficiently concrete. The very first dead soldier one sees, enemy or friend, takes war forever out of the category of abstracts."[9]

Although tempting, we should not read Gildersleeve's comment as a manifestation of the sobering effects of the passage of time. Shortly after the battle of Gettysburg, he wrote to a family friend of a profound war weariness that had overtaken him and his comrades. "Everybody in the army [...] is horribly sick of the war – Bad enough for the passengers to be seasick in a storm," he observed, "but still that is not dangerous." The situation becomes dire, however, when the "crew is sea-sick and the officers are sea-sick, and men lie about the deck so overcome with nausea that they care not whether they live or die." And this from the man who earlier in the same letter alluded to Pericles' Funeral Oration when imagining a Confederacy willing "to submit to any privation, to run any risk, to wait any time rather than to yield to the dictation of our enemies." Yet determination buckled under the weight of Confederate losses. He simply wanted the war to stop, "whether we are successful in this struggle or not."[10]

This might seem like a strange argument for a former Confederate to make, given the power of the myth of the lost cause that had permeated

[9] Gildersleeve, "Peloponnesian War," 330.

[10] Basil L. Gildersleeve to Socrates Maupin, Camp near Hamilton's Crossing, 10 September 1863, in *The Letters of Gildersleeve*, 39. See, for example, Thucydides, *History* 2.42.

much of mainstream American culture, or what Gildersleeve's contemporary, Mark Twain, had once called "Sir Walter [Scott] disease." The region "has not yet recovered from the debilitating influence of his books," Twain explained. "Admiration of his fantastic heroes and their grotesque 'chivalry' doings and romantic juvenilities still survives here [...] and traces of its inflating language and other windy humbuggeries survive along with it." And although no part of southern culture had been left unscathed by the disease's withering effects, its greatest damage, according to Twain, had been wrought on literary production. Twain had accused southern authors of writing "for the past, not the present;" of using "obsolete forms, and a dead language."[11] Gildersleeve was having none of it. True, Gildersleeve often peppered his essays with Greek, but he did not employ the language of chivalry. As America embarked a brutal imperialist enterprise, Gildersleeve most assuredly wrote for the present. Quoting Pindar, he concluded "A sweet thing is war to those that have not tried it."[12]

It is worth noting that Thucydides was having none of it, either. Recall the opening lines to his *History*: "Thucydides, an Athenian, wrote the history of the war between the Peloponnesians and the Athenians, beginning at the moment that it broke out, and believing that it would be a great war and more worthy of relation than any that had preceded it."[13] Thucydides invoked neither the muse of epic poetry nor the muse of history. From the outset, then, Thucydides rejected other, romanticized narrative frames and all their attendant tropes, conceits, and conventions.

Thucydides reiterated his realist point later in Book I, touting the virtues of his accountings of the war, undistorted by rhetorical excess. "Assuredly they will not be disturbed either by the lays of a poet displaying the exaggeration of his craft, or by the compositions of the chroniclers that are attractive at truth's expense," he promised, since "the subjects they treat of being out of reach of evidence, and time having robbed most of them of historical value by enthroning them in the region of legend."[14]

---

[11] Mark Twain, *Life on the Mississippi* (New York: Grossett and Dunlap, 1917 [1883]) 376-377.

[12] Gildersleeve, "Peloponnesian War," 331.

[13] *The Landmark Thucydides: A Comprehensive Guide to The Peloponnesian War*, Robert B. Strassler, ed., introduction by Victor Davis Hanson (New York: The Free Press, 1996) 3.

[14] *The Landmark Thucydides*, 15.

This stripping of rhetorical excess, this stated refusal to present war as adventure, as a test of wills fought heroically by worthy combatants, eager to prove their mettle, helps explain Gildersleeve's affinity with Thucydides. Listen to Gildersleeve's description of war: "Practical warfare is rough work. To frighten, to wound, to kill—these three abide under all forms of military doctrine," and, Gildersleeve asserted, are the only "essential processes" that wars share in common. "Whether death or disability comes by a Belgian ball or Spencer bullet, by the stone of a Balearic slinger, by the bolt from a cross-bow, is a matter of detail" which need not concern us. To be sure, "any two wars [...] will yield a sufficient number of resemblances in killed, wounded, and missing, in the elemental matter of hatred. These things are," Gildersleeve reiterated, "the essence of war, and the manifestations run parallel even in the finer lines." In other words, we can draw points of comparison between any conflict, often without difficulty. "One cock-pheasant finds the drumming of another cock-pheasant a very irritating sound, Chanticleer objects to the notes of Chanticleer, and the more articulate human being is rasped by the voice of his neighbor. The Attic did not like the broad Boetian speech," Gildersleve continued. "'Yankee twang' and 'southern drawl' incited as well as echoed hostility."[15]

For the next four pages of the essay, Gildersleeve delineates the commonalities shared by the Peloponnesian War and the Civil War, only to remind his readers that this exercise is bankrupt, little more than a parlor game. "Historical parallel bars are usually set up for exhibiting feats of mental agility," he cautioned. "The mental agility is often moral suppleness, and nobody expects a critical examination of the parallelism itself."[16] In other words, comparisons tell us little about the two things being compared and a lot about the person making the comparisons. "Iraq is another Vietnam," or "Saddam Hussein is another Hitler," says nothing about Iraq, or Vietnam, or Hussein, or Hitler; it does say something about the direction in which the speaker's moral compass is pointed.

"Such feats," Gildersleeve consistently maintained "imperil one's intellectual honesty. [...] To the sophist, an island is an island, a river a river, a height, everywhere." And anyone can play the game: "Sphacteria would furnish the model for Morris Island; the Achelous would serve indifferently for Potomac or Mississippi; the Epiloae for Missionary Ridge, Plataea for

[15] Gildersleeve, "Peloponnesian War," 332-33.
[16] Gildersleeve, "Peloponnesian War," 330.

Vicksburg, the harbor of Syracuse for Hampton Roads, and Thucydides' description of the naval engagement and the watching crowds would be made available for the fight between the Merrimac and Monitor."[17] No, no, no, no, no, Gildersleeve exclaimed. (Well, not in so many words, but certainly in spirit.) Gildersleeve was no geographical determinist, but perhaps more the point, he understood that analogies imply inevitability. To liken one naval blockade to another suggests the outcome of the latter was foreordained. Such a reading of events made no sense to Gildersleeve. Nor did it make sense to Thucydides. And for those on the ground level—the ones who were fighting, who were advancing on territory and who were retreating, those who were killing and dying—similarities were irrelevant. War is experienced by each generation anew. And it brings disruption and chaos, not continuity with times past.

Differences and discontinuities mattered to Gildersleeve; similarities in one area did not guarantee similarities in all areas, especially in those that mattered most. "Nicias in the Peloponnesian war," he insisted, "has nothing in common with General Scott, whose plan of putting down the rebellion, the Anaconda Plan, [...] bears some resemblance to the scheme of Demosthenes, the Athenian general, for quelling the Peloponnese."[18] Play all you want, you'll not come away with a better understanding of the Peloponnesian War or of the American Civil War.

So why, then, did Gildersleeve pen this essay, if not to point out that the Corinthians were just like the hot-headed secessionists or that Abraham Lincoln's Gettysburg Address sounded a lot like Pericles' funeral oration stripped to its core? This last point is worth dwelling on since so many historians have drawn parallels between the events at Gettysburg and at Athens. And yet it was not Lincoln who invoked Pericles during the dedication ceremony at Gettysburg, but Edward Everett, former U.S. Secretary of State and one of the foremost orators of the nineteenth century. Although a generation older than Gildersleeve, he shared with the Hopkins philologist a love of ancient languages; he, too, had studied at Gottingen, and he taught ancient Greek at Harvard. Everett is perhaps best remembered for speaking *before* Lincoln at the dedication of the National Cemetery at Gettysburg. "As a young man, Everett had tramped the fields of Greece's ancient glory," historian Gabor Borritt has written. "In a long lifetime he taught America the

[17] Gildersleeve, "Peloponnesian War," 335.
[18] Gildersleeve, "Peloponnesian War," 336.

greatness of the example of Greece. Now," in this speech, "he would use his learning to do for his countrymen what the ancients did for Athens."[19]

Pericles is perhaps most clearly evinced in the speech's conclusion: "Seminary Ridge, the Peach Orchid, Cemetery, Culp, and Wolf Hill, Round Top, Little Round Top, humble names, henceforward dear and famous—no lapse of time, no distance of space, shall cause you to be forgotten." Everett had, Borritt explains, "spoke to 'you,' the land around him." And then Everett turned to Pericles. "'The whole earth,' said Pericles, as he stood over his fellow-citizens, who had fallen in the first year of the Peloponnesian War, 'the whole earth is the sepulcher of illustrious men' All time, he might have added, is the millennium of their glory." Everett acknowledged "other noble achievements of the war," and offered to the Union's combatants "the warmest thanks and the richest rewards which a grateful country can pay." But even those who had fought elsewhere and had survived, Everett felt assured, "will join me in saying, as we bid farewell to the dust of these martyr-heroes that wherever throughout this civilized world the accounts of this great warfare are read, and down to the latest period of recorded time, in the glorious annals of our common country, there will be no brighter page than that which relates THE BATTLE OF GETTYSBURG.'"[20]

If Everett is remembered as having shared the stage with Lincoln, the content of his speech is long since forgotten. And so the elision occurs. And because Lincoln too talked about the war's dead, so the reasoning goes, then surely his speech echoed Pericles' Funeral Oration. Both Boritt, in *The Gettysburg Gospel: The Lincoln Speech that Nobody Knows* and Gary Wills, in his Pulitzer Prize-winning meditation, *Lincoln at Gettysburg: The Words that Remade a Nation*, devote considerable energy in parsing Everett's speech. Wills even includes the full text of Everett's oration in an Appendix, prefaced first by Lincoln's speech, and then followed by the funeral orations of

[19] Gabor Borritt, *The Gettysburg Gospel: The Lincoln Speech That Nobody Knows* (New York: Simon and Schuster, 2006): 101. For Everett's contribution to the Greek revival in early nineteenth-century America, see Gary Wills, *Lincoln at Gettysburg: The Words that Remade America* (New York: Simon and Schuster, 1992): 41-62.

[20] Borritt, *The Gettysburg Gospel*, 111. "Address of the Hon. Edward Everett at the Consecration of the National Cemetery at Gettysburg, 19th November 1863, with the Dedicatory Speech of President Lincoln and the Other Exercises of the Occasion; Accompanied by an Account of the Origin of the Undertaking and the Arrangement of the Cemetery Grounds, and by a Map of the Battle-field and a Plan of the Cemetery. (Boston: Little, Brown, and Co., 1864) 81-82.

Gorgias, Pericles, and again by Lincoln. Although neither of these scholars explicitly links Lincoln's Gettysburg Address to Pericles' funeral oration, they make it possible for others to do so. The elision between Lincoln and Pericles is thus almost inescapable.

"There is a certain irony [...] in the way that Lincoln has been best memorialized," Nicholas P. Cole has written. "Lincoln knew no Greek and little Latin," for example, although he did own an 1848 edition of Thucydides in translation.[21] Moreover, Lincoln's "style of speech was at odds with the classically inspired rhetoric of many politicians of his day and certainly reflected no formal training." Everett included the classical allusions and developed historical comparisons, not Lincoln.[22] And, as Gildersleeve suggested, those historical comparisons can be tricky business.

Let us return to Gildersleeve's assertion that all wars share three things—and only three things: the need to frighten, to wound, and to kill. The point is not to explain how *this* effort to terrorize resembles *that* effort to intimidate; how this military strategy over here looks just like that one over there. Rather, the point is to create a framework for understanding unprecedented death, destruction, and desolation. What Gildersleeve documents in his essay is the shattering of a worldview in the wake of warfare. Recall his experience as a young student studying abroad and his post-war response to the questions posed: "Is this your first ruin?' 'Is this your first nightingale?' I am not certain that I can place my first ruin or my first nightingale, but I can recall my first dead man on the battlefield." Thucydides well understood this shattering more than two millennia before Gildersleeve and his contemporaries grappled with the Civil War's consequences.

In early 1862, Ralph Waldo Emerson had jotted in his notebook that the Civil War had become "a new glass to see all our old things through."[23] For Gildersleeve, that meant, among other things, the classics. "I went from my books to the front and went back from the front to my books, from the Confederate war to the Peloponnesian war, from Lee and Early to Thucydides and Aristophanes." Significantly, however, Gildersleeve did not credit a

---

[21]Nicholas P. Cole, "Classical Democracy and the Gettysburg Address," in Sean Conant, ed., *The Gettysburg Address: Perspectives on Lincoln's Greatest Speech* (New York: Oxford University Press, 2015) 20; Robert Bray, *Reading with Lincoln* (Carbondale, Ill.: Southern Illinois University Press, 2010) 228.

[22] Cole, "Classical Democracy," 20.

[23] Ralph Waldo Emerson, *The Journals and Miscellaneous Notebooks of Ralph Waldo Emerson*, Linda Allardt, et. al., editor, (Cambridge, Massachusetts: Belknap Press, 1982) 163.

new way of reading familiar texts *solely* to his military service. "I fancy that I understood my Greek history and my Greek authors better for my experience in the field," he wrote, "but some degree of understanding would have come to me even if I had not stirred from home."[24] In other words, anyone who bore witness to the unprecedented scale of the Civil War's destruction saw their world refracted through this "new glass."

The Civil War made a mockery out of romanticism's tenets. And here it might be worth remembering that the generation that experienced the Civil War was born in the era of romanticism and thus shaped by its central concerns. The cultivation of the imagination over reason; the sense that the heart is a better judge of character than the intellect; the emphasis on the sublime and the transcendent; the sense that an individual's actions can affect outcomes; that history moves according to some divine will. It is all there. But here is the rub: the soul of genius mattered not a whit on the battlefield. Combat spared neither the coward nor the brave. What is more, there is nothing heroic about being picked off by a sharpshooter, by dying of dysentery or some other camp disease, or about having your bloated corpse picked clean by a hog.

What better way to understand contingency, randomness, and chance than by perusing Thucydides, which Southerners did with great avidity. Here, I will cite but one example. To borrow from Monty Python, nobody expects the plague. And yet the plague came, and its ruinous effect on on the Athenians' ability to wage war invited speculation. What gods had they angered; what oracle had they ignored? Here is Thucydides' accounting: "Such was the nature of the calamity, and heavily did it weigh on the Athenians; death raging within the city and devastation without. Among other things which they remembered in their distress was, very naturally, the following verse which the old men said had long ago been uttered: A Dorian war shall come and with it pestilence. So a dispute arose," Thucydides continued, "as to whether dearth and not death had not been the word in the verse; but at the present juncture, it was of course decided in favor of the latter; for the people made their recollections fit with their sufferings. I suppose, however," he interjected, "that if another Dorian war should ever afterwards come upon us, and a famine should happen to accompany it, the verse will probably be read accordingly." Here, Thucydides displayed keen insight into the human condition. The desire to fit an event or a phenomenon into a pattern, to

[24] Gildersleeve, "Peloponnesian War," 336.

make it accord with accepted wisdom, to give it an explanation or a reason or a purpose is often irresistible, perhaps especially in war. But Thucydides suggested throughout his *History* that the world simply does not work that way.

Gildersleeve understood. Let me conclude by returning us to his recollection of his first encounter with a dead body. "We were making an advance on the enemy's position [...]. Nothing, by the way, could have been more beautiful than the plan, which I was privileged to see; and as we neared the objective point, it was a pleasure to watch how column after column, marching by this road and that, converged to the rendezvous. It was as if," Gildersleeve continued, "some huge spider were gathering its legs about the victim. The special order issued breathed a spirit of calm resolution worthy of the general commanding and his troops. Nobody that I remember criticized the tautological expression, 'The progress of the army must be forward.'" But that plan, so beautiful on paper, had failed to materialize. In fact, a lot of things went wrong. "The advance on the enemy's position had developed more strength in front than we had counted on, or some of the spider's legs had failed to close in. A misleading report had been brought to headquarters. A weak point in the enemy's line had been reinforced. Who knows?" Who knows, indeed. "The best laid plans," Gildersleeve soon surmised, "are often thwarted by the merest trifles,—an insignificant puddle, a jingling canteen. This game of war is a hit or miss game," he concluded, "breeding a kind of fatalism that develops steadily as one acknowledges the horror."[25] Alluding back to the passage by Pindar, Gildersleeve wrote near the end of his essay what has to be one of the clearest examples of understatement, "The War was not an era of sweetness and light"[26] The Lost Cause mythmakers that Mark Twain had so caustically derided were no different than the Athenian elders who had tried to fix an explanation to something that has no explanation.

Thucydides' *History of the Peloponnesian War*, then, was not some relic from a remote past, incapable of speaking to an audience poised to ride a dynamo into the twentieth century. Thucydides had spared his readers nothing. Americans might have felt confident as they entered the new century, but a new brand of nationalism, religious fundamentalism, imperialism, and political factionalism all served to undermine any sense of stability. The Thucydides that Gildersleeve presented to his readers in 1897 understood

[25] Gildersleeve, "Peloponnesian War," 330-31.
[26] Gildersleeve, "Peloponnesian War," 341.

those threats. Gildersleeve did not use Thucydides as an antidote to progress, then. Instead, he used him as an antidote to hubris and to a kind of tortured naiveté that assumes a calculation or a formula could mitigate contingency, randomness, and chance. This might not have been the Thucydides that classicists wanted. But it was the Thucydides that Gildersleeve thought his readers needed. "A Southerner in the Peloponnesian War" is not an antimodernist response to the ills that plagued industrialized and mechanized America but rather a demonstration of the relevance of the classics in a modern world.

WHY OUR DEMOCRACY NEEDS THUCYDIDES NOW MORE THAN EVER

Laurie M. Johnson, Kansas State University

Most of my work on Thucydides has been about what his *History of the Peloponnesian War* could teach us about international relations. When I received this kind invitation from Mercer University, I realized this was an opportunity to revisit Thucydides in a new way. The conference topic was Thucydides and the American Founders, or more generally, what Thucydides could teach us about the American republic. And having pledged never again to write about the ancient historian in a way that reached only an academic audience, I decided I would turn to two immediate sources of inspiration—the *History* itself, of course, and the blogosphere.

With everything that had occurred within a few months of the conference, and being a fan of Thucydides, how could I not consider questions such as "Donald Trump—Cleon or Alcibiades?" or "How would Thucydides understand the concept 'fake news?' or (more seriously) "How would Thucydides measure the strength of our democracy?"

Here are some of the headlines I found: "The Mytilenean Dialogue from 428 B.C. Explains Who Really Won the Trump-Clinton Debate," "What Would Thucydides Have Thought About Donald Trump?" (same headline twice), "Can We Learn from Thucydides' Writings on the Trump of Ancient Athens?" "Thucydides on Donald Trump and 'New York Values,'" "U.S. – China Relations in the Age of Trump," and "To: Donald Trump. Love, Thucydides." There were more, but these are representative. Actually, it was quite refreshing to see that people thought enough of my favorite ancient historian to ask the questions, and that other people wanted answers. But this little excursion into the blogosphere led me to remember a piece I ran across shortly after 9-11, not a blog exactly, but an opinion piece from the Chicago *Tribune*, written by Danielle Allen, a political theorist at Harvard University.

Allen's work often juxtaposes ancient and modern democratic practices and concepts of citizenship.[1] Her Chicago *Tribune* contribution was "The

[1] "Danielle Allen," Edmond J. Safra Center for Ethics, accessed September 18, 2017, http://ethics.harvard.edu/people/danielle-allen.

Thinking Citizen: Why, When Entering a Crisis, We Must Not Check Our Brains at the Door." It was published a little over a month after two hijacked planes brought down New York's twin towers, another plane struck the Pentagon, and a final plane went down in a field in Pennsylvania. In this piece, Allen recalls her state of extreme indecision on that terrible day. She was visiting the University of Wisconsin-Madison to give a guest lecture on Thucydides, and not long before that class, the terrorist attacks began.

Listening to the shocking news on her radio, Allen had *that moment*. She knew that the entire world had changed, and at the same time she didn't know exactly what was going on or what kind of reaction she should have. I too was about to walk to a classroom where I would teach my scheduled Introduction to Political Thought class. I too hesitated at this unprecedented moment with a practical question—what should I do with this class? I went to the class, talked briefly and factually about what was unfolding (the towers had not yet come down, as I recall, by the time I had left my office), and then told the students to go home to be with their friends or families. That was my response. My thought was that in this way I would not be making the decision about how to react for my students—I'd be giving them that responsibility. I'm not second-guessing myself, but reading Allen's piece made me realize there were other possibilities.

Allen described in the *Tribune* piece the thought process involved in deciding to go ahead with the class on Thucydides, and what the effect was on her and the students to whom she spoke. A little more than a month out from 9-11, Allen was able to register a sense of meaning and hope that transcended and, in a sense got the better of, the terrorists' evil. She did that by exploring with that class the timeless insights of Thucydides.

Allen described her initial indecision about what to do. As she learned about the unfolding attacks, she would decide to head toward class, and then she'd change her mind and walk back to her radio. She went back and forth several times, in a daze, in effect standing still. "There is a Greek word for such behavior, this indecision," she wrote, "It is '*stasis*.'" As she explained, the most common meaning of *stasis* is "civil war," but it also means "paralysis and lack of motion." She was in a state of *stasis*—and, of course, so was much of the country. People in this situation are particularly vulnerable. Having been knocked off of their immediate agenda, having been perhaps also knocked off their foundational notions about things as fundamental as whether or not they are safe, whether they can count on being able to live like they have in the past, and whether their sense of identity can remain intact or has been forever altered, people are particularly susceptible to being told what to do.

As a friend reminded me not too long ago, this is what Naomi Klein refers to as the effect of "shock" in her book *The Shock Doctrine*.[2] Whatever we might think about Klein's thesis in that book, we can at least agree with her that when people are in *stasis*, they are more susceptible to being ordered about. The temptation to step into the void of *stasis* and use it for political purposes is not exclusively felt by any particular political persuasion, but it is certainly a real thing.

So, at a moment when her students could have been very vulnerable to simply being told what to do, Danielle Allen decided to go ahead with a discussion of a seemingly remote time, place and series of events. She justified her decision this way:

> If we really believe…that studying these old books is of any use, then now is surely the time to test that proposition. And if there is a book with which to test the proposition, it is surely Thucydides' "History of the Peloponnesian War." After all, it's mostly about what happens to democracies in times of crisis.

Allen's excellent point about the value of works like Thucydides' *History* especially during times of crisis was built upon by historian Paul Rahe, Professor of History at Hillsdale College and author of many books which, like Allen's, circle around ancient and modern democratic and republican institutions and practices.[3] Rahe came to Kansas State a full decade after the 9/11 terror attacks, to deliver a lecture to students of the program I direct, the Primary Texts Certificate. While Allen showed how keeping company with a classic primary text like the *History of the Peloponnesian War* could help us avoid *stasis* and continue to think, Rahe dwelled on how perhaps only through this kind of reading can we approach anything like objectivity. We need objectivity the most when we face unprecedented challenges, but we are the least likely to achieve it under those circumstances, unless we are trained and ready to resist the pull toward fear and instinctual reaction.

---

[2] Naomi Klein, *The Shock Doctrine: The Rise of Disaster Capitalism* (New York: Picador, 2007).

[3] Dakota Fuller, "Paul A. Rahe," Dr. Paul A. Rahe | Political Historian, accessed September 18, 2017, http://www.paularahe.com/books.html.

Rahe made the case for the liberal arts, and more particularly for learning through classic original works. He said that much of what we think we know is given and unquestioned. This, he said, the Greeks called *nomos* or custom. But we also have the capability of *ecstasis*, getting outside of ourselves and evaluating ourselves. People alone are capable of observing their customs, assumptions and opinions as such and deciding to change them. But how do we achieve this capability of stepping outside of *nomos*, to think in terms of *physis*, or nature? How do we ask the question of whether some *nomoi* are in accord with human nature and others less so? How, in other words, to escape the cave and come to see the sun?

Rahe noted that one way to gain some objectivity is the way of Herodotus, which was to travel, to see that not everyone thinks the way you do. But now we live in an increasingly globalized world. Traveling will no longer necessarily take you beyond your natural parochialism to the point where you can possibly think about things that are true and permanent. Rahe stated that when you go abroad you will find that "*nomoi* are being destroyed." In the future "there will be a universal *nomos*, and it will be very hard to escape from the bubble."

Rahe continues: "There is a kind of sameness creeping over the world...and the consequence is the entire world is becoming educated to be American...the fundamental pressure comes from us. The consequence is that when you travel today, you meet yourself."[4]

A somewhat humorous but hopefully helpful example of what Rahe was talking about happened on my first trip abroad, as a senior in Political Science, attending a model U.N. conference in Italy. Before getting there, I had a stop-over in Belgium for a day. After spending the night in a nicely appointed hotel room with different smells and (gasp) no washcloths, I went down for breakfast. The coffee was a bit different and the breakfast a bit lighter than the usual American fair. Outside, there was a small park still obscured by the morning mist. I was just getting into the charm of the slight differences between this experience and a similar one in America when I heard, coming from the restaurant's PA system, Billy Ray Cyrus singing "Achy, Breaky Heart." Well, the charm dissipated quickly, especially since I don't like country music. Then, in Italy, I again encountered the strange

[4] "Paul Rahe on Primary Texts in an Age of Globalization," YouTube, August 26, 2013, accessed September 18, 2017, https://www.youtube.com/watch?v=HnDNS7-aBsVo.

phenomenon of no washcloths and stronger coffee, but at night I went off with the girls to the disco, where all the music played was American disco music, only slower. Did I mention that the place had a mirrored ball flashing lights about? Did I also mention that disco music was already passé in the United States?

If you travel, you will no doubt find that wherever you go, unless you go to the wilderness, there is a McDonald's not too far away, that most of the television shows are from the United States, that American brands prevail in the upscale stores, and that you can get around more easily than others because there's more for you to read. The American way of life, brought to other countries via the globalized economy, has made the world much more homogenous. And in fact this is one factor in the current struggle within the Islamic world—which way shall they go, with Western culture and the secularism and materialism that entails, or with the older ways, represented by extremists as a return to the caliphate, and by moderates as an attempt to cling to faith and tradition, including culturally prescribed dress?

At any rate, for people in this country it is, Rahe would argue, particularly hard to escape themselves and get a more objective view via travel. In this situation, what is the way out of prejudice, the way beyond parochialism? Rahe's answer was this: "The avenue that is still open…is to travel through time. How do you do that? Primary texts."[5]

In the spirit of both inspirational figures, Allen and Rahe, I am drawn to the case of Corcyra related in the third and fourth books of Thucydides' *History*, with the hope of productively meditating on the causes and effects (and thus hopefully avoidance) of *stasis*. The Corcyraean civil war began in the fifth year of the war. Thucydides' description of this event is so granular that it can induce a sense of being overwhelmed and helpless in the reader (*stasis!*). At the same time, he avoids this effect by frequently stepping back and expounding on the timeless character of some of the events, a move which encourages readers to think about big questions such as the true nature of human beings and why they are prone to bouts of extreme violence.

The civil war began when a group of 250 Corcyraean oligarchs were captured by Corinth. The Corinthians released them on the promise that they would go back home and encourage their friends to revolt against the

---

[5] A similar point is also made by Martha Nussbaum, in her defense of a traditional liberal arts education, *Not for Profit: Why Democracy Needs the Humanities* (Princeton, NJ: Princeton University Press, 2016).

democratic party (referred to in my translation as "The People").[6] The former prisoners went home and lobbied their case with their fellow oligarchs. While remaining allied with democratic Athens, their arguments caused Corcyra to adopt a friendlier attitude toward the Corinthians and Spartans. This change in position knocked the population off its equilibrium, and from then on, the oligarchs and The People were at war. A series of events happened, none of which had to happen, but all of which pointed in the direction of all-out class warfare.

I will not run through all the details of these events, but highlight a few in particular that seem to have impressed Thucydides for their extremism and concentrate on what he took away from them.

First, the *stasis* that eventually engulfed Corcyra was instigated by an outside power aligned with Sparta, namely Corinth. The Corinthians deliberately sent oligarchic prisoners they held to foment a rebellion for their party in order to get Corcyra into the Spartan orbit. The ideological dimension of this move and the subsequent conflict always surprises students new to Thucydides. They tend to think that ideological warfare only got underway with the French Revolution, or with WWII and the Cold War, but ideological conflict was a big part of the strife not only in Corcyra, but in many of the Greek cities as the imperialistic war between Athens and Sparta expanded.

Second, a major threshold in the conflict occurred when The People decided to violate the rules of piety and risk the anger of the gods, tricking the oligarchic temple suppliants into foregoing their protected status only to slaughter them. This was fairly late in the civil war, which highlights that this was a truly meaningful "level up." In fact, prior to this abandonment of piety, The People had actually allowed suppliants safe passage to a nearby island so that they could be sure of controlling them better. They even supplied the prisoners in the temple with food so as not to anger the goddess Hera (3.75.5). At another point, they carried the suppliants back to the mainland, but still did not harm them. But as their Spartan allies sailed away and the Athenian fleet approached, The People felt emboldened and began to kill any oligarchs they could find, even those in the temple, leading many of the oligarchs to kill themselves:

---

[6] All quotations from Thucydides' History are from Thucydides, Richard Crawley, and Robert B. Strassler, *The Landmark Thucydides: A Comprehensive Guide to the Peloponnesian War: A Newly Revised Edition of the Richard Crawley Translation with Maps, Annotations, Appendices, and Encyclopedic Index* (New York: Free Press, 1996).

> Next they went to the sanctuary of Hera and persuaded about fifty men to take their trial, and condemned them all to death. The mass of the suppliants who had refused to do so, on seeing what was taking place, slew each other there in the consecrated ground; while some hanged themselves upon the trees, and others destroyed themselves as they were severally able. (3.81.2-3)

Afterwards, sins against the gods abounded—sons killed their fathers, and suppliants were murdered within temple walls. Thucydides' description of all this indicates, at the very least, that it was another indicator of just how badly normalcy had been overturned in favor of radical fear and self-destructive action.

The third event that exemplifies the extremism in the Coryrean *stasis* was the tendency for people on both sides of the conflict to use it as a cover for killing their personal enemies and settling old scores. The first hint that this might have been the case came when, as mentioned above, the Spartans sailed away and the Athenians arrived, allowing The People more freedom to do as they pleased. The way Thucydides puts it, they "slew such of their enemies as they laid hands on" (3.81.2). Not long after, he explicitly states private hatred and personal greed as motivations for the slaying. They "were engaged in butchering those of their fellow-citizens whom they regarded as their enemies: and although the crime imputed was that of attempting to put down the democracy, some were slain also for private hatred, others by their debtors because of moneys owed to them" (3.81.4). The ideological conflict itself became more and more tinged with the more personal motives of revenge, whether revenge for grievances that preexisted the current war or those created in the violence of the *stasis* itself.

Fourth, we find a growing abandonment of self-interest and ideology to simple pleasure in cruelty. This is the emotion that no good liberal wants to talk about—the total commitment to doing the most harm to one's enemies no matter what the cost, the idea that a happy death could come in the wake of simply slaughtering as many of one's enemies as possible.

An example of this is to be found in Book 4, as Thucydides tells us what eventually happened to the Corcyraeans. The Athenian fleet, after their victory at Pylos in 425 B.C., sailed to Corcyra on their way to Sicily. There they decided to help The People attack the oligarchs who had continued to harass them. The oligarchs surrendered to the Athenians. They were taken under a truce to an island where they would be held until they could sail with the Athenians to be judged in Athens. They agreed that if they tried to escape, the truce would be nullified, and they could be hunted down with impunity. But the Corcyrean people did not trust the Athenians to judge their enemies harshly enough, and they came up with a plan to trick them into breaking the truce. I will quote this passage at length because it exemplifies the warrantless cruelty that emerged late in the conflict.

> They gained over some few men on the island by secretly sending friends with instructions to provide them with a boat, and to tell them, as if for their own sakes, that they had best escape as quickly as possible, as the Athenian generals were going to give them up to the Corcyraean people.
>
> These representations succeeding, it was so arranged that the men were caught sailing out in the boat that was provided, and the treaty became void accordingly, and the whole were given up to the Corcyraeans. For this result the Athenian generals were in great measure responsible; their evident disinclination to sail for Sicily, and thus to leave to others the honor of conducting the men to Athens, encouraged the intriguers in their design and seemed to affirm the truth of their representations. The prisoners thus handed over were shut up by the Corcyraeans in a large building, and afterwards taken out by twenties and led past two lines of hoplites, one on each side, being bound together, and beaten and stabbed by the men in the lines whenever any saw pass a personal enemy; while men carrying whips went by their side and hastened on the road those that walked too slowly.
>
> As many as sixty men were taken out and killed in this way without the knowledge of their friends in the building, who fancied they were merely being moved from one prison to another. At last, however, someone opened their eyes to the truth, upon which they called upon the Athenians to kill them themselves, if such was their pleasure, and refused any longer to go out of the building, and said they would do all they could to prevent anyone coming in. The Corcyraeans, not wishing themselves to force a passage through the doors, got up on the top of the building, and breaking through the roof, threw down the tiles and let fly arrows at them, from which the prisoners sheltered themselves as well as they could. Most of their number, meanwhile were engaged in killing themselves by thrusting into their throats the arrows shot by the enemy, and hanging themselves with cords taken from some beds that happened to be there, and with strips made from their clothing; adopting, in short, every possible means of self-destruction, and also falling victims to the missiles of their enemies on the roof. Night came on while these horrors were taking place, and most of it had passed before they were concluded. When it was day the Corcyraeans threw them in layers upon wagons and carried them out of the city. All the women taken in the stronghold were sold as slaves (4.47-4.48.5).

Thucydides tells the above story of trickery, betrayal of trust and gratuitous cruelty in great detail because, for him, these are signs that civilization has completely broken down. And mentioned within this story are incidents in which at the height of the cruelty, people on the receiving end of that cruelty yet again chose to commit suicide. The oligarchs not only killed themselves out of despair, but also as a last attempt to have some control over their fate—that is, control over the way they would die—a reaction similar to that of the men and women who jumped to their death from the twin towers on September 11. In the case of the Corcyraean oligarchs, men who had previously thought that by their daring action they could gain complete control over their city were now reduced to grasping for one small bit of control over their lives.

The final example of extremism in the *stasis* that I'd light to highlight is Thucydides' emphasis on the radicalization of language in the *stasis*. Indeed, this is a point upon which he extensively editorializes, indicating that it was a very significant and troubling aspect of *stasis* for him. It is notable that he universalizes his observations about the changes in language during such conflicts:

> The sufferings which revolution entailed upon the cities were many and terrible, such as have occurred and always will occur as long as the nature of mankind remains the same; though in a severer or milder form, and varying in their symptoms, according to the variety of the particular cases" (3.82.2).

In other words, the radicalization of rhetoric, like so many of the emanations of this particular conflict, applies not only to the case of Corcyra, but to all events like it. Here he describes very well what Nietzsche would call (but with much less dismay) the "revaluation of values" that occurs during *stasis*:

> Words had to change their ordinary meaning and to take that which was now given them. Reckless audacity came to be considered the courage of a loyal supporter; prudent hesitation, specious cowardice; moderation was held to be a cloak for unmanliness; ability to see all sides of a question incapacity to act on any. Frantic violence became the attribute of manliness; cautious plotting a justifiable means of self-defense. The advocate of extreme measures was always trustworthy; his opponent a man to be suspected. To succeed in a plot was to have a shrewd head, to divine a plot a still shrewder; but to try to provide against having to do either was to break up your party and to be afraid of your adversaries" (3.82.4-5).

Beyond this incredible passage about the overturning of traditional values and hence traditional connotations of important words, Thucydides opines so much that I cannot quote it all here, but at this point I will just provide what I consider to be the most significant parts of two more pages of commentary (a rare amount of extended analysis by Thucydides) on radicalization during *stasis*:

> "...even blood became a weaker tie than party" (3.82.6).
>
> "Revenge also was held of more account than self-preservation. Oaths of reconciliation, being only offered on either side to meet an immediate difficulty, only held good so long as no other weapon was at hand..." (3.82.6).
>
> "...success by treachery won him the prize for superior intelligence. Indeed it is generally the case that men are readier to call rogues clever than simpletons honest, and are as ashamed of being the second as they are proud of being the first" (3.82.7).
>
> "Thus religion was in honor with neither party; but the use of fair phrases to arrive at guilty ends was in high reputation. Meanwhile the moderate part of the citizens perished between the two..." (3.82.8).
>
> "The ancient simplicity into which honor so largely entered was laughed down and disappeared; and society became divided into camps in which no man trusted his fellow" (3.83.1).
>
> "In this contest the blunter wits were most successful. Apprehensive of their own deficiencies and of the cleverness of their antagonists, they feared to be worsted in debate and to be surprised by the combinations of their more versatile opponents, and so at once boldly had recourse to action: while their adversaries, arrogantly thinking that they should know in time, and that it was unnecessary to secure by action what policy could provide, often fell victims to lack of precaution" (3.83.3).

Several authors have observed what Thucydides described regarding how language and attitudes changed is reminiscent of revolutionary "Newspeak," that is, the same kind of language inversion described by George Orwell in his famous dystopian novel, *Nineteen Eighty-Four*.[7] Walter Robert

[7] Orwell spent considerable time and effort imagining the lengths to which people could go to control thought through newspeak. See his appendix on "The Principles of Newspeak" here: O. Dag, "George Orwell: 'Nineteen Eighty-Four'," George Orwell: Nineteen Eighty-Four — Appendix: The principles of Newspeak, accessed September 18, 2017, http://orwell.ru/library/novels/1984/english/en_app.

Connor writes of it that "Language has now become an agent of violence, intensifying rather than alleviating the *kinésis* and the destruction. Revolutionary Newspeak makes violence seem simple and appropriate."[8] Delving back into the blogosphere, I found James Holmes lamenting something similar:

> Such turmoil, writes Thucydides, is especially cruel because it permits no one to remain neutral. Moderates swiftly perish. It pits citizen against citizen, kinsman against kinsman; old scores are settled with extreme prejudice. Indeed, a kind of Orwellian Newspeak prevails. Political factions garb themselves in lofty slogans while pursuing the basest of motives. Words mean their opposites. Prudence is cowardice, moderation effeminacy, indiscriminate violence manliness, treachery superior intelligence. Two plus two equals five![9]

Of course, this probably reminds us of something more immediately familiar. Recently we have been apprised of "alternative facts" (close enough to Orwell's Newspeak), "forgotten men and women," (a phrase straight out of Sinclair Lewis's *It Can't Happen Here*), and "enemies of the people" (a phrase Corcyraean democrats, French revolutionaries and Vladimir Lenin would have all recognized). In this era, which admittedly was a long time in the making, Thucydides' observations again remind us that what seems new, unsetting and even disturbing, is actually old—it is the latest manifestation of a particular tendency of human nature that comes out in times of high stress.

Journalist Tom Holland, reviewing Victor Davis Hanson's *A War Like No Other*, observed, "So it was, during the last century, that Thucydides' narrative of universal war, of Newspeak and class hatred, of terrorism, revolution and genocide, appeared all too bleakly contemporary. So it is too, in a new century, and amid the raging of a new war, that Thucydides still haunts the corridors of power in America."[10] It is with this realization of the incred-

---

[8] Walter Robert Conner, *Thucydides* (Princeton, NJ: Princeton University Press, 1984), 101.

[9] James R. Holmes, "Thucydides, War and Natural Disasters," The Diplomat, March 20, 2013, accessed September 18, 2017, http://thediplomat.com/2013/03/-thucydides-war-and-natural-disasters/.

[10] Holland, Tom. "Why the Future Looks Spartan." The Telegraph. January 15, 2006. Accessed September 18, 2017. http://www.telegraph.co.uk/culture/books/-3649344/Why-the-future-looks-Spartan.html.

ible timeliness of Thucydides' account of *stasis* that we turn to asking what he thought was the ultimate cause of radicalization or extremism.

Thucydides gives us his first answer to that question when he says that it is easy for people to have "better sentiments" in more peaceful and prosperous times because they do not feel cornered. But war "takes away the easy supply of daily wants and so proves a rough master that brings most men's characters to a level with their fortunes" (3.82.2). Going deeper still in search of what makes humanity descend into *stasis* to begin with, he says, "The cause of all these evils was the lust for power arising from greed and ambition; and from these passions proceeded the violence of parties once engaged in contention. The leaders in the cities made the fairest professions: on the one side with the cry of political equality of The People, on the other of a moderate aristocracy; but they sought prizes for themselves in those public interests which they pretended to cherish and, stopping at nothing in their struggles for ascendancy, engaged in direct excesses" (3.82.8).

So, Thucydides' opinion is that all the examples of extremism and violence in the Corcyraean *stasis* have happened and will happen again as a result of humankind's inherent capacity to change its spirit to one of faction, ideology, and cruelty, and that this capacity has at its root very solid and predictable foundations in greed and ambition. In his view, the fairer words of ideologies just cover up these more solid and predictable foundations.

For a contemporary example, and at the risk of being controversial, think of free-trade conservatives who don't call attention to our highly subsidized agricultural sector, and indeed regularly vote for farm bills that continue to control the lives of the few farmers we have left. Think also of the many advocates of socialism or communism who have tended to ignore the linkage between these ideas and 20th Century totalitarian oppression. For that matter, think of the populist leaders here and abroad who appeal to "forgotten men and women"[11] and then put people who are not so obscure into positions of power. It can seem like leaders want to discourage those who follow them from thinking outside of their ideological box, from asking questions like "Is that claim really true," or "what's in it for them?"—how could they keep ahold of their movements if citizens became healthy skep-

[11] "Trump: The Forgotten Men and Women 'Forgotten No Longer'," MSNBC, November 09, 2016, accessed September 18, 2017, http://www.msnbc.com/msnbc-quick-cuts/watch/trump-the-forgotten-men-and-women-forgotten-no-longer-804468291925.

tics? Now we're getting pretty close to the world of which Thucydides was familiar.

So why is it that in *stasis* ideological language covers up less lofty motivations?[12] Here are two suggestions. First, by covering up people's self-interest, fair words assuage any lingering sense of guilt or responsibility on the part of instigators. Second, fair words get credulous people who really have nothing to gain by getting involved to risk their lives for those who do. In fact, it is among them where we find the "true believers." It is among true believers that we are most likely to find those who are moved to such hatred of their ideological enemies that they exhibit the cruelty referenced above. That perhaps goes a bit farther than Thucydides explicitly goes in his narrative on the Corcyraean *stasis*, but it is very much where Hobbes went. Hobbes translated Thucydides' *History* and learned many important lessons from it, and definitely this one. In his analysis of the English Civil War, *Behemoth*, he takes this Thucydidean opinion of the dissenting preachers and demagogues who emboldened his country's People to move against the Crown and Church.[13]

But one last question remains. If Thucydides thinks that *stasis* was caused by negative aspects of human nature that are always present, does that mean that he also thought *stasis* is inevitable? Perhaps from the long view of history, yes, but in any particular case, no. He does not depict the evils of *stasis* as *determined* by nature. Thucydides' obvious tone of condemnation and lament suggests that free human choice was involved in the succumbing to the pressures and temptations that were presented in the Corcyraean case. Just because he thought that these events could recur throughout history does not mean that people are mere slaves to their impulses in any particular case. If that is the case, then there is always hope that we can recognize the signs of impending *stasis* and take appropriate action to contain and mitigate the effects of the selfish motives that lead to it. After all, Thucydides tells us at the beginning of his history that the future "course of human things must resemble" the past, and especially the Peloponnesian War which, at least up till his lifetime, was the greatest of wars. (1.22.4)

This seems to be a good enough reason why people who would be citizens should still read the *History of the Peloponnesian War*. Getting back to Danielle Allen's decision to hold her lecture on Thucydides while the crisis unfolded, I have to say that she made the wiser choice. She gave her students

[12] Called by those in the Alt-Right who virtue signal "virtue signaling."
[13] Thomas Hobbes, *Behemoth* (Oxford: Oxford University Press, 2010).

the chance to begin the process of thinking about those events in a more objective way, a way that would be less reactive, and that would be more likely to produce a rational response.

In *Not for Profit*, Martha Nussbaum carries the point made by Danielle Allen and Paul Rahe further by pointing out how, strangely enough, America's university education still has far more humanistic content, more required history, philosophy, literature, etc., than the average university education in Europe. However, Nussbaum reports that this type of education is under serious threat in the United States. American educational institutions have always leaned toward pragmatism, but in the past few decades they have been under severe pressure to produce (in the sense of factory production) students who get lucrative jobs. Now, there's nothing wrong at all with the goal of graduating employable students, but as Nussbaum points out, students who get mainly a technical education are actually less employable and promotable in the long run because they do not have the necessary ability to continue to learn, create and adapt. More to Nussbaum's main point, such students are not equipped to fulfill their roles as free democratic citizens who can exercise their rights to not only vote judiciously but to participate more fully in the life of their communities. This, she seems to be saying, is the main reason why communities are fraying and our political environment has become ever more dysfunctional.[14]

At this point, I hope you can see how the ability to contemplate the implications of history can make us better citizens. Through examining Thucydides' reaction to the Corcyraean *stasis* we not only are more able to recognize *stasis* in ourselves and in our society. We also become aware of the possibility that in times of crisis that we are the most vulnerable to self-interested elites, the most likely to give up our liberty and judgment and capitulate to those who are ready with ideas and the will to carry them out. Milton Friedman once famously pointed out that crises produce what we might call power vacuums, opportunities for those who want to move society forward (or backward) in some revolutionary fashion that the people would not willingly choose on their own. In his case, those ideas were about global free market capitalism, which he argued were good for all in the long run. In *Capitalism and Freedom*, he wrote, "Only a crisis—real or perceived—produces real change. When that crisis occurs, the actions that are taken depend on the ideas that are lying around. That, I believe, is our basic func-

[14] Martha C. Nussbaum, *Not for Profit: Why Democracy Needs the Humanities* (Princeton, NJ: Princeton University Press, 2016).

tion: to develop alternatives to existing policies, to keep them alive and available until the politically impossible becomes the politically inevitable."[15]

Whether you agree that free market capitalism is, in the long run, what is best for the world, you can at least admire Friedman's honesty and transparency in acknowledging that major revolutionary change most often comes from change-makers who are opportunistic. But what we can learn from Thucydides, especially his account of Corcyraean *stasis*, is that it is not acceptable to simply wave the white flag of surrender and allow elites the opportunity to do the thinking for us, whether those elites have good ideas or not. Instead, the fair words of ideology, especially in times of stress, need to be taken with some skepticism by those who want to hold on to their liberty, because there is always a chance that those words are being used not to enlighten but to divide, and to inflame the passions of those who will be on the front lines. Healthy skepticism, one outcome of a good education requiring us to read books like the *History of the Peloponnesian War*, does entail a loss of happy innocence, but is perhaps what it takes to make a democracy work even in the inevitable crisis.

Because we all can influence our government's actions, not only through our votes, but through direct and indirect political actions, democratic citizens absolutely cannot do without the type of education that writers like Thucydides can provide. On that terrible day when America was under attack, Danielle Allen's students were not victims of *stasis*, paralyzed and isolated. Instead, they were free members of a deliberative community, and they walked away with a greater ability to remain so. Indeed, community—the basis for any real democracy--is itself impossible if people cannot step back from immediate reaction and truly see their neighbors, their neighborhood, their city and their country, from a more objective perspective, from the point of view of past, present and future, from the vantage-point of the common good. If we are to keep democratic community alive and preserve it for future generations, we must pause and—yes—read a book, and not a book of the moment but a book with a long and great reputation for wisdom. There is no better book to turn to for this purpose than Thucydides' *History of the Peloponnesian War*.

---

[15] Milton Friedman, *Capitalism and Freedom* (Chicago, IL: University of Chicago Press, 2002) xiv.

INDEX